Leading Culturally Responsive Gifted Programs

Written by experienced leaders in gifted education, this book is a foundational guide for supervisors, administrators, and districts seeking to create culturally responsive and equity-focused gifted policies and programs.

Engaging chapters supported by real-world vignettes and interactive contemplation corners outline key elements of culturally responsive leadership and the administrative actions necessary for disrupting systems of oppression within gifted programs. Topics covered include culturally responsive gifted education, multitiered systems of support, authentic family engagement, the use of data to inform systemic change, and more.

Featuring authentic applications of culturally responsive gifted leadership practices and an innovative tool to evaluate gifted program inclusivity, this book is essential reading for all current and future leaders in gifted education.

Robin M. Greene is a national and international speaker, scholar, and practitioner. Dr. Greene is also the co-author of *Supporting Gifted ELLs in the Latinx Community: Practical Strategies, K–12* (Routledge, 2021) and is currently the supervisor of the Office of Gifted Education for the Colorado Department of Education.

Michelle Pacheco DuBois is a national and international speaker, scholar, and practitioner. Dr. DuBois is also the co-author of *Supporting Gifted ELLs in the Latinx Community: Practical Strategies, K–12* (Routledge, 2021) and is currently the coordinator of Gifted and Talented in Boulder Valley School District in Colorado.

Leading Culturally Responsive Gifted Programs

A Roadmap for Change

Robin M. Greene and Michelle Pacheco DuBois

Routledge
Taylor & Francis Group

NEW YORK AND LONDON

Designed cover image: © Getty Images

First published 2023
by Routledge
605 Third Avenue, New York, NY 10158

and by Routledge
4 Park Square, Milton Park, Abingdon, Oxon, OX14 4RN

Routledge is an imprint of the Taylor & Francis Group, an informa business

© 2023 Robin M. Greene and Michelle Pacheco DuBois

Library of Congress Cataloging-in-Publication Data
Names: Greene, Robin M., author. | DuBois, Michelle Pacheco, author.
Title: Leading culturally responsive gifted programs: a roadmap for change/Robin M. Greene and Michelle Pacheco DuBois.
Description: New York, NY: Routledge, 2023. | Includes bibliographical references. | Summary: Provided by publisher.
Identifiers: LCCN 2022058629 (print) | LCCN 2022058630 (ebook) |
ISBN 9781032276885 (hardback) | ISBN 9781032274690 (paperback) |
ISBN 9781003293729 (ebook)
Subjects: LCSH: Gifted children–Education. | Culturally relevant pedagogy. |
Educational equalization. | Multi-tiered systems of support (Education)
Classification: LCC LC3993 .G74 2023 (print) | LCC LC3993 (ebook) |
DDC 371.95–dc23/eng/20230301
LC record available at https://lccn.loc.gov/2022058629
LC ebook record available at https://lccn.loc.gov/2022058630

ISBN: 978-1-032-27688-5 (hbk)
ISBN: 978-1-032-27469-0 (pbk)
ISBN: 978-1-003-29372-9 (ebk)

DOI: 10.4324/9781003293729

Typeset in Palatino
by Deanta Global Publishing Services, Chennai, India

This book is dedicated to all the scholars and practitioners who have dedicated their lives to issues of social justice and inequities in gifted education. To the BIPOC leaders in gifted education and culturally responsive education who have paved the way and made this work possible, we are grateful. You have changed more lives than you know.

Contents

Figures

Foreword

Throughout my 30 years of experience as a classroom teacher, gifted specialist, literacy specialist, school administrator, state gifted specialist, national director of professional learning, and director of training and partnership development, I can attest to the dire need for greater emphasis on cultural responsiveness in teacher and leader preparation programs and staff development experiences. An unwavering advocate of equity, inclusion, diversity, and social justice, my strong beliefs can be traced back to my experiences as a student, when I knew some of my educators did not see my gifts or value my cultural differences.

For centuries, challenges to equitable access and services in education for minoritized student populations, most notably African American, have threatened the integrity and benefit of schooling. Not even Supreme Court decisions have resulted in a significant decline in the systemic, negative treatment of students of color. Over time, Native American students, neurodivergent students, LGTBQ+ students, students living in poverty, and twice and thrice exceptional (2e and 3e) students have also been on the receiving end of unwarranted mistreatment, disregard, and lack of access and equity in our nation's classrooms.

Not enough attention has been given to addressing the needs of the student diversity found in America's educational institutions. Concomitantly, there are educators charged with removing barriers for students considered "the least of these" who are hesitant or anxious about engaging in this work. In this timely publication, the authors share tips and describe the value in facing the reality of "place" in society with respect to race, culture, and privilege. The authors stress the critical need for school and district leaders to become well versed in culturally responsive leadership practices so they are better equipped to serve all students. The real-world examples and simple, effective tools provide educational leaders with explicit support to implement the strategies with fidelity.

Equity and social justice must be at the root of all policies and plans to increase access for students from all backgrounds. Quality gifted programming and talent development opportunities begin with plans for continuous evaluation and improvement of services. Careful and critical examination of identification and assessment protocols, data collection procedures, and multicultural curricular selections and practices must be a consistent part of an organization's culture in order to effect systemic and positive change. Leaders, far and wide, must espouse culturally responsive practices and policies to assure that all personnel under their direction receive targeted and engaged professional learning to execute a master plan to support, nurture, and instruct culturally and linguistically different students in inclusive and safe environments. To this end, the authors share tips to disrupt institutional and implicit bias and unpack personal feelings, even those steeped in family and institutional tradition. Albeit sometimes tough, ending the exclusionary practices that negatively impact the school experiences of culturally and linguistically different students is vital to their academic success.

Considering the multitude of students who are overlooked in America's public schools, educators need guidance in achieving equity in education and providing quality gifted and talented program services for all students. The authors meet this need through a discussion of both scaffolded support and advanced learning curricula for gifted and talented students via a culturally responsive lens.

In recent years, the term *culturally responsive leadership* has become more popular and taken on new energy. This publication is beneficial for educators in need of guidance in the implementation of culturally responsive strategies. Careful execution of the suggested strategies will transform the term from a popular buzz phrase to practical and beneficial application. While there is a wealth of information yet to be published on the topic, this text jumpstarts the critical conversations that can lead to greater impact in marginalized communities and populations.

Dr. Robin Greene and Dr. Michelle Pacheco DuBois, both scholars in the field, are dedicated to improving the experiences of students from culturally different backgrounds. Their personal and professional expertise is based on real-world experiences in gifted education, culturally responsive pedagogy, and culturally responsive leadership. The authors challenge educators to make a personal commitment to confront their positions of power and privilege. They share the value of embracing cultural differences among students, families, and school communities despite the potential challenges or setbacks that may be faced in the development of leadership pedagogies, practices, and policies to create inclusive schooling environments.

Leading Culturally Responsive Gifted Programs: A Roadmap for Change lays the groundwork for educational leaders, both within and outside gifted education, to address problems of practice and respond to thought-provoking questions that lead to proven solutions. A wealth of research-based strategies is shared with specific examples to guide classroom teachers and educational leaders on their pathway to equitable, culturally responsive practices. From local schools and districts to state and federal levels of leadership in gifted education, everyone should find value within this timely text. Equitable gifted program design options, identification and assessment practices, professional learning experiences for educators, and tips for quality program evaluation are shared. Educational leaders who are serious about engaging in equity work will find value in the user-friendly roadmap of viable and practical solutions to improve learning experiences and outcomes for all students, especially those from culturally and linguistically different backgrounds. This inclusive and comprehensive text will make an indelible mark on future scholarship and practices that improve the experiences of students, educational leaders, and institutions.

Dr. Erinn Fears Floyd, Founder
Equity and Excellence in Education, LLC
Director of Training and Partnership Development
The Consortium for Inclusion of Underrepresented Racial
Groups in Gifted Education (I-URGGE)

1

Overview and Introduction

Urgency and Need

Overview

Leading Culturally Responsive Gifted Programs has been written to serve as a foundational roadmap for school districts, administrators, and leaders of educational systems who want to create culturally, linguistically sustaining gifted education policies, practices, and programming that are antiracist. This book is a guide for individuals who are interested in effectuating tangible equity-focused changes for the learners in their own education context. In order for changes to occur, those reading this book must be willing to develop their cultural competency, critically examine the education system in which they are in (specifically gifted education), actively examine and work to dismantle institutionalized/systemic barriers in place for gifted students from historically marginalized populations, and recognize their own role in perpetuating systems of oppression. Those who read this book will find specific and immediate ways to make pivotal and sustainable changes. Furthermore, this book is also designed as a field guide outlining aspects of culturally responsive sustaining leadership and the administrative actions necessary for creating culturally responsive gifted education environments. Through experience-based leadership problems of practices, readers will engage in innovative and authentic applications of culturally

DOI: 10.4324/9781003293729-1

responsive gifted leadership to help support current and future leaders in gifted education.

To become a leader of culturally responsive gifted programs, you must be willing to become a culturally responsive leader, which involves embracing and expecting discomfort while actively working to dismantle systems of oppression. The "active" part of leading culturally responsive gifted programs lends itself to taking action steps that will develop antiracist behavior and ideas. Ibram Kendi (2019) describes an antiracist idea as "any idea that suggests the racial groups are equals in all their apparent differences—that there is nothing right or wrong with any racial group. Antiracist ideas argue that racist policies are the cause of racial inequities." To be an antiracist is to actively identify and eliminate racism by changing systems, organizational structures, policies, practices and attitudes so that power is redistributed and shared equally. Being culturally responsive while being antiracist means that you are honoring the cultures and the community of the staff, students, and families you serve while actively identifying and eliminating racist structures and systems.

Regardless of one's own ethnic/racial background, there are multiple pathways to get to becoming a culturally responsive and antiracist leader. Annalise Singh (2019), author of *The Racial Healing Handbook*, notes that becoming an antiracist for a white person includes acknowledging power and privilege, acknowledging feeling the need to promote multiculturalism, cultivating a desire for growth, etc. Becoming an antiracist for a person of color includes understanding that all racial groups are struggling in some way under white supremacy; acknowledging that there are class differences that can impact the degree of oppression people of color experience; challenging internalized white supremacy; and understanding that not all people of color are united in solidarity (Singh, 2019).

Throughout this book, as we engage in discourse regarding race, culture, ethnicity, equity, culturally responsive gifted leadership and antiracist behaviors, we may challenge some of your existing schemas regarding leadership, gifted programs, and possibly your own identity. For some of our readers, there *will* be moments when they experience cognitive dissonance. This dissonance will create varying emotional responses, uneasiness, and discomfort that are essential to individual growth towards cultural competency and developing as culturally responsive gifted leaders. If and when you feel uncomfortable, we ask that you take the steps we have as leaders to actively embrace the discomfort and learn from it by using these strategies that come from mindfulness and meditation: breathe, reflect, and adapt.

Strategy One: Breathe (Robinson, 2021). The first step in helping you embrace discomfort is to pause and take a deep, or diaphragmatic, breath that originates from the abdomen and specifically includes an exhalation that is longer than your inhalation. For example, when you come across something that causes duress, inhale deeply for four seconds and exhale slowly for five seconds or longer. We suggest you do this at least three times or until you feel calmer. The more you breathe, the more endorphins are released. Breathing when under stress is a mindfulness strategy that interrupts the body's flight-or-fight response. Breathing calms the parasympathetic nervous system and sends a message to the amygdala letting it know the body is not in danger, which then clears a proverbial path for the frontal lobe to allow you to reason and reflect. Breathing may sound simple, and still it may be hard to remember in the immediate moment. Breathing and taking a moment to pause are essential strategies in your culturally responsive gifted leadership journey that create a space for growth to occur and, when modeled, support others as they embrace discomfort.

Strategy Two: Reflect. The next immediate step you must take after breathing is to actively reflect upon the emotions that you feel and name them. Are you mad, frustrated, confused, sad, ashamed, or embarrassed? Why? What caused that emotion? Did we use words or phrases that are uncomfortable? Why are the words or phrases uncomfortable, and why do you think we chose them? Go back and re-read. Breathe. What in talking about race, equity, racism, cultural responsiveness, and/or gifted education causes those emotions to occur? In DiAngelo's (2018) book *White Fragility*, she shares that James Baldwin and W.E.B. DuBois wrote and spoke for years about the need for white people to look inward and to understand what it means to be white in a society that is divided by race. To develop cross-racial skills, one must sit with the "discomfort of being seen racially, of having to proceed as if our race matters (which it does)" (DiAngelo, 2018). In our years leading culturally responsive gifted programs and our continual development as culturally responsive leaders, we have learned that in discussing equity, racism, culture, antiracism, race, and gifted education, many emotions surface that originate from guilt, white fragility (DiAngelo, 2018), cultural mismatch, miscommunication, anti-intellectualism, and more. These emotions happen to people of all communities, and every time we have experienced these emotions, we have embraced them as learning opportunities in ourselves and in others.

Annalese Singh (2019) states, "To understand how racism works, it's important to know about your racial identity and your racial identity development." Therefore, regardless of your cultural identity, it is critical to understand your racial identity because that is your frame of reference. So as you read and reflect on any discomfort, take note of your emotions and ask: "Why am I feeling this way? How am I physically reacting to this, and why? What about my thoughts, beliefs, and/or actions are incongruent with my beliefs? How will I move forward with the new information? How will I create space for new information?" In asking yourself these questions, you are engaging again in mindfulness, allowing your body a moment to pause so that you can create space for emotional regulation and displaying resilience.

Strategy Three: Adapt. Adapt your behaviors, thoughts, and/or actions. After you have reflected upon your discomfort, the next step is to think about which behaviors, thoughts, and/or actions can or should be adapted. Remember, your reaction was data for you to notice about yourself and it is not to cause further guilt or shame—it is data. It is also possible that in the immediate moment, nothing needs to be adapted, other than your breathing, to help bring you back into the present moment. However, when you encounter cognitive dissonance regarding your identity and deeply held beliefs that may not be congruent with antiracist policies and practices or culturally responsive leadership, then it is critical to deeply think about why you are reacting in a specific way and what is within your locus of control that you can change.

These adaptations will range in size and type from technical quick fixes to adaptive/behavioral changes, and they do not always have to be large-scale changes to positively impact you on your journey towards creating culturally responsive gifted programs. For example, an adaptation may be countering a thought that you have with another and creating a different narrative when the thought comes back up. Remember that for as many moments as you feel uncomfortable when confronting leadership problems of practice and equity challenges, you will also have moments of joy, pride, and excitement. You will have moments as you read and think, "Yes, I am doing that, or I am doing it differently!" It is equally important to hold on to those emotions and reflect as well. You want to make sure that you can continue to create those emotions by creating systems and structures that sustain those positive responses.

Organization of the Book

Leading Culturally Responsive Gifted Programs is organized into eight chapters, with each of the chapters focusing on elements needed to help readers create and sustain culturally responsive gifted education programs. Through the use of *Contemplation Corners*, culturally responsive leadership scenarios, and snapshots of culturally responsive gifted leadership derived from the authors' professional and lived experiences, each chapter is designed to help readers reflect upon their own practices and determine action steps, if appropriate, for the development of culturally responsive gifted education programs within their local context. The first chapter serves multiple purposes. As you are reading now, the first chapter provides an overview of the book as well as explaining how to use this book to support your continuous learning and growth. Chapter 1 also presents the current state of affairs in gifted education in America, including the complex sociopolitical climate in which gifted learners and gifted programming are often at the center of debate. Chapter 1 focuses on the importance and need for culturally responsive leaders in gifted education and challenges readers' thinking about how to lead change in the context of some of the most volatile rhetoric in gifted education's history.

The second chapter develops readers' understanding of how leaders of culturally responsive gifted programs can intentionally create culturally inclusive learning environments. Chapter 2 shares the deep history of culturally responsive classrooms and their connection and their importance for creating inclusive spaces. Additionally, the chapter discusses the critical nature of understanding one's own cultural identity and how that identity shapes how educators perceive what learners and families are able to do, as well as how leaders perceive what their educators and students are capable of doing. The chapter includes discussion on how to recognize and interrupt implicit bias as key components to creating inclusive learning environments.. Chapter 2 helps leaders recognize, support, and implement the elements necessary for students and families to see their cultures and their neurodivergence as strengths that contribute to the physical, instructional, and psychological learning environments. Specific examples of designing culturally responsive lesson plans and creating culturally responsive gifted programming, both social emotional and academic, are shared to help leaders identify and create similar programs in their context.

Chapter 3 examines the role and responsibilities of administrators as designers of culturally responsive systems—designers who help nurture their staff members, students, and families and specifically support others in their culturally responsive journey by working towards cultural competency. Chapter 3 shares specific leadership dispositions necessary to lead culturally responsive gifted programs found in servant leadership. Utilizing Liberatory Design (Anaissie et al., 2021) mindsets that are the result of a collaboration between social justice and community activists across the United States and the National Equity Project (n.d.), the authors provide personal experiences as culturally responsive leaders. These examples of mindsets include building relational trust, practicing self-awareness, recognizing oppression, embracing complexity, focusing on human values, seeking liberatory collaboration, working within fear and discomfort, attending to healing, working to transform power, exercising creative courage, and encouraging transparency in ideas. The chapter focuses on specific ways in which leaders become culturally responsive and antiracist while centering on the needs of the community. Chapter 3 also addresses the role of implicit bias, microaggression, and systemic racism in leadership and helps leaders navigate through systems of oppression that are both internalized and externalized. Finally, Chapter 3 helps leaders understand how to manage both change fatigue, and Racial Battle Fatigue (Smith, 2004) by sharing examples of how to create culturally responsive and sustainable systems for gifted learners and the adults who support them.

Chapter 4 synthesizes the DuBois Greene Culturally Responsive Gifted Education Framework (Dubois & Greene, 2021), the Checklist for Culturally Responsive Gifted Best Practices (DuBois & Greene, 2021), and the National Association for Gifted Children's (NAGC) Master Checklist of Gifted Program Elements for Self-Assessment (Neumeister & Burney, 2012) into a Gifted Program Inclusivity Evaluation tool (G-PIE). The G-PIE was designed to be used as a model for creating and examining culturally responsive practices within gifted programs. Chapter 4 discusses each area of the G-PIE and outlines ways in which changes can be made when leaders in gifted education focus on leading cultural shifts within their systems.

Chapter 5 explores the importance of data and how it can be utilized to positively and proactively address discrepancies and increase access for students of color to gifted education services. This chapter explains how data can help determine root causes of disproportionality among student groups and significantly change the way educational systems respond with action steps. The authors give examples of easy and specific tools that have been used in our practice to support readers' own understanding of how to determine the root cause of disproportionality within their own context. Chapter 5 also shares the role of equity audits and the types of data that leaders can collect to determine the inclusivity of their programs. Chapter 5 also explores Donna Y. Ford's (2013a) equity allowance formula and how it can highlight discrepancies within systems and guide leaders to create equity goals focused on equitable access to gifted education services for culturally and linguistically diverse students.

In Chapter 6, the authors will guide readers as they think about systems and structures that are needed to develop and sustain culturally responsive gifted programs. Chapter 6's focus on systems includes asking readers to examine the local district and state-level systems that must be in place to develop an inclusive network of support. Chapter 6 includes a focus on Culturally Responsive Multi-Tiered Systems of Support, or CR-MTSS (Collins, 2021), and how CR-MTSS can be used as a strength-based approach for making data-based decisions for gifted services within a complex multilevel organization.

A critical element in leading culturally responsive programs is ensuring that family engagement is a continuous and authentically integrated component of the gifted program. Chapter 7 will help leaders recognize that in order for gifted programs to truly be culturally responsive, leaders must intentionally create space to listen to, hear, and respond to families to lead continuous improvement. This chapter examines the term *family engagement* and discusses how family engagement should not be treated as an event or something that happens *to* the community; engagement happens *with* the community. Chapter 7 will guide leaders to recognize antiquated family engagement tropes and adapt traditional Eurocentric family engagement into family engagement practices that will meet the needs of the multiple cultures within their communities. A discussion about comparing individualistic cultures to communal cultures and demonstrating how school administrators can adapt traditional Eurocentric family engagement methods to support the different cultures and cultural norms present in their school community. This chapter will give examples of ways to bring families into conversations when developing or refining gifted programs so that they represent the need of the learner, and how to build community awareness and advocacy for gifted programs using the strengths of the community as the foundation. The authors will share how to develop authentic family engagement opportunities, such as creating family-facilitated learning communities to build understanding of giftedness and advocacy opportunities, assessing community needs through empathy interviews and authentically listening, developing advisory committees, and using interpreters and translators in all community languages at every event and in every communication so as to show language as a strength.

The concluding chapter, Chapter 8, invites the reader to explore authentic leadership problems of practice by engaging them through a series of culturally responsive leadership scenarios and equity challenges. Each one of these scenarios has been experienced by the authors, and we invite readers to reflect on how they would solve the equity challenges faced. Through these experience-based leadership problems of practice, the authors share innovative and authentic applications of culturally responsive gifted leadership to help support current and future leaders in gifted education. Questions will be posed to the reader for further reflection, and recommendations will be outlined for future practice based upon our experiences.

How to Use This Book

Leading Culturally Responsive Gifted Programs is designed for educational leaders at the school, district, and state level as well as the gifted and general educators they serve, who are committed to impacting and redesigning systems so they can create culturally responsive and sustaining gifted programs. The authors want to challenge readers to be actively engaged while reading. The ideas in this book can be used in a variety of ways that can be differentiated to meet the specific needs of the reader for their learners and their families. It is up to the reader, however, to self-select the most appropriate way to differentiate their own learning and process. There are two different ways to approach learning with this guide. Firstly, you can choose to read each chapter by itself, stopping to reflect and use the elements that are most pertinent for your specific and immediate needs as you develop and lead culturally responsive gifted programs; or, as a second option, you can choose to read the book in its entirety, engaging with each activity, scenario, and program review with a holistic approach while using prior learning from the chapter before to think deeply about how your current systems, practices, and policies can be redesigned to authentically meet the needs of the learners in front of you. The application of what you read and learn in *Leading Culturally Responsive Gifted Programs* will be critical for your personal and professional growth.

This book should be utilized in professional learning environments such as workshops, professional learning communities, and small group and individual book studies for school, district, and state leaders and administrators, as well as with practitioners who work with gifted and advanced learners. The topics in the book will act as a guide to support staff training, coaching conversations for continuous improvement, and engaging families by supporting the entire community. Each chapter provides questions that can be used as part of ongoing professional learning or coaching sessions. As stated previously in the chapter, school leaders and district and state administrators who are committed to creating antiracist gifted education by changing systems and providing equitable educational access to culturally responsive gifted services for learners and their families will find the book's content useful in their equity journey and practice.

Although this book is written for those who work primarily with or are leading programs and programming for gifted and advanced learners who are historically marginalized and not included in gifted programming, there are many universal educational truths within the information presented in this book. These truths can be adapted across multiple programs (general education, special education, multilingual education, etc.), preschool through 12th grade (P-12), by leaders interested in creating, nurturing, and sustaining culturally responsive education programs and developing antiracist policies. Every educational leader can take the tenets in this book and apply them across different contexts to honor every student's culture by developing policies and practices that celebrate the diversity of experiences within the community and the nation. Additionally, as part of a continuous improvement cycle, school districts or leaders will find this book helpful as a template for examining their services for these learners and how they support equitable access of opportunity to rigorous programs.

Additionally, because this book is the first of its kind, this book may be used as a foundational text for graduate-level university classes in educational leadership, curriculum and instruction, etc., with a concentration on neurodiverse and special populations such as gifted and talented learners. Furthermore, this book can also be used as supplementary text for university courses focusing on gifted and talented education, culturally responsive leadership within education, leadership of gifted programs, and special education, and by others interested in pursuing antiracism in educational practices.

Finally, we have designed this book for you to write in and take notes as you would in a workbook, and as an essential tool to add to your own educational-equity and social justice toolkit for vulnerable populations of learners that cannot continue to be overlooked. Therefore, we ask that you engage with the text as you read. Annotate. Use highlighters, use sticky notes, keep a journal, or record your thoughts and reactions using whatever tools and technology help you capture your thoughts.

Earlier in the book, we discussed the need to be mindful of the emotions you are experiencing. It will be critical to note any emotions you are feeling as you read. When or if you notice an emotional reaction, write when that reaction surfaces, in relation to what topic, and what, if anything, about your behaviors or actions as a leader needs to be adapted. As you read, talk to others about what you are reading and engage them in the same conversations about specific leadership equity challenges. Ask them about some of the problems of practice and equity challenges posed in the book, or develop your own to accompany the ones in the text. Solicit diverse viewpoints and thoughts to challenge your thinking and intentionally create moments of cognitive dissonance.

Because this book will be a part of your educational equity and social justice toolkit as you work daily to battle against implicit and explicit biases while redesigning educational practices with the strengths of culturally and linguistically diverse learners to guide you, you must actively work towards cultural competency and be a culturally responsive leader yourself. Therefore, in every chapter, there are places for you to reflect upon what you have read, what you may have learned about yourself, and what steps you may need to take on behalf of yourself, your students, and or your staff and community to apply new learning. These sections in the chapters are titled *Contemplation Corners*.

Answer the questions and reflect upon some of the authentic leadership equity challenges that we, the authors, have experienced. Ask other colleagues some of the questions we ask in the book. In order to lead culturally responsive gifted programs and disrupt systems of white supremacy and racism, you have to engage others in conversations about race and educational equity. Have brave conversations with others and yourself. Be honest with yourself about your role in the system of education and how you can be a part of the change process. However you choose to use this book, it is our hope that the content will be inspiring and helpful to readers to motivate them to make a pivotal change in their systems toward providing access and opportunity for culturally and linguistically diverse gifted learners.

Introduction

Current National Context

Equity. As we write this in the year 2022, the P–12 public education system in the United States is at a watershed moment in terms of how we choose to embrace the intersectionality of race, gender, class, language, ability, and equity. There are multiple private-interest groups that are loudly influencing the future of education. Their influence includes, but is not limited to, what books are placed in libraries and classrooms, the curriculum being taught, policies created, and imposing ideological belief systems that oppress and silence the voices of the students, families, and educators for whom our schools are meant to protect; including Black Indigenous People of Color (BIPOC), gifted and talented students, students within the LGBTQIA community, and those in poverty. The loudest groups are utilizing a familiar trope within white supremacy culture that Jones and

Okun (2001) noted as the right to comfort. Specifically, those in power have the right to psychological and emotional comfort, and they scapegoat those who cause discomfort. The opportunity to attain educational equity is causing discomfort for some in power.

Currently, the phrases *equity, diversity and inclusion*, and *social emotional learning* are becoming weaponized by politicians and lobbyists focused on K–12 settings who are creating policies that directly dictate curriculum standards and education practices impacting what and how millions of students learn across the United States. In addition to equity, diversity, and inclusion, there are political action groups vociferously conflating Critical Race Theory with educational equity and have been able to convince many families that schools are "indoctrinating their children with a woke agenda" (Florida Government, 2021), thereby putting many of the equity-focused initiatives that school districts, school committees/school boards, and educational organizations had planned in a holding pattern. Some groups, such as the Massachusetts Association of School Committees, have taken a proactive role in dispelling myths to help their families understand the difference between CRT and equity so that families are informed (MASC, n.d.). Critical Race Theory is a theoretical framework first developed among legal scholars in the 1970s to analyze the impact of race on the legal system. That theory is now being applied to education, and most recently gifted education, with the introduction of GiftedCrit in Greene's (2017) seminal work as a way to analyze the impact of racism in gifted education. Equity, in particular educational equity, is a K–12 term that is associated with the legislation of the 2002 No Child Left Behind Act (NCLB) (U.S. Department of Education, n.d.), and with its renewal under the new name, the Every Student Succeeds Act (ESSA) (U.S. Department of Education, n.d.) in 2015. That legislation tasked public education to disaggregate data based on student demographics to close achievement and excellence gaps (Plucker & Peters, 2016). From that legislation, Department of Education agencies in each state put guidance in place for school districts to develop equity initiatives to help close achievement gaps between BIPOC and white learners. NCLB and ESSA specifically name gifted and talented students as students who must also be recognized and on whom data must be collected and disaggregated to monitor achievement.

Although there is a loud minority of voices trying to instill fear and hold on to power, by focusing their efforts on school boards and committees, curriculum, and standards, there are other groups countering those voices so that BIPOC students will get the education that they need. Equity organizations like The Gemini Group, The National Equity Project, and others are national groups devoted to informing families about the beauty of diversity, equity, and inclusion, so that all students are seen for their cultural values and the contributions that they bring to the classroom and society each and every day. They are working directly with educational institutions, businesses, lawmakers, and communities and community activists to help advocate for all people to be included and valued.

Equity and Gifted Education

The most current data from the Office of Civil Rights shows that over 3.3 million students are identified as being enrolled in gifted and talented programs (Office of Civil Rights, 2018); however, this number only encompasses those who are formally identified and not those learners who are gifted and talented but who have not met the threshold or set of parameters the school, district, or state constructed for identification/enrollment. Of the 3.3 million learners, the disaggregated data tells the more accurate story of who gets to be identified in America. Within those numbers, 8.2% of those learners are Black, 18.3% are Hispanic, 9.9% are Asian, 0.7% are Indigenous Americans, 58% are white, 0.2% are Native Hawaiian, 4.2% identify with two or more races, 2.8% are served under IDEA, and 2.4% are English Learners (Office of Civil Rights, 2018). Because sexuality or genders other than male and female are not documented (and we are in a social climate where that may still be dangerous for some of our students), we do not have accurate statistics for students who identify as members of the LBTQIA community. An emerging body of research, however, is showing that "the population of gay, lesbian, and bisexual students may be much higher than previously realized" (NAGC, n.d.), and we must ensure that we are working to include all learners in gifted programs.

Through equity audits of policies and practices to close achievement and excellence gaps, school districts and even government officials are continuously reviewing educational programs and programming that are creating disparate outcomes for learners. In some areas of the United States like New York City, New York and Seattle, Washington, leaders are looking at programming that is not representative of the greater population they serve, and it is their gifted programming, like so many others across the country, that remains overwhelmingly white and affluent (Wright et al., 2017; Ford, 2013a, 2013b; Orfield et al., 2014). Thus, what we are witnessing is the term *gifted and talented* becoming more taboo by the day, and gifted programming across the United States is not only under scrutiny; some programs are being dismantled completely in the name of equity. Rather than dismantling the system that we already have and denying access to Black and Brown learners, it is our moral responsibility to instead dismantle systems of white supremacy and create structures that are grounded in culturally responsive practices; therefore we need culturally responsive leaders in gifted education leading culturally responsive gifted programs. "Eliminating gifted programs is the highest form of discrimination, suggesting that underrepresented populations cannot BE gifted. It is a shrewd, rapidly spreading bias. Affluent families will always find a way to get their students what they need" (Davis, 2021).

The razing of gifted programs under the guise of equity is what Wright and Ford refer to as "smoke and mirrors" and does not address the root cause of the systemic and structural racism that are "like many U.S.-created institutions normed on whiteness and grounded in racism" (Wright & Ford, 2021). In order to shift the narrative for Black Indigenous People of Color (BIPOC) in white-dominant systems throughout education, specifically gifted education, it is essential that district and school leaders ensure that they are culturally responsive gifted leaders. Scholars within the field of gifted education have been discussing creating culturally inclusive spaces for gifted learners for over 40 years, and the work around characteristics and culturally responsive classrooms has helped move the field slightly; however, there is still a component that the field has yet to examine in detail: culturally responsive gifted leaders. Culturally responsive leaders are administrators who are capable of guiding others at the school, district, and state levels to make systemic changes, creating pathways for BIPOC learners to engage in enriched and accelerated learning opportunities in culturally responsive and sustaining systems.

Our gifted students of color must have culturally responsive antiracist leaders who are devoted to actively creating systems in which equity, diversity, and inclusion thrive. This includes leaders who honor and center community-based perspectives of historically marginalized communities by creating policies that are antiracist and challenge deficit thinking of students and who recognize that gifted potential exists in all socioeconomic, ability, ethnic, racial, cultural, and linguistic groups of children. Why is this important? The United States population is becoming a more diverse and linguistic group of people. The Pew Research Center (2022) noted that the U.S. Hispanic population reached 62.1 million in 2020, which is an increase of 23% over the previous decade. The Black population is also expanding in the United States. In 2019, 46.8 million people in the U.S. identified their race as Black, either alone or as part of a multiracial or ethnic background, which is an increase from 2000, where there were 36.2 million (Tamir, 2021). More and more immigrants are moving into the U.S. from other countries for various reasons from war torn countries or countries where crime is forcing families to flee in order to not succumb to ideals that they do not share. We can no longer, as a society, be allowed to continue to look at the color of a person's skin or their language and measure their worth or ability on that basis. This practice in schools begins with educators changing mindsets and shifting the paradigm of deficit thinking about students that are not from the majority culture. Leaders must examine their personal belief systems and engage with their staff in a collaborative dialogue to challenge thinking about BIPOC learners in their school settings. They must purposefully build the capacity of others to identify and disrupt inequities in their buildings, districts, and state levels.

A Brief History of Culturally Responsive Education

In order to become a culturally responsive antiracist leader in one of the most diverse and rapidly changing demographic educational systems the United States has seen, leaders must understand the history of culturally responsive education and gifted education and where the two intersect. However, as we begin a leadership journey together, it is important to have the timeline of this work as it lays the groundwork and serves as a crucial reminder of what is pedagogically sound for all of the learners in our classrooms. As Harmon (2012) states while referencing the work of scholars such as Donna Y. Ford, Gloria Ladson-Billings, and Geneva Gay, "Culturally responsive education is one of the most effective means of meeting the learning needs of culturally different students."

The term *culturally responsive teaching* was first introduced by Gloria Ladson Billings in 1995 as she investigated the pedagogical practices of exemplary African American teachers of African American students. She describes culturally responsive teaching as a pedagogy that recognizes the importance of including students' cultural reference in all aspects of learning (Ladson Billings, 1995). Since that research, numerous qualitative and quantitative research studies have shown that students from diverse backgrounds learn best in environments that are "relational and personal, have high expectations for self and others, and are similar to what is present in an extended family" (Harmon, 2012).

Culturally responsive and relevant pedagogy has had multiple names throughout research and has been referred to as *culturally responsible, culture compatible, culturally congruent, culturally relevant* and *multicultural education* (Harmon, 2012). For the purposes of this, text the authors are using Geneva Gay's (2000, 2010) description stating that culturally responsive pedagogy uses "cultural knowledge, prior experiences, frame of reference, and performance styles of ethnically diverse student to make learning more relevant and effective ... It teaches to and through strengths of the students. It is culturally validating and affirming" (Gay, 2000, p. 29).

Every student, BIPOC and white, comes to the classroom with a culture that must be recognized and valued, and the work of

Ladson Billings and researchers who came after her showed that students perform their best when they feel safe. Students feel safe when their school supports and recognizes their culture. This support may or may not be explicitly understood by the student, and that is where the hidden curriculum can enfranchise or disenfranchise entire groups of learners.

Schools and the Hidden Curriculum

Schools are microcosmic versions of society, and we, as leaders, must instill in our students that they are part of a community that reflects the larger society. Even as far back as 1907, John Dewey stated, "Each one of our schools is an embryonic community life, active with types of occupations that reflect the life of the larger society and permeate throughout with the spirit of art, history, and science." The school is the society and each building has a set of stated and unstated rules, or norms, that children must adapt to and work with, just as they do with the norms of society. Schools are cross sections of society representing varied cultural, linguistic, socioeconomic, and neurodiverse learners. In a mini society, children start learning to live with others, share their sorrows and happiness, and develop the qualities of cooperation, tolerance, love, friendship, and sympathy, which are very necessary skills in society (Partap College of Education, 2017).

If our schools are mirroring society, then we must acknowledge and address the hidden curriculum that operates within our schools. The hidden curriculum refers to the unwritten, unofficial, and often unintended lessons, values, and perspectives that students learn in school (The Glossary of Education Reform, 2017). This includes educator and administrator mindsets, implicit bias, and behaviors that they model on a daily basis for students. The hidden curriculum is different from the school curriculum, which encompasses lessons, skills, and knowledge taught through direct instruction. It is not taught through direct instruction; it is learned through observation and informal instruction. The hidden curriculum consists of the unspoken or implicit academic, social, and cultural messages that are communicated to students while they are in school (The Glossary of Education Reform, 2017).

In its most damaging form, the hidden curriculum is the unintentional manifestation of educators' and the education system's implicit bias and systemic racism, ableism, sexism, and classism. It is critical that leaders recognize and evaluate their own implicit bias and the hidden curriculum that is within their school, district, or state organization because the values and lessons reinforced by the hidden curriculum are often accepted as the status quo. The implicit message becomes that practices and messages aimed at students from historically marginalized populations do not need to change—even if they are contributing to undesirable behaviors and results, whether it's bullying, conflicts, or low graduation and college-enrollment rates, for example (The Glossary of Education Reform, 2017). These accepted status quo practices and messages in the hidden curriculum are centered around social expectations of gender, language, behavior, and morals.

A hidden curriculum has the potential to either positively or negatively impact students and learning environments. For example, if a hidden curriculum values English and Eurocentric values and negates the heritage languages of students, this can have a negative impact on students who are emerging bilinguals as they can feel forced to assimilate into the majority culture. Across the United States, the hidden curriculum can also be observed as a separate classroom of English learners isolated from their English-speaking peers throughout the majority of the day, or students with disabilities in windowless classrooms, or gifted education classrooms that are primarily white while general education classrooms are racially and ethnically diverse. These hidden curricula expose organizational decisions that have been made that send unintentional messages to learners about their cultural worth, belonging, and academic potential.

These organizational decisions may be rooted in implicit bias or in unconscious unintentional assumptions people make, or they could be part of a larger systemic bias and have an impact on how educators view learners as well as how learners view one another (Gonzalez et al., 2018). Morris (2005) in "Tuck in that Shirt!" points out that perceptions of race, class, and gender guide educators' assumptions of which students lack cultural capital and reinforce race, class, and gender stereotypes. He argues that the hidden curriculum in schools forces young people of color to act and dress like white people. In being forced to "act white," the message that is sent to students is that one culture is more superior to others, thus reinforcing white supremacy in a very subtle way.

Another example of a hidden curriculum might be the message that students of color or with a disability have less academic skill or potential than students from other cultures. This can be seen at the micro level within a classroom and the types of rigorous materials that an educator gives to their student, the importance they place on Eurocentric values like individualized work and extra credit or sitting still (Glossary of Education Reform, 2017), the books in the classroom, the language on the wall, how the educators speak to the learners, who in the classroom is praised for asking questions and or being quiet, and if there is inflexible ability grouping and tracking. At the meso level, the hidden curriculum can further be observed in how the school leader structures the overall schedule and assigns those in historically marginalized populations to educators and specific classrooms. It can also be explored at the macro level of the entire school system. When looking at a school district, urban or rural, identify which students are receiving resources and supports that affirm the students' cultural worth and sense of belonging. When there is an obvious disparity in funding between schools or districts, there is room to interpret a negative and pernicious hidden curriculum assigning value to historically marginalized learners. This may not be the intent; however, it is the impact nonetheless.

Alternatively, the hidden curriculum might mirror the ideals and vision of a school messaging the integrating and celebrating of the multicultural diversity of the student body by inviting students and parents to share stories about their home country, for example, or by posting and publishing informational materials in multiple languages (The Glossary of Education Reform, 2017). The espoused theory and the theory of action demonstrating an inclusive and affirming hidden curriculum will be seen at the school and by the district whose secondary building, for example, ensures that it has honors classes, general education classes, classes for students with special education needs, multilingual learner classes, etc. on the same floor if possible, and allocates the same funding and quality materials. Furthermore, as seen in schools with supportive hidden curricula, there will be evidence-based practices such as ability and flexible grouping while using culturally responsive practices and intentionally creating opportunities for student and family experiences to be included (Greene, 2017).

Investigate and observe the hidden curriculum in your organizational system. Does it reflect diverse ways of thinking about students of color? Does it honor students' heritage languages? Does the hidden curriculum align with the organization's cultural and equity beliefs? A hidden curriculum can reinforce the lessons of the formal curriculum, or it can contradict the formal curriculum, revealing hypocrisies or inconsistencies between a school's stated mission, values, and convictions and what students actually experience and learn while they are in school (The Glossary of Education Reform, 2017).

Embracing Culturally Responsive Leadership

So what are the next steps in this equlty leadership journey? First, continue reading this book. We are going to take you on a journey towards leading culturally responsive gifted programs that includes you taking action to create or refine culturally responsive gifted programs and becoming a culturally competent leader, which, as was mentioned before, includes discomfort. Second, remain open to experience and reflection as you read this book. Think about your context and how the situations we describe apply to you. Engage with the tools we have given you to reflect and take time to truly understand the emotions you are feeling as they relate to the work that you are doing to support gifted culturally linguistically diverse learners. Next, analyze your current hidden curriculum, bias, leadership problems of practice, policies, practices, and the behaviors that drive them. It is also equally important not to allow yourself to become mired in the analysis for so long that you cannot make a decision as to what to do next. Then, reflect where you can take accountability for supporting the hidden curriculum and perpetuating bias; everyone has a role to play in the microcosm of education and society and no-one is absolved. After you have analyzed, reflected, and taken accountability, the last piece of the puzzle is to act. Think: What are the action steps you can take as a leader of culturally responsive gifted programs in your building or your organization to build the capacity of others? This book will give you tangible steps within your locus of control to create antiracist micro, meso, and macro systems for gifted students from historically marginalized populations that will create opportunities for all of the learners in your classrooms.

As stated earlier, in addition to gifted education and programming coming under scrutiny, words like *culturally responsive, social emotional learning, critical race theory*, and even the term *equity* itself have faced challenges from various political organizations who intend to influence curricula and school boards. Our intent is not to politicize any of these words because when we deal with the lives of children and the future state of the world, we must remain focused on research and practical application that has proven to result in an increase in student scores and improvement in student and teacher morale, and supports the nurturing of the whole child—the main charges of education and the Department of Education. Instead, we intend to follow the words of Lord Robert Baden Powell, and help leave the world better than we found it based on personal experiences and research. The timing of this book, however, is critical for leaders of gifted education programs because it helps give the language and tangible tools to develop culturally responsive antiracist practices and policies during a time when equity is being overtly politicized and helps eliminate distractions for those on a mission of inclusion. This book lays the foundation by giving guidance on how to develop the reader's own culturally responsive leadership and create culturally responsive gifted education programs.

Key Points

♦ Self-reflection is an important piece of an educational leader's equity journey.

- Engage others in conversations about race and educational equity.
- Gifted potential exists in all socioeconomic, ability, ethnic, race, culture, and linguistic groups of children.
- Build the capacity of others to identify and disrupt inequities in your systems.
- Culturally responsive pedagogy is inclusive of all cultures and is a critical component in educational success for BIPOC learners.
- Eliminating gifted programming in Black and Brown neighborhoods is a racist act and continues to deny gifted Black and Brown learners access to the high-quality instruction afforded to their white peers.
- Recognize and understand the positive and negative hidden curricula within your schools, district, and state level.
- Equity leaders must be willing to become antiracist in their journey to eliminate systems of oppression.
- To become a leader of culturally responsive gifted programs, you must be willing to become a culturally responsive leader, which involves embracing and expecting discomfort while actively working to dismantle systems of oppression.

References

Anaissie, T., Cary, V., Clifford, D., Malarkey, T., & Wise, S. (2021). *Liberatory design*. http://www.liberatorydesign.com

Collins, K. H. (2021). *Servicing 2e and 3e learners using Collin's culturally responsive multi-tiered system of support*. https://www.sengifted.org/post/3e-learners

Davis, J. L. (2021, November 12–14). *Eliminating gifted programs increases inequity* [Conference session]. National Association for Gifted Children Conference, Denver, CO.

Dewey, J. (1907). *The school and society*. University of Chicago Press.

DiAngelo, R. (2018). *White fragility: Why it's so hard for White people to talk about racism*. Beacon Press.

DuBois, M. P., & Greene, R. M. (2021). *Supporting gifted ELLS in the Latinx community: Practical strategies K–12*. Routledge.

Florida Government. (2021, December 15). *Governor DeSantis announces legislative proposal to stop W.O.K.E. activism and critical race theory in schools and corporations*. https://www.flgov.com/2021/12/15/ governor-desantis-announces-legislative-proposal-to-stop-w-o-k -e-activism-and-critical-race-theory-in-schools-and-corporations/

Ford, D. Y. (2013a). *Recruiting & retaining culturally different students in gifted education*. Prufrock Press.

Ford, D. Y. (2013b). Gifted underrepresentation and prejudice-learning from Allport and Merton. *Gifted Child Today, 36*(1), 62–67.

Gay, G. (2000). *Culturally responsive teaching: Theory, research, and practice*. New York: Teachers College Press.

Gay, G. (2010). Acting on beliefs in teacher education for cultural diversity. *Journal of Teacher Education, 61*, 143–152.

Gonzalez, C. M., Garba, R. J., Liguori, A., Marantz, P. R., McKee, M. D., & Lypson, M. L. (2018). How to make or break implicit bias instruction: Implications for curriculum development. *Academic Medicine: Journal of the Association of American Medical Colleges, 93*(11S Association of American Medical Colleges Learn Serve Lead: Proceedings of the 57th Annual Research in Medical Education Sessions), S74–S81.

Greene, R. M. (2017). Gifted culturally linguistically diverse learners: A school-based Exploration. In *Perspectives in gifted education: Influences and impacts of the education doctorate on gifted education* (Vol. 6). Institute for the Development of Gifted Education, Ricks Center for Gifted Children, University of Denver.

Harmon, D. A. (2012). Culturally responsive teaching though a historical lens: Will history repeat itself? *Interdisciplinary Journal of Teaching and Learning, 2*(1), 12–22.

Jones, K., & Okun, T. (2001). *Dismantling racism: A workbook for social change groups*. Change Work.

Kendi, I. X. (2019). *How to be an antiracist*. One World.

Ladson-Billings, G. (1995). Toward a theory of culturally relevant pedagogy. *American Educational Research Journal, 32*(3), 465–491.

MASC. (n.d.). *Understanding the difference between critical race theory (CRT) and educational equity*. https://www.masc.org/images/news/2021/ MASC_CRT_2021.pdf

Morris, E. W. (2005). "Tuck in that shirt"! Race, class, gender, and discipline in an urban school. *Sociological Perspectives, 48*(1), 25–48.

National Association for Gifted Children. (n.d.). *LGBTQ diversity toolbox for administrators – Introduction.* https://www.nagc.org/lgbtq-diversity-toolbox-adminstrators-introduction

National Equity Project. (n.d.). https://www.nationalequityproject.org/

Neumeister, K. S., & Burney, V. (2012). *Gifted program evaluation: A handbook for administrators & coordinators.* Prufrock Press.

Office of Civil Rights. (2018). *2017–18 state and national estimations.* https://ocrdata.ed.gov/estimations/2017-2018

Orfield, G., & Frankenberg, E. (with Ee, J., & Kuscera, J.). (2014). *Brown at 60: Great progress, a long retreat and an uncertain future.* The Civil Rights Project/Proyecto Derechos Civiles.

Partap College of Education. (2017). *School as a miniature society.* http://partapcollege.org/national-seminar-on-school-as-a-miniature-society/

Pew Research Center. (2022). *U.S. Hispanic population continued its geographic spread in the 2010s.* https://www.pewresearch.org/fact-tank/2022/02/03/u-s-hispanic-population-continued-its-geographic-spread-in-the-2010s/??

Plucker, J. A., & Peters, S. (2016). *Excellence gaps in education: Expanding opportunities for talented students.* Harvard Education Press.

Robinson, S. (2021). *White antiracism & racial healing: Racial healing in community.* https://aea365.org/blog/White-antiracism-racial-healing-racial-healing-in-community-by-lenka-berkowitz-libby-smith/

Singh, A. A. (2019). *The racial healing handbook: Practical activities to help you challenge privilege, confront systemic racism & engage in collective healing.* New Harbinger Publications, Inc.

Smith, W. A. (2004) Black faculty coping with racial battle fatigue: The campus racial climate in a post-civil rights era. In D. Cleveland (Ed.), *A long way to go: Conversations about race by African American faculty and graduate students at predominately white institutions* (pp.171–190). Peter Lang Publishers.

Tamir, C. (2021). *The growing diversity of Black America.* https://www.pewresearch.org/social-trends/2021/03/25/the-growing-diversity-of-black-america/

The Glossary of Education Reform. (2017). *Hidden curriculum*. https://www
.edglossary.org/hidden-curriculum/

U.S. Department of Education. (n.d.a). *Every student succeeds act (ESSA)*.
https://www.ed.gov/essa?src=rn

U.S. Department of Education. (n.d.b) *No child left behind*. https://www2
.ed.gov/nclb/landing.jhtml

Wright, B. L., & Ford, D. Y. (2021). *Smoke and mirrors: Challenging the
elimination of gifted and talented education under the guise of universal
access for all children*. https://www.diverseeducation.com/opinion/
article/15279782/smoke-and-mirrors-challenging-the-elimination
-of-gifted-and-talented-education-under-the-guise-of-universal
-access-for-all-children

Wright, B. L., Ford, D. Y., & Young, J. L. (2017). Ignorance or indifference?
Seeking excellence and equity for under-represented students of
color in gifted education. *Global Education Review, 4*(1), 45–60.

2

Creating Culturally Inclusive Learning Environments

Culturally Responsive Gifted Teaching Overview

When gifted students of color walk into the school or classroom every day, "half of the curriculum walks in the door with the students" (Emily Style, 1982). Leaders of culturally responsive gifted programs must have teachers who understand the essential components of culturally responsive education and teaching and its intersectionality with gifted education. The term *culturally responsive teaching* was first coined by Geneva Gay (2002), who wrote, "when academic knowledge and skills are situated within the lived experiences and frames of reference for students, they are more personally meaningful, have higher interest appeal, and are learned more easily and thoroughly." Culturally responsive teaching is a pedagogy that recognizes the importance of students' cultural references in every aspect of learning by using the students' customs, experiences, and perspectives to drive the learning environment and experiences. This type of teaching helps create a sense of belonging for students of color in academic and traditionally white spaces. To understand how to teach with culturally responsive gifted practices, it is critical to review the history of culturally responsive education and the intersectionality of gifted education.

DOI: 10.4324/9781003293729-2

The Roots of Culturally Responsive Education

The roots of culturally responsive pedagogy and teaching can be traced back to the emergence of African American schools during the period of Reconstruction in the United States.

Early African American schools were using culturally responsive teaching and culturally congruent practices long before the 1954 Supreme Court case, *Brown v. Board of Education* (National Archives, n.d.). In the 1960s, multiethnic basal editions of children's books were created at Banks Street College in New York to help provide mirrors and windows for learners. The pedagogical practice of culturally responsive education gained momentum in the 1970s with the work of Abrahams and Troike (1972), who stated that "Teachers must capitalize on the cultural differences as a resource to help build the dignity of the learner" (p. 6).

During the same time period, culturally responsive teaching was redefined as *multicultural education*, focusing on the belief that all people have intrinsic worth and recognizing human diversity through the elimination of prejudices, biases, and stereotypes based on sociodemographic variables (Ford, 2011). Multicultural education centers around instructional practices, classroom experiences, and school environments that are inclusive and embody the lived experiences of racially, ethnically, and linguistically diverse learners (Gay, 2010, 2018; Ladson-Billings, 1995).

Throughout the 1970s and into the mid-1990s, scholars and researchers continued to explore the impact and importance of culturally responsive practices in classrooms. During this time, Gloria Ladson-Billings began examining the practices and reflections of pedagogical exemplary teachers of African American students. This work led to the development of a framework outlining culturally responsive and culturally sustaining pedagogy practices (Ladson-Billings, 1995). Her framework continues to inform current thinking and instructional practices regarding culturally responsive educational practices today (DuBois & Greene, 2021) and includes attention to outcomes based teaching, authentic assessment techniques, high expectations, authentic learning activities, and the integration of student learning styles.

There are multiple layers that intersect between multicultural education and gifted education. Ford (2011) suggests the two fields are more similar than different and when combined form multicultural gifted education based on the fundamental beliefs that (a) gifted education must integrate the philosophy of diversity from multicultural education, and (b) multicultural education must incorporate the philosophy of an elevated curriculum by challenging culturally different students cognitively and academically. As educators and administrators, we have seen how closely the two tie together and have used these practices within our work, both in the classroom and at administrative levels across the organization.

An example of culturally responsive and gifted education practices working together can be seen in *A Culturally Responsive Equity-Based Bill of Rights for Gifted Students of Color* (Ford et al., 2018). The ground breaking work of Drs. Donna Y. Ford, Kenneth Dixon, Joy Lawson Davis, Michelle Trotman-Scott, and Tarek Grantham was written to "effect change based on equity and cultural responsiveness" (Ford et al., 2018). It demonstrates a commitment to families of culturally diverse students and affirms the rights of students of color to an education that offers them opportunity and access to rigorous coursework and culturally relevant experiences. The Black scholars who united to create the Bill of Rights are renowned experts in the fields of gifted education, special education, and multicultural education. For leaders of culturally responsive gifted programs, the Bill of Rights is a holistic approach outlining what is necessary to desegregate gifted education and advanced learner programs to support and advocate for students of color (Ford et al., 2018).

Another example of culturally responsive gifted practices from NAGC is the *2019 Pre-K–Grade 12 Gifted Programming Standards* (NAGC, 2019). These standards outline the design guidance for an exceptional gifted education program. The standards are viewed by gifted educational leaders as the gold standard to reach in their gifted education programs. There are multiple student outcomes within the standards that have embedded culturally responsive practices such as Standard 4 learning environments in which the cultural competence student outcome states:

- Students with gifts and talents value their own and others' languages, heritages, and circumstances.
- They possess skills in communicating, learning, and collaborating with diverse individuals and across diverse groups.
- They use positive strategies to address social issues including discrimination and stereotyping (NAGC, 2019).

The Professional Learning standard student outcome for ethics states:

- All students with gifts and talents, including those who may be twice exceptional, English language learners, or who come from underrepresented populations receive equal opportunities to be identified and served in high-quality gifted programming as a result of educators who are guided by ethical practices (NAGC, 2019).

These are just a few examples of culturally responsive gifted education practices that are making a difference in the identification practices and gifted services for our students of color.

Contemplation Corner

What other scholars are you familiar with that have laid the foundation for culturally responsive gifted pedagogical practices? How has their work informed your practice?

Recognizing Implicit Bias

The mention of recognizing implicit bias is most important here in this chapter as educators' perceptions and implicit biases regarding their students, families, and cultures continue to impact not only how they see and treat students of color, but also the educational environment and ultimately the success of students. Therefore, it is critical that leaders recognize implicit bias and work with educators and other personnel to identify and interrupt implicit bias. Zaretta Hammond (2015) defines implicit bias as the unconscious attitudes and stereotypes that shape our response to certain groups. You might be saying to yourself right now that you do not have any bias towards students of color or that you see all students as the same color. Everyone has biases of some sort that are either intentional or implicit. Implicit bias occurs involuntarily, often without your awareness or intentional control; this is different from explicit racism, which is an intentional behavior intending to harm a person based upon the color of their skin (Hammond, 2015). Implicit bias is rooted in neuroscience and how your brain processes large amounts of incoming information by using a shortcut we know as stereotyping, which is the overgeneralized belief about a particular group of people (Hammond, 2015). This could be something such as the belief that all tall people play basketball, all Latinx people enjoy eating tacos, or all gifted children earn high grades in school. It is important to remember that everyone has stereotyping impulses. This is an evolutionary trait (Hammond, 2015).

It also critical to recognize implicit bias and actively interrupt these thoughts. So seek counter narratives to those thoughts, because if you do not counter those thoughts once you recognize them, then you are no longer engaging in implicit bias—you are being explicitly biased. Taking a few courses on social justice and equity, or having your staff take a few courses on justice and equity, does not make you culturally competent and bias-free. You must continue to remind yourself to not be complacent in your thinking. Instead, be introspective and reflect upon how you perceive students and their families. Are you an asset-based or deficit-based thinker?

Understanding Your Cultural Identity

Creating a culturally inclusive environment is not something that you do to students through culturally responsive teaching alone. In order to have a truly culturally inclusive environment, you must have the mindset of including cultures in all aspects of your work. Before you can engage in understanding your students' culture, you must begin with your own. An important step in creating culturally inclusive environments is examining your beliefs by understanding your cultural identity. Your cultural identity impacts how you view the families, students, and fellow educators with whom you work. It impacts how you react and respond to people, the environment, and your own thoughts. Furthermore, your cultural identity (your self-perception and self-conception based on your culture) can act as an open or closed door to inclusive environments for culturally linguistically diverse learners without you even realizing what is happening. Hammond (2015) uses the metaphor of a tree when talking about cultural identity. However, you may be familiar with the cultural iceberg model developed by Hall (1976) where if the culture of a society was an iceberg, then there would be some aspects visible, above the water, but there is a larger portion hidden beneath the surface. The authors acknowledge Hall's model and its importance, but we prefer Hammond's tree as a visual icon because it portrays cultural identity as part of a bigger ecosystem that shapes and impacts its growth and development. As we examine the parts of Hammond's culture tree, reflect on your own cultural identity and your students' and families' cultural identities.

Contemplation Corner

How might reflecting upon your own cultural identity change the way you look at students and families of color?

On Hammond's culture tree there are three levels: surface, shallow, and deep. Hammond (2015) describes surface culture as the observable fruit that the tree bears. *Observable* is the key word here. Surface culture is anything that you can visibly see. The surface level has a low emotional charge and centers around concrete elements such as food, dress, music, and holidays (Hammond, 2015). This is often the level of culture that schools will focus on when they believe that they are being culturally responsive. This typically results in students bringing in food or celebrating holidays around the world in class. While this is one aspect of culture, it is egregious to stop here and does not truly explore the elements of someone's culture. Staying at this level also creates opportunities for stereotypes to form and students from culturally linguistically diverse backgrounds getting reduced to stereotypes.

Shallow culture is visualized as the tree branches and the bark of the tree. On this level are the unspoken rules around everyday social interactions and norms such as courtesy and attitudes towards elders, the nature of friendships, concepts of time, personal space between people, nonverbal communications, rules about eye contact, and appropriate touching (Hammond, 2015). For instance, in some cultures when speaking with a person you make direct eye contact, and in other cultures direct eye contact is considered disrespectful and rude. Some cultures consider being late as an impolite action and other cultures think of time as not a fixed concept but a flexible one, so they often arrive after a stated time. The shallow level does have a strong emotional charge because some behaviors can be considered as disrespectful, offensive, or hostile (Hammond, 2015). Thus, students may be doing something that in their culture is the norm but in your culture might be considered rude. So how do you react to these cultural differences? Do you reprimand the student or do you learn more about the student's culture so that you understand why the behavior occurs and then you can adapt and change your expectations to reflect the value of the student's cultural background?

Deep culture acts as the foundation for how we approach problem solving and define relationships with one another, our own self-concept, what we deem to be fair, and even whether or not we prefer competition or cooperation. Deep culture is one of the most important levels as it is one that cannot be seen and carries our deep cultural beliefs and behaviors. Deep culture is similar to the root system of a tree and is what grounds us as individuals and nourishes our mental health (Hammond, 2015). This is how two people can look at the same event and have very different reactions based on their deep culture. For instance, in many eastern cultures, the color red is a symbol of good luck, but in western cultures it is a symbol of bad luck. While our individual culture grows and evolves, our deep cultural roots help our brain make sense of the world; when this is challenged, we experience some dissonance. Sometimes with that dissonance we grow—and sometimes we retreat and dig down deeper. When creating culturally inclusive environments for students and staff, you cannot retreat and dig down deeper, nor can you afford to have your families and staff dig down and retreat. Instead, you must actively model how you are learning about your cultural identity, demonstrate empathy and curiosity for others' cultural identities, and work through cultural mismatches and misunderstandings based on those previously mentioned levels of Hamond's tree, together.

Collectivism and Individualism Cultures

Although cultures may visibly be different at the surface and shallow levels, there are many common values at the root system of the tree that are present. These roots offer educators another dimension to look at students through a set of commonalities or cultural constructs that were first introduced by Dutch sociologist Geert Hofstde, known as collectivism and individualism (Brewer & Venaik, 2011). Collectivism and individualism reflect "fundamentally different ways the brain organizes itself" (Hammond (2015). While our brains are hardwired towards a communal view of the world for survival, as people moved from rural communities to urban communities, people became more individualistic. Collectivistic societies tend to emphasize the importance of interdependence within communities, relationships, and cooperative learning. Individualistic societies tend to emphasize the importance of independence and self-sufficiency. In the United States, the dominant culture is individualistic; however, the cultures of many of the students in our classrooms who are Black, African, Latinx, and Indigenous are collectivist. The dominant culture of those who have made laws and set up our modern education system, and even the gifted education system, came from individualistic cultures (European cultures) and are at a cultural mismatch with the very students we serve.

Understanding collectivism and individualism informs how students in the classroom may prefer to work, compete, view world problems, problem solve, and ultimately interact with one another. It may also inform how you as a leader prefer to lead your staff and create systems, and what you expect from your programs and the types of programming you offer for your learners. Understanding the different cultures in your building and similar root systems will allow you to help educators create inclusive spaces and work through potential cultural mismatches, as they may or may not have been raised in a collectivist environment. In grouping cultures together based on similarities in value systems, we do not want to oversimplify nor stereotype. Remember that no culture is a monolith, and that even within individualistic and collectivist cultures, there are additional dimensions that could have communities within those groups adopt different characteristics seen across cultures. This is especially true as different cultures connect to one another and marry, sharing traditions and blending cultures and values. There are also different degrees of individualism and collectivism within cultures. However, understanding the overall values associated with collectivism and individualism can help you lay a strong foundation for inclusion and build empathy across your building.

Culturally Responsive Gifted Learning Environments

Leaders of culturally responsive gifted programs recognize that every aspect of the learning environment is an integral part of a student's success in school. Learning environments not only include the space for learning but also encompass the cultures of the classroom, the school, and the district. There are three types of learning environments that we will discuss here: physical, psychological, and instructional (Watts, 2022). The physical learning environment begins when you walk onto a school campus. Is the school inviting and welcoming of diverse learners? Are the languages of the families in the school visible and used throughout the building for all to see? Are there pictures of the students and families in the hallways, in the school office, and in any common spaces, including the teacher's lounge? Is student work visible immediately? Are collectivist culture values exhibited, such as teamwork, working for the good of the community, and celebrating one another's success?

In the classroom, the physical learning environment consists of the lighting, furniture, the layout of the classroom, the arrangement of tables and chairs, how the learning materials are arranged, the breakout spaces, the color of the walls, the materials on the walls and whiteboards, etc. The images displayed should reflect culturally different students, ideally representing those whose cultures are within the classroom and community, and the materials on the wall should be in the students' heritage languages. It will be filled with student-created materials so that the students have a voice that is readily visible in the classroom. For classrooms in which students are acquiring English, sentence stems with critical thinking statements are an excellent support to have. This will help all learners in the classroom thrive, not just those who are learning an additional language.

The physical learning environment must be a safe and accepting space so that learners are able to express themselves as they are, not as they might pretend to be in order to fit into a classroom where the culture may be different than their own. The addition of fidgets, wiggle chairs, resistance bands, sensory tools, and multiple types of seating options are supportive of neurodivergent learners as well and helps create a safe space. There should be no use of negative or stereotyping phrases that refer to individuals or groups of students. The environment must not only espouse cultural acceptance, neurodivergent acceptance, and trust among students; it must also cultivate belonging. Additionally, there should be space to allow and encourage the verve of students who may display that in their learning. Culturally responsive teachers and administrators know how to create an environment that the brain perceives as safe and nurturing, which allows the brain to relax, let go of any stress, and focus on learning (Hammond, 2015), and this begins when students enter the door.

The psychological learning environment is the way in which administrators and teachers form welcoming spaces by the warmth of their tone, the temperament of their personality, and their emotional dispositions, which are the foundation of all learning. Educators' relationships that are built on trust and rapport among students makes students feel safe and inclusive and allow for students to be open to learning. Gay (2010) says that positive relationships are one of the major pillars of culturally responsive teaching and are as important as the curriculum. When we think about our families who come from collectivist, community-based cultures where relationships are the bedrock of all social, political, and cognitive endeavors, it resonates how powerful and valued relationships are to these families (Hammond, 2015).

A positive psychological learning environment allows for students to take risks, ask questions, and receive feedback without experiencing judgment or the feeling of not being heard. Students react positively to warm demanders, or educators who "expect a great deal of their students, convince them of their own brilliance, and help them to reach their potential in a disciplined and structured environment." Ware (2006) showed that warm-demander pedagogy can create a culture of achievement for African American students. This idea of being a warm demander creates a sense of respect and trust among teacher and students. Forming trusting relationships with students is vital to providing students with a sense of belonging. When students feel safe, their brain produces a hormone called oxytocin, which stimulates the brain to want to make connections with others (Hammond, 2015).

One way to form positive trusting relationships with students is to let them know that you care about them through words and actions. Making personal and authentic connections with students is vital to the success of students who are culturally different. Teachers and administrators may need additional training in how to support students whose cultures are different from their own and how to create a psychological safety net where students can be themselves. Later in this chapter, we will discuss how leaders of culturally responsive gifted programs can specifically ensure that educators and other administrators create psychologically safe environments by focusing on their own perceptions of gifted culturally linguistically diverse learners and biases.

Instructional learning environments, including the specific instructional practices utilized by educators, play significant roles in students' access to schooling and social-emotional security within their classrooms and schools. These settings should embrace and value the cultural assets that students bring to school and recognize the importance of their cultural wealth. Chapter 7 digs deeper into cultural wealth and the cultural assets that students of color and their families bring to the school community. Culturally responsive classrooms and schools have materials and books within their instructional settings that contain rich stories and portrayals of culturally different people highlighted in a positive way and not stereotyped in a negative way—which is historically the way culturally different people have been portrayed in history books. They will tell the stories of Black and Brown members of society and will offer counternarratives to a white European view.

Often, our Black and Brown students are given learning materials in which they do not see themselves in the stories or content. They do not see any aspects of their culture, beyond heroes and holidays, included in content and stories. However, when students are able to see themselves in content being taught, they become more invested in their own learning. Emily Style in her 1988 monograph "Curriculum as Window and Mirror" first referred to students being able to view content through their own culture as a "mirror." The term *mirror* represents the reflection of yourself that you can see in the content you are receiving. Style (1988) suggests that all students deserve a curriculum that mirrors their own experiences and their own culture, thus validating and building their identity. The term *window* refers to content that students can see through the experiences of others that are different from their own experiences. Stories and content rich with culturally linguistically diverse experiences and perspectives provide all students with cultural understanding that can lead to discussions about social justice and antiracism (Synder & Fenner, 2021).

Culturally responsive educators hold high expectations for all of their students. They view each student as a successful and productive member of their classroom as well as a partner in their learning journey. They see learners as having the ability to be independent critical and creative thinkers and have deep appreciation for the students in their classroom. Educators must check their implicit bias and how it might be impacting their students' learning. Are students of color receiving less rigorous content because the expectation of the teacher is that these students will be easily frustrated with more rigorous content? Is the expectation of the teacher based upon a student's skin color or culture? These are questions that educators and administrators must routinely ask themselves in an ongoing internal conversation to ensure that they are working with students of color at the same level of instruction as other students from the majority culture.

Contemplation Corner

As a culturally responsive leader of gifted programs, what are two strategies that you can implement within your context to create learning environments that positively impact culturally linguistically diverse learners?

Culturally Responsive Gifted Instructional Practices

Culturally responsive gifted instructional practices are those practices that are focused on students' assets and strengths, which includes recognizing the value of students' language, culture, and life experiences while incorporating best teaching practices in gifted education (DuBois & Greene, 2021).These practices are beneficial for all students but are necessary for gifted students to be successful students and humans who are the next generation of intellectual and creative thinkers in the world. In this chapter, instructional practices will be broken down into sections: social-emotional and academic. These sections are not meant to be extensively detailed as the authors have provided additional content focused on instructional practices in Chapter 4 and in their previous book, *Supporting Gifted ELLs in the Latinx Community: Practical Strategies, K–12*. Instead, these practices are meant to remind you about what should be in place, what evidence-based practices we have used that work, and to begin thinking about structures, systems, and professional learning needed in your context to ensure that culturally linguistically diverse gifted learners have access to inclusive learning environments.

Social-emotional

As we write this book, the social-emotional needs of gifted students have become increasingly urgent. It is clear that our world has become a constant barrage of conflict not limited to racial injustices, gender discrimination, educational inequality, political chaos, human rights injustices, and the social-emotional fallout from the pandemic for our students. As adults we are struggling to navigate our way through the injustices that surround us on a daily basis. Can you imagine how our culturally different gifted students with high emotional intelligence and a sense of social justice are doing this? We must consider that culturally different students are challenged every day in their school environments with implicit bias remarks or microaggressions from classmates, teachers, and administrators. These students may choose to assimilate to the majority culture in their school, which can cause conflict within their native peer group. So how do we empower culturally diverse gifted learners to develop their social-emotional competencies? Leaders of culturally responsive programs can create opportunity and access for culturally inclusive environments by supporting students' social emotional needs by embedding evidenced-based social emotional strategies in their school or district environments and providing training to educators and administrators on these strategies.

Bibliotherapy

One strategy that can be effective in addressing the social-emotional needs of gifted students is bibliotherapy, which is the use of literature to help students connect with characters and situations

that are familiar to them. Books that represent culturally different characters can guide students to recognize that their gifted
characteristics and behaviors are not unique to them but that
there are other people like them who have the same experiences.
Bibliotherapy can be an effective way for students to develop
problem-solving skills, increasing compassion, growing empathetic understanding, and enhancing self-awareness (Pehrsson
& McMillen, 2007). Bibliotherapy is particularly impactful when
students see themselves and elements of their deep and shallow
culture in the main characters and story. These books are what
Rudine Sims Bishop (1990) refers to as mirror books. Bishop notes
that the "dominant social groups have always found their mirrors
in books, but they, too, have suffered from the lack of availability
of books about others. They need books as windows onto realities … that will help them understand the multicultural nature of
the world" (Bishop, 1990). By providing mirror books for culturally linguistically diverse learners, the learners receive messages
about their value and worth, from their language and speech
patterns to their traditions. Literature that depicts authentic culturally linguistically diverse characters and authors who are
culturally different portraying success and positive characteriza-
tion can be powerful. It can encourage others to reflect on themselves and to think inwardly. Bibliotherapy can clarify values and
instill cultural identity and ethnic pride in students (Pehrsson
& McMillen, 2007). Leaders of culturally linguistically diverse
gifted programs can have their educators, librarians, and fellow
administrators search on the internet or in their local library for
mirror and window books with culturally linguistically diverse
characters, or books by BIPOC authors, to ensure that students
see themselves and their peers represented in the classroom.

Mentorships

Mentorships are partnerships that have the ability to transform
lives by nurturing the passions of gifted culturally different
students (DuBois & Greene, 2021). They have been researched
extensively in gifted education research and have been used
in the authors' practice as ways to support culturally linguistically diverse gifted learners' psychosocial and career needs. The

mentor can serve as a role model and advocate for their mentee's psychosocial needs by sharing common experiences, offering windows into different experiences, transferring values, and offering moral support by establishing a friendly and supportive relationship with the mentee. The impact a mentor can have on career supports includes coaching, supporting internships, opportunities for career development in a specific field, accessing scholarships, helping prepare for interviews, and carrying out daily tasks associated with careers, as well as considering the challenges gifted culturally linguistically diverse learners will face in a chosen field of study or interest (Vrabie & Cretu, n.d.). Pairing mentors with students that have the same interests and passions can elevate the partnership because of converging interests. For students of color, mentors can be helpful in boosting students' self-confidence and heightening their aspirations as the relationship grows and develops (Berger, 1990). Mentors sometimes become tightly connected to the students they work with and they may follow up with families about the students' lives even after the mentorship is discontinued. Mentorships, when intentionally created, facilitate the development of racial and ethnic identities, and research has shown that they can combat the effects of discrimination. In multiple studies, ethnic identity is linked to positive outcomes for learners of culturally diverse backgrounds (Peifer et al., 2016). This positive outcome is linked when students are paired with mentors who are culturally competent, and it can happen in cross-cultural relationships as well as in mentorships among members of the same race and ethnicity groups (Sánchez & Colón, 2005)

Affinity Groups

Affinity groups are groups of people who come together because of a similar purpose, cause, interest, or ideology. There are times when culturally different students need a platform to voice racial concerns and develop their racial and ethnic identities. They need a safe place where they can speak freely among their cultural peers who may be facing some of the very same racial stress and social concerns they are facing. Affinity groups can serve students in this way and allow them to gather together with others who share the same cultural identity. A place where they can talk about issues related to that identity, and transfer that discussion into action, will make for a more equitable experience at school (Bell, 2015). When students' cultural identities are valued and respected, they have an openness to learn and thrive. It is equally important for families and staff members to have affinity groups as well so that they are able to speak about specific concerns and issues they are facing as culturally linguistically diverse individuals with gifted children or gifted students. When thinking about creating inclusive environments, leaders must also consider the impact on staff and include every member in the building.

Self-Advocacy

Self-advocacy is a powerful tool that students can use to voice their educational needs to schools, in districts, and at the state level. Davis and Douglas (2021) have developed a new and expanded definition of self-advocacy specifically for the gifted students who are also part of one or more special populations:

- Self-advocacy is the dynamic process that enables high potential students to claim their right to an education that addresses their unique intellectual, academic, psychosocial, and cultural needs without endangering their self-esteem or that of others.
- It is a compilation of culturally responsive and inclusive empowerment strategies that open opportunities for positive academic and life outcomes previously precluded for some students due to stereotyping, systemic biases, and limited access to resources (p. 3).

When students learn self-advocacy skills and are able to use these skills to advocate for their own needs to those who work with them, they can become the creator of their own learning environments. Too often in high-school settings, culturally different students are guided to take grade-level classes and not advanced grade-level courses. There are multiple reasons why this practice takes place, which include low expectations, bias, and systemic oppression. Therefore, it is important to start teaching self-advocacy skills early for culturally linguistically diverse gifted learners. Teaching them how to say what they need as soon as they can speak is critical because many students from collectivist cultures and those who are gifted are worried about being a burden for their teacher. Or they may have had a negative experience when asking for help or sharing what they needed to learn (i.e. movement, laughter, accommodations). As a leader of culturally responsive gifted programs, your job is to help educators understand how different cultures may or may not advocate for themselves without stereotyping these cultures.

When you create a culture where culturally linguistically diverse gifted students become aware of their assets and their challenges, while giving them the language scaffolds to advocate for their needs as they continue to grow, you are also teaching the educators who work with them how to respond to students as they continue to voice their needs. This also gives teachers who may not have been taught self-advocacy skills in their childhood and youth the opportunity to learn what positive self-advocacy looks like and how to advocate not only for their students, but for their needs as educators in the building. In essence, you are helping build self-efficacy for your entire community. When we give our culturally different gifted students self-advocacy skills we give them a voice and a choice to change these practices. Self-advocacy skills are one of the most powerful tools that students of color can have in their toolkits.

Attending to Intersectionality

The concept of intersectionality describes the ways in which systems of inequality based on race, gender, sexual orientation, disability, and class intersect and create dynamics that are unique to that individual person. We see this in gifted education, for example, when a gifted Black female with dyscalculia wearing a Hijab is denied access to advanced classes despite the body of evidence showing her ability. We cannot overlook how she might be discriminated against, nor disassociate any of her identities, such as being Muslim, Black, having a disability, being female or being gifted, from one another, because together they create her unique perspective and view of the world. Each identity may also be the cause of a form of discrimination for the student.

The culturally inclusive environment will affirm and validate intersectionality for the learner. Another way in which the gifted education field has been diving into intersectionality is by looking further at students who are thrice exceptional (3e). 3e students are those students who display three exceptional conditions: being culturally diverse (members of a socially oppressed group), being gifted, and simultaneously being identified by or having another disabling condition (such as a learning disability) (Davis & Robinson, 2018). It is important to recognize that intersectionality among 3e students has a significant impact on the social-emotional wellbeing of these students. These students can have low expectations for themselves due to their complex multidimensional profiles. They may be bullied or ostracized as they try to fit in at school. Teachers may not recognize or understand the complexities of being 3e and may instead choose to not notice that these students have different needs both academically and emotionally. What can we do as culturally responsive gifted educators and administrators? We can have high expectations for these students, speak to their strengths, and put academic and social emotional supports in place so that they can be successful throughout their educational journey and thrive.

Contemplation Corner

As culturally responsive leaders in gifted education, what are some practices that you can implement in your building and or at the district/state level to address culturally different students' social emotional needs?

We must consider that our students from culturally diverse backgrounds have experienced racism and oppression throughout their school years, which has affected their sense of self identity and worth. In order to support culturally different gifted students, we must put in place culturally responsive social emotional engagement practices to support these students' sense of self-worth and cultural identities—practices that ensure that students feel culturally and linguistically safe to be themselves in their classrooms and schools.

Academic

The authors believe that a culturally responsive teaching environment displays Gay's (2018) eight distinguishing qualities of culturally responsive teaching. These qualities are:

- *Validating,* seeing cultural differences as assets, incorporates multicultural information, resources, and materials in all subjects
- *Comprehensive and inclusive,* teach to the whole child, committed to students maintaining their cultural identities
- *Multidimensional,* wide range of cultural knowledge, experiences, contributions, and perspectives across contents
- *Empowering,* infrastructures that support student confidence to take academic risks and experience success
- *Transformative,* actively engages students to become social critics and change agents committed to greater equality among ethnic groups
- *Emancipatory,* authentic knowledge about different ethnic groups accessible to students allowing students to be liberated both psychologically and intellectually
- *Humanistic,* concerned with the human welfare, dignity and respect of various individuals and groups
- *Normative and ethical,* parallel rights and opportunities to historically marginalized ethnic groups that are historically reflective to the Eurocentric culture (pp. 36–46)

These traits are reflective in culturally inclusive environments where culturally different students' heritage cultures are respected and valued. There are high expectations for all students; these are not based upon the color of their skin or the culture they represent. The content delivered in the classroom portrays different cultures in respectful and positive ways. While it is important to have ethnic content in school curricula, it is equally important to combine the ethnic content with instructional strategies that emphasize inquiry, critique, and analysis rather than rote memory and regurgitation of factual information (Gay, 2018). Authentic learning is the basis of culturally responsive classrooms. They incorporate project-based and interest-based learning with real-world applications that are culturally relevant. There is programming embedded with authentic social justice dilemmas in which culturally linguistically diverse students can see themselves reflected in the content. Instructional strategies are used to support increasing curricular challenges such as the upper levels of Bloom's Taxonomy, the Depth and Complexity Framework, and Webb's Depth of Knowledge Framework. Developing a student's critical and creative thinking skills should be embedded into all of the content areas. Access for students to books in which they can see themselves and their cultural ancestors demonstrates that these culturally different students are valued and respected.

Snapshot: Affinity Group

BIPOC and Gifted

This group was created by students who were interested in talking about the intersectionality of being Latinx, Black, and Indigenous and being identified as gifted. The students wanted to meet after a talk on being bright, talented, and Black, but the students wanted to expand it to other students of color.

The group met weekly and were multiage high schoolers. They even set up online meetings for students who could not attend in person. The students spoke about what it meant to be identified as gifted and the pressures of being gifted within their family or cultural group. They shared that just being together in a safe space was important for them. They opened up one meeting once a month to Allies to come and support them to help provide windows into their world so as to have advocates and build common understanding of their experiences.

Designing Culturally Responsive Lessons

When thinking about how to support educators in a building or district, leaders of culturally responsive gifted programs must also think about how to approach education with their gifted culturally linguistically diverse learners as learning experiences, and therefore should think of lesson planning as an opportunity to design experiences for their diverse learners. Stembridge (2020) provides a framework for lesson planning with equity in mind. Stembridge suggests that educators design experiences for culturally linguistically diverse learners with beliefs and goals for conceptual understandings. Leaders of culturally linguistically diverse gifted programs can have their educators, instructional specialists, gifted specialists, and more do this by having their them begin with the following questions:

- What are our beliefs about students?
- How does culturally responsive education inform our practices and our thinking?
- What conceptual or profound understanding do we want for our students to walk away with?
- In what types of authentic ways will students demonstrate their understanding?
- What types of instructional practices are planned for students?
- Before, during, and after the lesson, how do we want learners to feel? (adapted from Stembridge, 2020)

When asking educators to confront their beliefs about what students are able to do prior to the start of planning a lesson, Stembridge highlights the importance of educators bringing forward their implicit and explicit bias. By starting off a lesson with this thinking, educators can begin to ground themselves in asset-based thinking. Do educators really think that their students are capable of doing higher level work? How do they know? Have the educators pre-assessed the learners in an authentic demonstration of learning and in their heritage language if necessary, or are they making assumptions?

As educators are thinking about the overarching goals and essential understandings of the lesson that they want their learners to understand, they must also consider the impact of their own instructional moves and how being culturally responsive in their approach will create an equitable environment for the learner. This is the heart of culturally responsive lesson planning and designing with equity in mind, because Stembridge's framework asks teachers to truly consider the culture of each student and meet them where they are at while keeping high expectations. The framework outlines six themes that must be a part of every lesson for the lesson to be considered culturally responsive and engaging: cultural identity, relationships, asset-focused factors, vulnerability, engagement, and rigor. These concepts are detailed here:

Cultural identity: The focus of cultural identity is to ensure that students' culture is validated and affirmed, and that it is a positive experience. Questions leaders can have their educators ask when planning lessons include:

- How does instruction specifically make reference to culture?
- How does instruction allow students to draw from their cultural roots, traditions, values, etc.?

Relationships: This portion of the framework is focused on how the instructional design can build relationships and strengthen the classroom community. Questions leaders can have their educators ask when planning lessons include:

- How does this lesson build community in the classroom?
- How do teachers leverage existing relationships, or build new ones, with students at different levels of engagement?

Asset-focused factors: These are students' strengths that are not limited to cognitive or achievement ability alone. They could include students' interests, affects, personality, and passions. Leaders can have educators ask questions such as the following when planning lessons:

- How are students' strengths appropriately leveraged in education (across all domains)?
- How does the lesson help students understand their strengths and patterns as learners to allow potential for growth?

Vulnerability: This is about creating moments for vulnerability and risk taking to exist in your experience. This is an important lesson for students to learn from one another, and from the teacher and administrator. Questions that leaders can have educators ask when planning could include:

- What are some of the environmental risk factors this student faces (poverty, taking sister to school three times a week early, trauma, etc.)?
- What protective factors (resilience, nurturing and attachment, etc.) are in place to increase risk taking during the lesson or after?
- What does risk-taking look like for the student or for the educator?
- How does the lesson and instructional design encourage risk-taking?

Engagement: This is the ability to hold students' interest and have them interact with the material and curriculum behaviorally, affectively, and cognitively. Leaders can help educators dive deeper into this section by having educators ask themselves:

- How does the instruction truly engage students within all three domains of interest?
- How does it model what engagement looks like?
- How is it differentiated?

Rigor: This is the final component of Stembridge's framework and refers to accelerated and more sophisticated levels of Bloom's Taxonomy to ensure that all students have access to higher order thinking skills. Rigor also requires a bit of cognitive dissonance and pushing students outside of their zone of proximal development. Leaders can sit with their educators and think about rigor layered with culture and equity by considering the follow questions:

- How does the instructional design move students along Bloom's beyond recall and apply?

- How can instructional design incorporate the Bloom-Banks Matrix (Ford, 2011)?
- In what ways do students construct their own meaning and grapple with cognitive dissonance?
- How does the instruction lead students to make new connections and evolve their understanding of the concept?

Creating a culturally inclusive environment in the classroom utilizing lesson design in this way will take time and planning. As a leader of culturally responsive gifted programs, it is imperative that you create time and help your educators design lessons in this way and teach administrators the core components of this work.

Conclusion

As a leader of culturally responsive gifted programs, you must be able to create culturally inclusive learning environments, recognize inclusive learning environments when you see them, and help build the capacity of others to create inclusive learning environments as well. The most immediate and tangible place where this can be seen is at the school level within classrooms. The work to create culturally inclusive learning environments cannot stop at the school level; otherwise the work will not be sustainable. Leaders must work on establishing systems and structures at the district level for district-wide adoption of some of the evidenced-based strategies we shared earlier, such as culturally responsive bibliotherapy, culturally responsive gifted education with trained educators and administrators, acceleration policies, dedicated collaboration across departments to teach general education teachers how to design culturally responsive lessons, and ongoing implicit training and conversations around race. Without this, the foundation for culturally inclusive learning environments will be built on shifting sands that will not outlast the leader nor support culturally linguistically diverse gifted learners.

Key Points

♦ There is no formula for creating culturally inclusive environments, but there are key ingredients.

♦ Both leaders and their teams must examine and interrupt their implicit bias.

♦ An essential component of culturally inclusive environments is recognizing that cultural identity and the impact it has on students and families is an important step towards cultural competency.

♦ Understanding the different types of cultures and the values that different cultures may bring to the classroom will help build relationships.

♦ It is important to recognize that intersectionality among 3e students of culturally different gifted students has a significant impact on the social-emotional wellbeing of these students.

♦ There are high expectations for all students; these are not based upon the color of their skin or the culture they represent.

♦ Culturally inclusive environments must be present at all levels of the educational organization so that systems of oppression can be disrupted.

References

Abrahams, R. D., & Troike, R. C. (Eds.). (1972). *Language and cultural diversity in American education*. Prentice-Hall.

Bell, M. (2015). *Making space*. https://www.learningforjustice.org/magazine/summer-2015/making-space#:~:text=This%20example%20of%20collective%20action,a%20more%20equitable%20experience%20at

Berger, S. L. (1990). *Mentor relationships and gifted learners*. https://www.hoagiesgifted.org/eric/archived/e486.html

Bishop, R. S. (1990). Mirrors, windows, and sliding glass doors. *Perspectives: Choosing and using books in the classroom 6*(3), ix–xi.

Brewer, P., & Venaik, S. (2011). Individualism—Collectivism in Hofstede and GLOBE. *Journal of International Business Studies, 42*(3), 436–445. http://www.jstor.org/stable/29789431

Davis, J. L., & Douglas, D. (Eds.). (2021). *Empowering underrepresented gifted students: Perspectives from the field.* Free Spirit Publishing.

Davis, J. L., & Robison, S. A. (2018). Being 3e, a new look at culturally diverse gifted learners with exceptional conditions. In Kaufman, S. B. (Ed.), *Twice exceptional: Supporting and educating bright and creative students with learning difficulties* (pp. 278–289). Oxford University Press.

DuBois, M. P., & Greene, R. M. (2021). *Supporting gifted ELLs in the Latinx community: Practical strategies, K–12.* Routledge.

Ford, D. Y. (2011). *Multicultural gifted education.* Prufrock Press.

Ford, D. Y., Dickson, K. T., Davis, J. L., Scott, M. T., & Grantham, T. C. (2018). Culturally responsive equity-based bill of rights for gifted students of color. *Gifted Child Today, 41*(3), 125–129.

Gay, G. (2002). Preparing for culturally responsive teaching. *Journal of Teacher Education, 53*(2), 106–116.

Gay, G. (2010). *Culturally responsive teaching: Theory, research, and practice* (2nd ed.). Teachers College Press.

Gay, G. (2018). *Culturally responsive teaching: Theory, research, and practice* (3rd ed.). Teachers College Press.

Hall, E. T. (1976). *Beyond culture.* Anchor Books.

Hammond, Z. (2015). *Culturally responsive teaching & the brain: Promoting authentic engagement and rigor among culturally and linguistically diverse students.* Corwin.

Ladson-Billings, G. (1995). Toward a theory of culturally relevant pedagogy. *American Educational Research Journal, 32*(3), 465–491.

National Archives. (n.d.). *Brown v. Board of Education, 347 U.S. 483 (1954) (USSC+).* https://www.archives.gov/milestone-documents/brown-v-board-of-education

National Association for Gifted Children. (2019). *2019 pre-k–grade 12 gifted programming standards.* NAGC.

Pehrsson, D., & McMillen, P. (2007). *Bibliotherapy: Overview and implications for counselors (ACAPCD-02).* American Counseling Association.

Peifer, J., Larence, E., Willism, J., & Leyton-Armakan, J. (2016). The culture of mentoring: Ethnocultural empathy and ethnic identity in mentoring for minority girls. *Cultural Diversity and Ethnic Minority Psychology, 22*(3), 440–446.

Sánchez, B., & Colón, Y. (2005). Race, ethnicity, and culture in mentoring relationships. In D. L. DuBois & M. J. Karcher (Eds.), *Handbook of youth mentoring* (pp. 191–204). Sage Publications Ltd.

Snyder, S., & Fenner, D. S. (2021). *Culturally responsive teaching for multilingual learners: Tools for equity.* Corwin.

Stembridge, A. (2020). *Culturally responsive education in the classroom: An equity framework for pedagogy.* Routledge.

Style, E. (1988). *Curriculum as window and mirror.* https://nationalseedproject .org/Key-SEED-Texts/curriculum-as-window-and-mirror

Style, E. J. (1982). *Multicultural education and me: The philosophy and the process, putting product in its place.* University of Wisconsin Teacher Corps Associates.

Vrabie, T., & Crețu, C. M. (n.d.). Impact of the mentoring relationship on the development of talented students – A narrative review. *Journal of Educational Sciences*, XXII, *1*(43), 44–62.

Ware, F. (2006). Warm demander pedagogy: Culturally responsive teaching that supports a culture of achievement for African American students. *Urban Education, 41*(4), 427–456.

Watts, S. (2022). *What is a learning environment in education?* https://study .com/learn/lesson/learning-environment-types-importance-what -is-learning-environment.html

3

Culturally Responsive Leadership

Culturally Responsive Leaders

The culture in which we live and work and that is a part of everyday inevitably influences our view of leadership (Hofstede, 1993). That view of leadership impacts how we ultimately support those whom we are serving and why we are drawn to leadership roles. Some in positions of leadership are drawn to leadership for more individualistic and egocentric purposes such as title and positional authority, and they believe that the individual can make changes via a "top down" approach. This philosophy is the antithesis of a culturally responsive leader. Culturally responsive leaders embrace a more collectivist philosophy of leadership by following the concepts and tenets of an idea first described by Robert K. Greenleaf in 1970 as *servant leadership*. Servant leaders are those who are "called" to lead, and their leadership is an act of caring and service. Their focus is on the growth and wellbeing of the people and communities with which they are associated and has a positive impact on the organization, and, in the case of our work in education, our school system. The culturally responsive leader serves by listening and building relationships to understand what individuals need to grow and better their organization based on the unique cultural needs of the people in the organization and the community.

DOI: 10.4324/9781003293729-3

Culturally responsive leaders demonstrate the following ten servant leader skills:

- Listening: They listen without judgment and are receptive to what is being shared with them. They are wholly focused on the person/people, concern, challenge, and or need that is being presented. By listening in this completely accepting manner, they build relationships across cultures.
- Empathy: Striving to understand others' intent and their viewpoints is a critical skill in building relationships, specifically across cultures.
- Healing: One of the great strengths of both a culturally responsive servant leader and an organization that embraces a servant leadership model is the ability to heal relationships. This also includes healing oneself. Emotions impact how we interact with one another and the decisions we make daily.
- Awareness: In his essay, Robert K. Greenleaf (2002) states "Awareness is not a giver of solace—it is just the opposite. It is a disturber and an awakener. Able leaders are usually sharply awake and reasonably disturbed. They are not seekers after solace" (p. 41). Awareness helps culturally responsive leaders understand issues involving the dynamics within the community, the immediate organization, and relationships between the people they serve and themselves. This awareness helps them understand issues involving ethics, power, and values and then work with those they serve to solve challenges they face.
- Persuasion/influence: When making decisions, culturally responsive leaders embrace the skill of using persuasion to impact change rather than their positional authority. They seek to convince people to embrace a new policy or practice rather than coerce, and they are typically effective at building consensus in groups.
- Conceptualization: To conceptualize is to look beyond the day-to-day realities of the organization or challenge and conceptualize what the solution "could be" by setting

long-term goals and a vision. These goals may be hard to attain, but they differ from those in traditional leadership structures where there is traditionally a focus on short-term daily objectives. Both goals are necessary for the success of the organization. However, it is critical for the servant leader to lean into conceptualizing, specifically for culturally responsive work within white supremacist structures.

- Foresight: Skilled culturally responsive leaders are able to intuit what the community or organization needs and what may happen (to a certain extent) in the organization or the community if a specific policy, statement, or practice is put in place. This is based on lessons from the past and the realities of the present.

- Stewardship: Culturally responsive leaders are good stewards of their organization's resources. They bear responsibility and take ownership for how resources are used, and when considering what resources to allocate (funds, human resources, time, etc.), they do so mindfully, resourcefully, intentionally, and ethically with the purpose of bettering the system, students, educators, and families/community.

- Building community: Culturally responsive leaders understand that it is critical to build their community—not only their immediate community with their employees, but with their families, students, community, and additional stakeholders such as central office employees. They may have multiple communities in which they identify, create, and connect to one another with the purpose of creating a sense of belonging and commitment to one another. Culturally responsive leaders not only help create this community/communities with their stakeholders, but they are deeply committed to these communities as well and also feel a sense of belonging to them.

- Commitment to the growth of people: Culturally responsive leaders embrace the servant leadership philosophy that people have intrinsic value other than just what they can physically produce. These leaders understand that their employees' cultures, ideas, beliefs, career desires, and needs are essential and valuable. Because of this belief, culturally responsive leaders value developing other employees and finding supports to support the growth of their team members and the community. When the team learns, the organization benefits.

As a culturally responsive leader of gifted programs, you are in a unique position to design and influence systems, structures, and organizational and community cultures that perpetuate inequities and systems of oppression. A culturally responsive leader of gifted programs is one who is attuned to their community and builds upon the community's strengths to create gifted programming that is inclusive of the community's voice and reflective of its values. You are in a position of power and privilege by the nature of the role to impact gifted learners from historically marginalized communities and disrupt systems and patterns of oppression. You can do this in several ways by collaborating with other departments at the district and state level to solve equity challenges such as the lack of teachers of color being hired or students of color not being identified for gifted services. These are all challenges that leaders can approach on the basis of the tenet that ongoing systemic change is a part of culturally responsive leadership.

In our ever-changing world, leaders are forced to adapt and pivot when the unexpected happens or when policies and initiatives evolve. Culturally responsive leaders are able to do this as they reflect and adapt in these situations while also implementing practices that are culturally responsive. So what makes leaders able to do this work? What are the critical traits that culturally responsive leaders need to possess? Table 3.1 displays critical traits needed for a culturally responsive leader.

TABLE 3.1
Traits of a Culturally Responsive Leader

• Exhibits servant leadership	• Liberatory Design mindset (Anaissie et al., 2021)
• Reflective of personal bias and works to actively interrupt biased thoughts	• Reflective of system biases that exist and actively works to interrupt systems of oppression
• Action-oriented equity	• Continually engages in conversations regarding race
• Up to date with the most current research practices and literature regarding the community they serve and support	• Has depth of knowledge of how giftedness manifests in the cultures for whom they serve, and/or seeks out knowledge about the way in which giftedness manifests
• Develops others leadership capacity, cultural competency, and understanding of gifted pedagogy	• Develops an equity vision • Conducts equity audits (see Chapter 5)

Contemplation Corner

Which traits in Table 3.1 are you already exhibiting? Which traits are opportunities for growth?

Cultural Competency

Cultural competency is a critical trait that can be nurtured by culturally responsive leaders throughout all levels of an educational organization by developing what Cross et al. (1989) described as "a set of congruent behaviors, attitudes, and policies that come together in a system, agency or among professionals and enable that system agency or those professionals to work effectively in cross-cultural situations" (National Center for Cultural Competence, n.d.). This set of behaviors, attitudes, and policies are based on an awareness, respect, and integration of cultures different from one's own. When leaders of culturally responsive gifted programs work towards cultural competency, then they are also striving to create an environment where cultural competency can occur in the classroom, school, or district or at state level. The Cross Framework (Cross et al., 1989) emphasizes that the process of achieving cultural competency occurs along a continuum and sets forth six stages including: 1) cultural destructiveness, 2) cultural incapacity, 3) cultural blindness, 4) cultural precompetence, 5) cultural competency, and 6) cultural proficiency. Cultural destructiveness occurs when attitudes, policies, structures, and practices within a system or larger organization can actually cause harm to a cultural group. The 2013 Supreme Court case *McFadden v Board of Education for Illinois School District U-46* (United States District Court, 2013) was one of the first legal cases to highlight cultural destructiveness in gifted education when practices, policies, structures, and attitudes cause harm to a group of learners. In this case, the learners in School District U-46 were Hispanic English learners. School District U-46 created separate criteria for qualification for gifted programs for learners based on their language proficiency, and in a review by the Office of Civil Rights, the gifted programs for English learners were also qualitatively different in content and rigor. Additionally, the court found that when students became proficient in English, students were exited from their program and were not able to transfer into another gifted program in the district because the district had a different set of criteria for the students with the host language (English). The school district was found guilty of intentionally segregating Hispanic English learners from their non-Hispanic English-proficient peers.

> The court ruled that District U-46 violated students' civil rights by separating gifted Hispanic students from their white peers, thus perpetuating the cultural distinctions and barriers to assimilation that our nation's civil rights laws are dedicated to prevent. That this segregation occurs at the stage of a child's education and life when he is most vulnerable to identifying his opportunities by cultural differences only aggravates an otherwise disparate impact on these children.
>
> (United States District Court, 2013)

Cultural incapacity refers to the incapacity of the system to be able to respond effectively to the needs, interests, and differences of culturally linguistically diverse groups. Examples include disproportionally allocating resources to one cultural group over another, systemic bias, discriminatory hiring practices or classroom practices, and more. Cultural incapacity currently exists in many education systems in how funding is distributed, who is hired to teach, and the credentials required to teach. For leaders of culturally responsive gifted programs, the key is to begin finding flexibility within the system so as to move it towards cultural competency. For example, if you are a leader of culturally responsive gifted programs and you have the ability within your budget to allocate resources, it is critical to do an audit to see which schools in your district are getting more money than others. Then it is essential to determine if those funds need to be redistributed. It also includes looking at your hiring practices and working to recruit teachers and leaders who are culturally linguistically diverse to work with students who are culturally linguistically diverse.

Cultural blindness is an expressed racial ideology that purports that discrimination can end if all people are treated the same, thus ignoring the unique lived experiences, cultures, and value that every person brings to their environment. This ideology in education is dangerous. It's dismissive and perpetuates racism because it gives permission to those in power, specifically white educators and administrators, to not "see" a student's race. By not seeing a student's race, we are not recognizing the inequities that they face or will face in education such as access to gifted education, opportunities to access advanced math classes, opportunities to take Advanced Placement courses, and access to scholarships and specific career training. A colorblind approach allows white educators to deny uncomfortable racial differences such as why the majority of children identified for gifted programming are white, or why the majority of teachers of gifted learners are also white. This discomfort is not good or bad. It is data that we must face and discuss so that we can work to build culturally responsive and culturally proficient systems that allow culturally linguistically diverse gifted students and their teachers the ability to thrive.

Cultural precompetence is a stage that many of the leaders of gifted programs we speak with find themselves in as they work towards cultural competency. This is a level of awareness from the leader that the system and organization within which they work have areas of cultural strength and that areas of growth still remain in which to respond appropriately to the needs of culturally and linguistically diverse populations. For example, the leader of gifted programs who is expressing cultural precompetence may be focused on increasing identification of gifted culturally linguistically diverse learners, but they may not have a plan to get there. They may also hire culturally linguistically diverse teachers to support their gifted programs; however, they may not be able to retain them because they have not created additional structures such as mentorships and support for the teachers as they enter a predominantly white field. Cultural precompetence can still be harmful to learners and educators because inconsistencies can create mistrust and perpetuate stereotypes—especially stereotypes about gifted culturally linguistically diverse learners. For example, a culturally precompetent leader of gifted programs may want to create an Advanced Placement (AP) Mathematics course in a Title I high school for the first time in the school's history and allow any student who chooses to enter the class. On the surface, this sounds like an idea that is creating opportunity and access to learners. However, it will be critical to ensure that there are scaffolds in place for the learners from the school to understand how to approach a class like AP. If this is the first of its kind that learners have taken, then the students at this school may need to have scaffolds to help them access the course content and cope with the rigor and pace of an AP classroom. In order to move from precompetence to competence, the leader needs to consider what additional courses must be offered in middle school and elementary school and what training is appropriate for the teachers to have so that learners are prepared to take this type of course while still offering scaffolds to those in the class currently.

Leaders of culturally responsive gifted programs are striving for cultural competence so that their systems and organization demonstrate respect and accept cultural differences through some very specific actions that are focused on strategic change and implementation. In this case, the leader is trying to not only be culturally competent, but is working to make the organization culturally competent. This is a large task that will need multiple layers of support. It begins by creating a mission statement grounded in equity that articulates the principles and rationale for cultural and linguistic competence in all areas of the organization. In gifted education, this ranges from the state level to the school building and leaders are able to articulate what this looks like. Additionally, they include evidence-based culturally competent practices in their work. For example, this would include using culturally responsive education practices and curricula, while also ensuring that anti-bias hiring practices take place. Furthermore, a culturally competent leader will also practice community engagement in which they seek to solve equity challenges with the community and to ensure that reciprocal learning is taking place (National Center for Cultural Competence, n.d.). Leaders at this level will provide financial support and allocate resources to develop cultural competency for all members of the organization, regardless of their position. Lastly, leaders at this level will also ensure that they are collecting data and have the capacity to review data for a cycle of continuous improvement towards cultural competency. For leaders of culturally responsive gifted programs, this is a whole program to think of and develop. This includes budget, hiring, training, curricula, policies, practices, attitudes and beliefs, data collection, and the ability to change course when needed. How can you be a good steward of your resources while conceptualizing a vision?

Cultural proficiency is the last stage of the continuum. Cross et al. (1989) refer to this stage as advanced cultural competency or cultural proficiency, the most positive end of the scale. This is the stage where attitudes, policies, and practices are embedded with culturally responsive tools.

Being culturally proficient is a mindset shift in which all settings, policies, practices, and attitudes hold culture in high regard. Culturally responsive leaders lead with intention and focus on advocating for cultural competence throughout systems to recognize and value cultural differences.

Because this is a continuum, you may find yourself in different places on different days. Do you know everything there is to know about every culture on the planet? In order for anyone to really become culturally competent, we have to explore our own cultures, and it all starts with introspection. Can we ever get to cultural proficiency? If you are looking at all students the same way and are unaware of the students' individual cultures, then you may miss their verve, their excitement, or even their need to be quiet and have physical space. When missing those cultural cues, adults can mistake aspects of a student's culture as a behavior concern because those aspects differ from the teacher's culture and are considered a cultural mismatch.

Confronting Equity Challenges

Equity challenges are the institutionalized racist, classist, and sexist challenges faced by a person or groups of people based on their race, class, gender, language, sexuality, economic status, ability, or other identifying factors. It is the BIPOC community that is disproportionately impacted by equity challenges. When we add in ability and consider giftedness and twice exception-ality and the intersection of this diversity, culturally responsive leaders of gifted programs have a unique opportunity to deeply impact the educational trajectory for gifted learners of color, their families, and the educators with whom they work and who face equity challenges directly with their community. A culturally responsive leader of gifted education is ready to embrace equity challenges and disrupt over 100 years of systemic racism by working with their community to design solutions for the chal-lenges faced by the community.

When working with gifted programs in communities of color who have been disenfranchised from the school system, leaders of culturally responsive gifted programs need to try approaches that are outside of the traditional educational box to disman-tle oppressive systems and structures by being bold and using a transformative and liberating design for problem solving: Liberatory Design for Learning (Anaissie et al., 2021). Many of the systems and structures and even the culture of gifted education in the organization or school you work within may represent an inherited system perpetuating oppression for gifted historically marginalized populations. An antiracist culturally responsive leader of gifted education is one who actively seeks to disrupt systems of oppression, including any role they themselves may have in perpetuating systems and structures of oppression for access to gifted education.

Liberatory Design is a creative problem-solving approach that is focused on equity and design solutions for the liberation of people from systems of oppression. It is an antiracist way to approach problem solving and an avenue for change manage-ment that relies on some of the best practices in design thinking and human-centered design to shift the way in which historically marginalized populations engage with the world. Liberatory Design is constructed using what the authors of the process refer to as mindsets and modes. Mindsets invoke attitudes and values that ground and focus design practice, and modes provide guid-ance for the process (National Equity Project, n.d.).

While this design process is appropriate for all aspects of educational and systemic racism, it is especially useful in gifted education as it truly creates bridges for those who are the most impacted to have a voice and to co-design solutions. As gifted education has a history deeply intertwined with racism (DuBois & Greene, 2021), this liberatory design focus is yet another practice that can help reshape the narrative for families whose voices are instrumental in shaping the future of gifted education: Black and Brown families and teachers.

Finally, as a culturally responsive leader, if you truly want to support those learners from the most marginalized groups of learners in our gifted programs, then you must critically reflect on your role in perpetuating systems of oppression. The Liberatory Design process is a model that creates self-awareness to also liberate the designers of the equity solutions from habits that perpetuate continued oppression within gifted education; it shifts relations and shares power while creating conditions for relationships to thrive and a common understanding to occur.

The next portion of this chapter will highlight the Liberatory Design model and examines how we, as culturally responsive leaders of gifted programs, have used this process in our work to disrupt systemic racism and change the minds and hearts of those making decisions about gifted education so that systems are disrupted.

Liberatory Mindsets

Tania Anaissie, David Clifford, and Susie Wise, in collaboration with the National Equity Project, developed 12 *Liberatory Mindsets*, or values and beliefs, that are meant to help bring attention and intention to the design process while recognizing oppression in daily life and realizing alternate ways of doing work. The mindsets are a set of guiding values and beliefs that act as a framework for anyone who is looking to design a solution for a complex problem of practice to expand their frame of reference for what could be possible and inspire creative courage and liberatory collaboration with others. The next section will discuss each mindset and how culturally responsive leaders of gifted programs can utilize them, as we have in our practices.

Relational Trust

When building relational trust, culturally responsive leaders of gifted programs are investing in relationships intentionally with their staff members and their families, finding commonalities and connecting across their differences. They are honoring the stories and diverse perspectives and practicing empathetic listening without forming judgments. In Liberatory Design, relational trust is critical because when working on difficult and challenging topics, such as solving for disproportionality among ethnic groups in gifted education programs, teams must invest in each other to develop trust, share openly, and authentically collaborate. Leaders must be vulnerable with their team and model how to process emotions while also creating opportunities for healing and prevent distortion of work based on miscommunication, cultural mismatches, or misunderstandings, which become distractions from the ultimate goal.

Building relational trust with families of gifted learners of color and with staff members working with gifted families or students can be achieved in multiple ways. This can be done in a staff meeting or in a one-on-one session by inviting people to share what matters to them personally through authentic social emotional check-ins and team building. It includes dedicating time and space in meetings with staff, coworkers, or even with families to allow people to bring forward their full identities without judgment. Leaders also begin developing relational trust by illustrating the importance of nonjudgmental listening. Ask about your staff members' beliefs about gifted education and what it means to be gifted and Black, or gifted and Latinx. Do not judge; listen.

Ask your families what giftedness means to them in their culture. How does it manifest, or what does it "look like"? When working with the community, create physical and emotional space for the community to reflect and process any emotions. As the leader, you receive those emotions without defensiveness. Finally, in all spaces, the leader cultivates a culture that invites dialogue without fear of repercussion, and collective sense-making without fear of judgment. All of these pieces, when put together, create relational trust and a sense of belonging.

Practice Self-Awareness

A second mindset in Liberatory Design that culturally responsive leaders of gifted programs must engage in is actively practicing self-awareness. Our cultures and the accumulation of our lived experiences determine who we are and how we design. Therefore, it is important for us to deeply examine our own implicit biases, the emotions we are experiencing, the values we hold, and those we espouse while we are working on complex problems. Anaissie et al. (2021) state that "Practicing self-awareness increases our capacity to work with humility, curiosity, and courage."

Practicing self-awareness and examining our own implicit bias is especially important when working with vulnerable populations such as gifted learners, culturally linguistically diverse learners, learners from poverty, and learners who are twice or thrice exceptional, because the implicit bias that we may have can act as hidden spots impeding us from being able to effect real change for gifted learners from historically marginalized populations. It is a check on our privilege and thoughts. Practicing self-awareness happens when we acknowledge and challenge our own assumptions about what we are experiencing and what we are feeling. It also occurs by proactively seeking out knowledge about privilege and oppression and expanding one's own understanding of equity across multiple contexts. For example, do you find yourself thinking that the family from an impoverished part of town will not agree to be a part of the design committee on family communications because you assume that they will be working during the time of the committee meetings? Did you ask them?

Additionally, culturally responsive leaders must begin looking at how their identity and their position and privilege are impacting their perception. Anaissie et al. (2021) offer the following questions for leaders engaging in Liberatory Design to ask themselves:

- "How does my identity—my race, class, gender or another identifier—position me in society relative to privilege and oppression?"
- "How might my identity impact people and process?"

As you practice self-awareness, it is critical to remember that you will not have all of the answers for the equity challenges you face, and that is okay. It is also important to remember that there may be times, if you are a culturally responsive white leader, that you may experience some cognitive dissonance, and even some white fragility. Again, recognize that and name that. Ask yourself why you think that is occurring and take a moment to breathe. If you are a culturally responsive leader of color, you are also practicing self-awareness and recognizing your proximity to race, class, and privilege, and you may also need some time to breathe and attend to healing. All of these pieces in self-awareness are part of your equity journey and helping design liberatory systems for gifted historically marginalized learners.

Recognize Oppression

Oppression occurs individually, intrapersonally, interpersonally, institutionally, systemically, structurally, and across various forms of identities. Culturally responsive leaders of gifted programs understand that inequities do not exist in silos or in single moments in time. Instead, inequities are historical, organization, and systemic and it is critical that leaders recognize and name oppression so that they can work to dismantle it. Gifted education is one part of the education system in which oppression occurs, and both the current education and gifted education systems in the United States were founded on racist and classist principles. It is your job as a culturally responsive leader of gifted programs to recognize oppression in all its forms and help others recognize it as well.

In order to understand and see oppression, culturally responsive leaders must actively look for and name identity-related patterns of inequity when they see them. Culturally responsive leaders must listen to the experiences of those who are most negatively impacted by any level of oppression. This means that culturally responsive leaders of gifted programs are listening with empathy to gifted teachers and gifted families of historically marginalized populations to understand what oppression in systems looks like for them.

Then leaders must begin to identify what structures, practices, and policies within gifted education from the school and or district have, over time, produced the results, whether intentionally or unintentionally. This process is not to lay blame on the leader, or anyone before them; it is to understand the perspective of those within gifted education who are being impacted and take action. If the leader created the policy or practice that is causing oppression, this is an opportunity to repair harm. If not, this is still an opportunity to repair harm.

Lastly, culturally responsive leaders must recognize how their own positional power shapes the world they experience and how they frame equity challenges for gifted education. Engage in dialogue about the oppression you have recognized related to gifted education for students of color and the impetus of the oppression. Be brave and discuss any role in perpetuating oppression for gifted learners. When you start naming the way you have unintentionally oppressed learners, you are beginning to break down the walls of white supremacy culture and engage in antiracist work.

Embrace Complexity

Culturally responsive leadership within gifted education and the equity challenges you face are incredibly complex. The potential solutions to the equity challenges that you face will be equally complex and potentially numerous, and they will not be solved quickly. Therefore it is critical to recognize that any of the gifted equity challenges you face as a leader, whether its increasing identification for Indigenous students in poverty, bringing communities of color together to advocate for equitable gifted programming, creating antiracist policies, working with school leaders on developing high quality gifted programming in schools that have a high population of culturally different learners, being a school leader working with educators in the building on culturally responsive gifted instructional practices, etc., there are no quick fixes when race and implicit bias are part of the equation. These problems will be messy, and powerful, thoughtful design emerges from the messiness, not from avoiding it (Anaissie et al., 2021).

As a culturally responsive leader of gifted programs you may get pressure from the leaders above you to "fix" decades of inequities in gifted education—inequities that stem from larger sociopolitical contexts that are out of your control. However, remember to take a deep breath and practice mindfulness when this occurs. Complex challenges such as academic excellence gaps among Black and Brown gifted students, however, don't have ready-made solutions, and part of being a culturally responsive leader is understanding the unique complexities of each situation and the various factors at play. This will also mean helping your staff members and families embrace complexity as well.

Many of the staff members we have worked with have wanted "answers now" to problems they are facing that don't have quick and ready answers. The need to have immediate answers and urgency is a vestige of white supremacy culture (Jones & Okun, 2001) that is embedded in every organizational system and structure originating from Europeans, including education. Your job as a culturally responsive leader is to recognize that and disrupt it. The need for quick answers is something that you will run into as well, and at first this will feel very uncomfortable for staff members who are not used to dealing with these types of situations. Therefore, when this happens, acknowledge the confusion and discomfort brought forward by ambiguity present in equity work.

Empathize with those who want answers. Then, bring together multiple perspectives on the challenge—especially from those most harmed or the most vulnerable groups, because it opens up ways of thinking. For example, if someone wants you to quickly fix the excellence gaps between gifted students of color and white students, this is an equity challenge in which you will need time to bring multiple perspectives and review data. Then you will need to create an opportunity for sense making before decision making. That is, make sense of the concern or problem at hand. What is really going on? Then, how do you work together to come to a solution?

Focusing on Human Values

In order to be a culturally responsive leader of gifted programs supporting very complex and diverse communities, it is critical that you get to know the community you are designing for in as many different ways as you can. This goes back to building relational trust, and this includes placing relationships at the center of the work. You are a leader of culturally responsive gifted programs, so you need to know the cultures of the various learners and the families in your communities. Your work is to respect those cultures and the cultural wealth the families, learners, and educators bring with them. To do this work, you must invest the time and effort to understand a community and recognize the expertise of the people who are closest to the issues being addressed in the design challenge that is presented.

When focusing on human values, leaders understand that they are not the expert. They should approach conversations with the community with humility and acknowledge that. It is also critical to verbally honor the stories, experiences, and emotions that the community is sharing with you. Show emotion with them. Actively take part in sense making with the community. At this point you are working to shift power dynamics with them and show that their voice is just as important in the work that you are doing.

Seeking Liberatory Collaboration

When a culturally responsive leader of gifted programs seeks liberatory collaboration, they are actively recognizing the differences in power dynamics and identity and are designing "with" the gifted community instead of "to" the gifted community. Liberatory Design is only effective when relationships between leaders and the communities with which they are working are reframed as equity partnerships. Therefore, culturally responsive leaders of gifted programs must create the conditions in which liberatory collaboration with the gifted community can occur. Those conditions include:

- Actively and continuously seeking out diverse identities, roles, skill sets, education levels, and experience in building a design team or problem-solving team for the gifted community's problem of practice
- Acknowledging and building upon the strengths and skills of your problem-solving team
- Acknowledging the stories of team members as strengths and that their knowledge will help add to what is needed for gifted education systems
- Creating clear and specific conditions for collective learning
- Creating clear conditions for collective risk taking as a gifted community
- Creating clear conditions for collective action when working with gifted equity challenges
- Framing questions such as "How might *we* as a gifted and twice or thrice exceptional community create equitable gifted services?"
- Putting a protocol in place to ensure the "*we*" in your sentences is inclusive of the diversity of the stakeholders, and asking members of your gifted community to hold each other accountable to the diversity
- Using language such as "calling one another *into* conversations" about equity rather than "calling one another *out*"

Working with Fear and Discomfort

When embracing ambiguity and complex problems, as well as talking about problems about race and systemic and institutional racism that impact gifted education, fear and discomfort are to be expected. These challenges are high stakes for the culturally linguistically diverse learners and their families that we support, and cause stress for all involved. White educators, administrators, and families may feel as if their identity is attacked when discussing race and diversity. Gifted families in general may feel as if their program or their identity as gifted families are being attacked when changes to equity and equity practices are occurring. This again is what Robin DiAngelo refers to as white fragility—it is a cognitive dissonance that comes out of fear and discomfort. However, fear and discomfort are essential for growth in any antiracist work. Fear and discomfort are anticipated parts of equity and design work because, as Anaissie et al. (2021) expressed, "the journey through an equity challenge is ambiguous."

Fear and discomfort are great opportunities for growth that can be used by culturally responsive leaders of gifted programs as leverage by creating and holding space to process emotions regarding the fear and discomfort that is present. This can be done by establishing protocols to help name the fear and by having antiracist and social-emotional resources ready to support staff, family, and community members to get additional support to work through discomfort they might feel. An important question for a leader to consider is how much time to spend discussing the fear and discomfort and whether or not the fear is hindering the team's creativity or if it is fueling it. If the fear is indeed hindering and harming creativity for the group, then you will need to devote more time to processing what is happening, practicing self-awareness, and going through a protocol about the possible risks and rewards of the work that you all are doing together.

Attending to Healing

Culturally responsive gifted leaders attend to healing when harm is done, regardless of the situation. Equity work, in particular, is challenging and emotional, and may be triggering, especially when we are talking about gifted education and when children and lives are involved. For people of color with whom you work, the equity work may trigger memories of prejudice and racism in schools or by gifted educators or gifted program leads directly tied to themselves or their child, or they could experience microaggression and overt racism while engaging in discussions with the team collaborating to help dismantle systems of oppression within gifted education and the education system as a whole. For white staff and family members with whom you work, they could be experiencing guilt, defensiveness, anger, white fragility, and other emotions as they remember their own experiences in school or hear the stories of members on the committee about their children in gifted education. Trauma, past and current, is a factor that cannot always be seen that impacts how people trust one another on teams. Therefore, culturally responsive leaders must attend to their team's wellbeing and healing on a consistent basis. Training for your team will be essential in microaggression, implicit bias, recognizing intent and reconciling with impact, and attending to healing.

Attending to an individual's or the team's wellbeing will look different for different leaders. Some examples that the authors have used include:

- Establishing protocols with your team when someone feels pain. "I am feeling_____. I heard_____. Could you tell me more about what you meant when you said_____?"
- Establishing protocols to name when there is an opportunity for healing. " Do you have a moment? I wanted to clarify something that I felt yesterday and talk with you about what was said or done and talk about how we can move forward and heal."
- Modelling healing in a group setting
- Practicing healing in a private setting
- Checking in with individual team members
- Incorporating healing into your design process as a protocol by leaving time to attend to healing at the end of the meeting or during lunch
- Considering using restorative justice and using a trained restorative justice trainer to help you or a team member process and heal

Working to Transform Power

Power hoarding is an attitude and behavior of white supremacist culture, or white dominant culture, that shapes organizations and is embedded into our institutions (Jones & Okuna, 2001). Culturally responsive leaders of gifted programs understand that gifted education has had a stronghold in power hoarding related to scores and program selection for gifted education, and in many places, it still does (DuBois & Greene, 2021). In order to dismantle systems of oppression, gifted education cannot continue to power hoard and must shift the power dynamics among teams and distribute among stakeholders. One way to do that is to explore where power and decision making can be shared across structures and systems within gifted education at the school or at the district level. Culturally responsive gifted leaders also understand that transforming power structures within a team or organization can create a sense of shared purpose, greater self-direction, and stronger commitment because when people share power they have the ability to challenge inequities in their interactions (Anaissie et al., 2021).

Culturally responsive leaders of gifted programs can transform power dynamics in some simple ways that will not take major organizational shifts or cost additional funds, but it may challenge some gifted education and general education employees' perceptions of hierarchies, and that could take time getting used to for them. Some ideas for transforming power that the authors have used include:

- Intentional pausing and reflecting on team dynamics, asking the team members questions like, "How are we working together as a team on this equity problem of practice?"
- Asking, "Are we including the voices of the most impacted for our gifted learners?"
- Including feedback about team dynamics in one-on-one conversations with team members privately
- Creating a strategy to transform power in conversations, meetings, and decision making by distributing leadership among the team members

You can continue to transform power by also asking how you are working with those in the gifted community who are most impacted by the decisions and to what extent the design solutions you are suggesting transform power for them.

Exercising Creative Courage

Over time, oppression for any group creates fear of change, and that fear of change quiets the creativity that is needed to tackle equity challenges. Therefore, culturally responsive leaders of gifted programs must encourage their teams to exercise creative courage in solving gifted equity challenges. Encourage teams to think of bold ideas to push past the dominant culture's status quo. Encourage teams to think of courageous ideas that will cause others fear and discomfort and might even cause the ones suggesting the idea some discomfort at the time.

In order for your team to think creatively, you will have to cultivate an environment where risk taking is celebrated and that inspires curiosity and the courage to think, feel, and act creatively. You will know this when you hear your staff come to you with ideas, maybe even what you consider to be "wild ideas," on how to solve equity problems of practice within your school or district. You will work with your team to define what creativity looks like, feels like, and means for your team and in gifted education in your setting. Celebrate and share wild ideas that come as well as share in the mistakes that will come with trying those ideas. Develop the capacity to listen with curiosity.

Taking Action to Learn

As a culturally responsive leader of gifted programs, you want your team to take risks and experiment as a way for them to think and learn without making their own personal sense of worth dependent on the outcome. That means that you as a leader are not making your personal value or your team's value dependent on the outcome. Oppression and white supremacy culture thrive on risk-averse behavior and the perfectionistic need to get things right the first time (Jones & Okun, 2001). Because we have been conditioned as a society to this form of white dominant culture, and gifted dominant culture celebrates and closely identifies with it, your job as a leader of gifted programs will be to help your team take small low-risk actions that enable them to learn without placing a large risk on the physical or emotional wellbeing of a person or the community.

Instead, you will model appreciation and that mistakes are opportunities for learning (Jones & Okun, 2001). Appreciation for risk taking is in direct opposition to white supremacy culture, and it will feel difficult for many of your team members at first. However, when creating low-risk opportunities for high success and supporting mistakes, you help build your team's self-agency and their ability to offer more creative ideas. An example of a low-risk activity where a team member at a school takes action is when someone on the design team is solving for the equity challenge of creating a sense of belonging for monolingual Vietnamese speaking families, with an idea to have a family Gifted Education night in Vietnamese for the first time in the school's history. While the organizer remembers interpreters, they forget to have childcare, so the design team adapts on the spot and supports the families with childcare. At this point, the culturally responsive leader would show appreciation for the innovative idea and that the Vietnamese community was included in a way that had not been tried before. The culturally responsive gifted leader would also then say that now they know they will need childcare for future events, which will increase the capacity of people to attend and staff to engage.

Sharing, Not Selling

The last behavior of Liberatory Design is that culturally responsive leaders of gifted programs and their gifted design teams share their work with others by inviting them into the process as collaborators instead of trying to convince them of the value of the work. In gifted education this is a lesson that the authors have had to practice as we have often felt that we are trying to "sell" others on why gifted children are of value and important. However, when we adopted this mindset and invited those with additional decision-making abilities to collaborate with us about systems and structures that were impacting gifted learners of color, we were able to show them the unique cognitive and social emotional needs of these learners. They learned with us, and we weren't talking at them anymore. They also had an ownership in the process. By sharing the work with them, we also invited questions from them that allowed us to understand what myths and misunderstandings they held about our department or school. It was an opportunity for us to also reflect on the bias we had about them. When sharing, remember the following:

- Sharing is an opportunity to learn with your team
- Be transparent about your team agreements, goals, narratives around gifted education, and expectations for work
- Earn the trust of each other through your actions and set that same standard for them
- Share all protocols with them and explain the process of Liberatory Design that you have undergone

Liberatory Design Modes

In addition to the 12 *Liberatory Design Mindsets*, there are 8 *Liberatory Design Modes* (Anaissie et al., 2021) that culturally responsive leaders will use when processing problems of practice or working as a community to solve equity challenges. Liberatory Design Modes provide guidance for teams and help leaders and teams intentionally take time to pause and reflect upon any potential white dominant cultural habits that are contributing to inequity. The design process can begin with any mode at any time and move in any direction (to another mode). Prior to diving deeper into each mode, we would be remiss if we did not mention the three core components that keep all of the modes tethered together: Notice, Reflect, and See the System (Anaissie et al., 2021).

Noticing

To notice is to actively practice the Design Mindset of self-awareness. This mode is essential for practicing self-awareness or helping build systemic awareness in yourself or with your team and collaborators. It is also helpful when exploring the historical context of equity challenges and naming the power dynamics that exist. The following questions are critical to ask yourself or your team as you engage in this mode:

- Who am I?

- Who am I in this work or in this setting?
- Who are we collectively as a team in our work together?
- What is my relationship to privilege and opportunity as well as institutional and systemic power?
- How does my power and privilege relate to that of those most impacted by the equity challenge we are trying to solve?
- What is our team's relationship to privilege and opportunity as well as institutional and systemic power?
- How does our power and privilege relate to that of those most impacted by the equity challenge we are trying to solve?
- Do we understand the realities of both the opportunities and the constraints that must be addressed in this work? What do we need to know?

Reflecting

As a culturally responsive leader, reflection is a key foundation to help keep you grounded when you engage in self-awareness and practice collective sense making. Reflection is crucial because it is not just for you to process what you are feeling and any internal conflict you are noticing, but it allows you as the leader to continuously connect with your team and your communities to help them process any conflict they are having, actively name emotions, and rethink aspects of work to see what might need to be modified. Reflection is also an active practice that your team and communities can do with one another. It is key to reflect before, during, and after each mode. The following are possible questions to consider asking before, during, and after each mode:

- Are our processes liberatory? Do they feel liberatory? How do we know? If not, why? What and how should we adjust?
- How do our emotions and our emotional states impact us and how do we show up for one another and in our work?
- How might white dominant culture create unconscious bias?

- Are there unconscious biases impeding our relationships or work?
- Is there a way to release harmful or distressing emotions so that we can move forward together as a team and heal while still caring for one another?

Seeing the System

Culturally responsive leaders of gifted programs must be able to identify the potential equity challenges that exist within the system in which they work. Being able to see the system within their work, what the system is producing, and when it is perpetuating equity challenges, as well as what is needed to learn more about the challenges as leaders engage in empathy work, is crucial to move forward with solving equity challenges. Seeing the system is not always an easy feat when you are a part of the system itself. It is like telling a fish that they are swimming in water and the fish asks, "What is water?" Seeing the system means seeing the water and recognizing what you are swimming in.

When you are starting a design process, it is critical to step back to better understand the context and history that impacts the current challenge; you need to understand what parts of the educational system you are in that have created the current challenge. You may also need to understand what sociopolitical structures and systems have helped create equity challenges that you are also trying to help solve with the community. However, as a leader, it may not be possible to truly see the system until after you have conducted empathy interviews or completed additional empathy work so that you can see the system through the eyes and from the perspectives of those who are disproportionately impacted. This level of seeing is needed for those wanting to make systemic changes. The following are some questions to consider when engaging in the design process:

- What patterns of inequity do you notice?
- Are there patterns of inequitable outcomes and inequitable experience that we can see in our system? What data do we have to support our answer?

- What else about the organization or relationships within the organization are relative to these patterns that you notice? What data do we have to support our answer? Is this perception or reality?
- What are the structures, systems, and power dynamics that could be contributing to the inequities?

Empathizing

At its core, empathy is the ability to understand and share the feelings of another person. To empathize is to show empathy. When you are designing solutions to equity challenges impacting gifted communities, culturally responsive leaders of gifted programs must empathize. That is, they must design opportunities to deeply understand the "experiences, emotions, and motivations of the person or community you are designing with." (Anaissie et al., 2021). Empathy, furthermore, must be done with an openness to experience, with respect for the community you are designing with, and without judgment.

Empathy interviews are one way in which you and your team can better understand the lived experiences of the community with which you are designing equity challenges. While empathy interviews are one way to empathize, asking questions to better understand your community does not have to take place formally. Here are some questions to consider when empathizing:

- How can we learn from our communities?
- How can we learn by creating relationships with one another rather than transactional experiences? Who is the most impacted by our decisions and this equity challenge?
- Who is being harmed? Who is the closest to pain?
- Who is the furthest away from power and has the least decision-making ability?
- Who is the closest to power?
- How might the lived experiences of the community I am working with see me and therefore impact the level of trust/ability to build trust?

Defining

In this Libertory Mode, the culturally responsive gifted leader is working with the members of their community to develop a common understanding and point of view about the challenges and needs with the community. This phase of the process when you have data needs to be synthesized and made sense of. This data can be collected from empathy interviews with staff, families, students, etc. The data could also be observational, after watching how staff interact and/or how students interact. It could be quantitative, looking at family sense-of-belonging surveys with the gifted program, or a deep dive into gifted students' test scores. Regardless of whether the data is quantitative, qualitative, or both, your data should be able to give insight into the problem or problems at hand.

This particular part of the Liberatory Design model is helpful for leaders who may have a very broad equity challenge, helping them narrow it in order to begin. For example, if you want to solve for disproportionality at the district level, that is a really large equity challenge worth solving. It is also very broad in scope. So, you need to dig deeper. The following questions could help you define and narrow your equity challenge focus:

- What do people within the gifted community identify as their core needs and equity challenges?
- Are we considering the local and historical contexts of the gifted community? Have they tried to solve this challenge before? What have they tried?
- Is this a challenge that we understand well enough to feel comfortable designing solutions for, or is there more to understand before we begin?
- How and to what extent is this in our sphere of influence? With whom do we need to connect or collaborate with to ensure we have a sphere of influence to design for change?
- Whose seat is missing from the table? Who else do we need to bring in—possibly not from the immediate gifted community—that will bring a different perspective and allow for collaborative sense making?

Inquiring

As a culturally responsive leader of gifted programs, you will be embracing fear and discomfort when things are ambiguous or unclear. Your role, as we discussed earlier, is to help others also embrace ambiguity. When designing solutions with the gifted community, one of the modes you will want to engage in to help process solutions and embrace ambiguity to help reach a solution is inquiry. You will need to inquire when the path forward is not clear. Asking questions can help refine the challenge and provide clearer directions before your team offers solutions and begins piloting/testing them.

The authors of Liberatory Design define inquiry as "navigating the ambiguity and uncertainty of 'not knowing' by taking 'safe to fail' actions." (Anaissie et al., 2021). Those actions create a space for the collective risk taking promoted by the Liberatory Design Mindsets and shift power dynamics to those in the group. Individuals within the group also develop self-agency and feel enfranchised. Inquiry is also an important part of the process when you do need more clarity on how and where to go next with your team. Questions to use with your gifted teams are:

- Is there something that we still need to better understand about our _____ (families, students, teachers, gifted leaders) that is creating inequity?
- What about the gifted education system, or the greater school system that we are in, do we need to better understand?
- What is creating the inequities in our gifted community that we are focused on?
- What small things can we try?

Imagining

At some point in the design process, you and your team may feel blocked or "stuck." This is the point where you need to notice how you are feeling, reflect on what is causing the block, and take a moment to imagine and brainstorm as many ideas as you can to attack the problem. We have embraced imagining as part of the process because it allows for creativity and inclusion of multiple perspectives within your gifted community. It also allows you to revisit any issues that came up as a result of another part of the design process (e.g., someone may have surfaced a solution to gifted information being communicated differently to families that was overlooked and needs to be revisited). The following are some questions to consider to help your team imagine:

- Have we cultivated an environment for the multiple perspectives in our community to truly feel included as part of the design process?
- Have we cultivated an environment where everyone in the design process is able to share ideas without fear of judgment from other collaborators or team members? How do we know?
- How big are we going with our ideas? Are we really giving ourselves permission to push boundaries and move past the status quo? Are we considering those options that do not feel possible within our current system? Are we truly imagining ideas that would disrupt systems of oppression for gifted learners and our gifted community?

Prototyping

When you are at the prototype phase of the design process, you and your team are ready to take your ideas and make them tangible and testable. By prototyping, you are also going to be in a place to receive feedback because you will want to understand how the solution that you just designed with members from the community is actually going to impact members of the community. In creating a prototype, you are not fully rolling out a solution, but you are putting your first, and second, and third, etc., versions of the solution together and are close to testing them out in the community. Perhaps the prototype is a new website based on the feedback you and your team have received from Black and Brown families, which was designed with some community members so that all information will go out to families at the same time. Before you begin, and as you working on the prototype, you will want to ask your team the following questions:

- What will we learn about the inequities, system, or problem we are trying to solve for?
- Are we able to build a prototype that will elicit and invite our gifted community's interaction?
- Do we think that the design we created actually supports the idea of cocreation and liberation for equity? How will those who are most impacted be liberated, and how will we have disrupted inequity?

Trying your Prototype

What good is a prototype if you cannot try it out? The last Liberatory Design Mode process is to try the prototype. The reality is you can develop a prototype and try it out at any point in the process because Liberatory Design is meant to be fluid and nonlinear, and there is no one particular way to work this process except for the way that works for your team and is authentic for your stakeholders and community. Trying your prototype is appropriate when you are ready to gather authentic feedback for your prototype and to check your own assumptions and intentions. Feedback provides an opportunity for you and your design team to continue to improve the design and ensure that it is aligned with your stated equity goals.

You may want to try your prototype as soon as your team has fully articulated what it wants to learn about its prototype. Perhaps it is a new hiring practice for teachers of color and there is a set of interview questions going out to interviewees that was developed with your current teachers of color. Your design committee wants to see how this new set of questions is received and understood as well as how it attracts new candidates to the position. You may also want to try your prototype early in your process when you have created a rough draft version of it and just want to know if you are headed in the appropriate direction or if you will need to change course. For example, we as leaders have done this when working with Advisory Councils to create prototypes of surveys, and asked a small group of families to pilot them to see if the questions asked were clear and if answers about equity were being yielded. When deciding if you and your team are successful in the "try" phase, consider some of the following questions:

- How are we including our most impacted by inequity in a feedback loop and letting them know about success and failures in the design challenge?
- How are we able to engage the most impacted by the system or problem we are solving for the opportunity to give us feedback in the process of adapting the prototype?

TABLE 3.2

Equity Challenges Revealing Systemic Inequities and Racism for Liberatory Design

District	School
• Inconsistent identification rates for multilingual learners across K–12 schools in the same school district • Implementation of district guidance on best practice for gifted learners is based on whether the school leader "believes in" gifted education or not • Gifted education is in some district communications but not others, yet information about Special Education and English learners is in every communication • Teacher pay: Teachers receive stipends for working with vulnerable populations and gifted is not considered a vulnerable population • Schools with affluent families receive all communication from the district sent home on time while those in Title I schools receive information a day or two after the affluent schools, often missing important deadlines for mentorships, GT programs, events, and even scholarships	• Family events are held only during the day • School leader sends information home in English only about gifted programming or forgets to send information home at all • School leader in a school with a student population of primarily Black learners refuses to send information about magnet gifted programming because he doesn't want students who get good grades leaving (even though it is still a choice to leave the school and gifted programming can happen in the school) • The Indigenous learners in your school do not feel a sense of community in the gifted classroom

- How are we creating the conditions so that it is safe to fail and ensuring that we are not causing additional harm to our highly impacted gifted community, or for those for whom we are designing?

Liberatory Design In Practice

Chances are that after reading these Liberatory Design Mindsets and Liberatory Design Modes, you have thought "I've done some of those" or "I use _____ when I do____." The critical piece of Liberatory Design for culturally responsive leaders of gifted programs is that these mindsets and modes are specifically designed to be used with your community. Now your community is going to have multiple equity challenges that exist that are unique to your population of learners and your needs. Table 3.2 shares examples of equity challenges that you may be familiar with or may have experienced directly yourself. Review the practices that are exemplified below that are directly impacting Black and Brown learners.

Contemplation Corner

Which of the scenarios in Table 3.2 have you experienced, if any? How have you solved for this? What two mindsets could you start and who do you need from the community to help solve for your equity challenge?

The Liberatory Design process does not have to be sequential. However, many leaders find that completing the process sequentially or in a cycle is helpful. As the leader of your gifted programs you should, along with your team and the needs of the project, determine which steps to take next. Because we often have multiple problems of practice happening at once, it is helpful to have a specific mode or set of modes to help you. For example, you may be working on solving for disproportionality and family engagement at the same time; if that is the case, you may have to define and imagine or you could be working in different phases of equity challenges at the same time. Make sure that you practice the mindsets and model the mindsets for everyone on your design team.

Change Management

As you are developing your culturally responsive leadership skills, another piece to consider is how you manage the multiple changes in an ever-changing educational environment. Change fatigue is the resistance or passive resignation to organizational changes by stakeholders. It is insidious by nature because it acts in opposition to equity work and dismantling systems of oppression. Therefore, it is critical for leaders to balance how many initiatives are moving forward at once and what signs of change fatigue look like when it occurs. This is exhibited through resistance, anger, and even fear when new initiatives are brought forward. For example, if the educators with whom you work seem to react with anger when you send an email out about a change to a naming convention on a student's identification file, before you react emotionally, stop and ask what other changes are happening that may cause the educators to react in such a manner. Are there multiple changes happening in your system? Are the educators being asked to implement a new literacy curriculum, follow post-COVID pandemic protocols, or work with a new attendance system—perhaps they are doing all three? If so, their reaction is most likely related to change fatigue. They are tired with the multiple education initiatives that are handed to them to the point that even something that feels insignificant to you as the leader will feel quite large to them. The same can be said for families when changes happen continuously. Therefore, it is critical to manage change proactively for all of your stakeholders in a culturally responsive manner. You can use the tools described above in Liberatory Design so that you are already engaging the community and stakeholders who are a part of the change and will better be able to help you anticipate how the community and additional stakeholders will react.

Signs of change fatigue due to a saturation of change include, but are not limited to:

- Noise
  - Louder and more frequent complaints about change without engaging in conversations about solutions
- Apathy
  - Educators and or families grow disengaged and stop asking questions completely, and thus stop exercising creative courage
- Burnout
  - Educators are visibly tired
- Cynicism and negativity
  - This cynicism can spread and is counterproductive to equity initiatives
- Skepticism from individuals about the success of the change
- Resistance to change
  - This may be active or passive in nature

Racial Battle Fatigue

Lastly, it is imperative that as part of your culturally responsive practice and managing change that you are aware of and prepared for Racial Battle Fatigue, a term first coined in 2003 by social psychologist Dr. William Smith (Goodwin, 2018). Racial Battle Fatigue (RBF), as defined by Smith, is the "cumulative result of a natural race-related stress response to distressing mental and emotional conditions. These conditions emerged from constantly facing racially dismissive, demeaning, insensitive and/or hostile racial environments and individuals." It is the impacts of racial micro and macro aggressions that Black Indigenous People of Color (BIPOC) face daily. Culturally responsive leaders understand the constant microaggressions, or comments and actions that are hostile or demeaning towards historically marginalized groups, that create toxic stress for BIPOC individuals. Leaders of color who are experiencing RBF themselves must also watch for signs that they are experiencing the stress of fighting the daily micro and macro assaults. It is critical that you work to ensure that your leadership takes into consideration how RBF impacts your stakeholders, and, if you are a culturally responsive leader of color yourself, how RBF can impact how you lead and effectively manage change.

Common signs and symptoms of RBF for BIPOC individuals as adapted from the Counseling Center at Minnesota State University include, but are not limited to:

- Poor academic performance/inconsistent academic performance
- Anger
- Anxiety
- Apathy
- Distress
- Depression
- Emotional or physical detachment
- Exhaustion
- Hopelessness
- Internalization of racism
- Muscle tension
- Nausea
- Sleep deprivation or disturbances (night terrors, sleep walking, etc.)
- Verbal, non-verbal, or physical combativeness (Minnesota State University, n.d.)

The physiological, social-emotional, and physical manifestations of RBF will impede progress towards creating culturally responsive gifted programs and shifting mindsets about gifted learners. If you as a leader are experiencing RBF, or you realize that your stakeholders are experiencing it, then you must first name what is happening and bring the impacted individuals together to give them strategies to cope. Strategies such as breathing exercises, journaling, exercising (if possible), and creating counter-stories to the narrative they are telling themselves is key to continuing to move stakeholders and whatever change initiatives you have forward.

Conclusion

When embracing the tenets of servant leadership and liberatory mindsets, culturally responsive leaders are continuously putting their community and those whom they serve, including their employees, at the center of their work. Leaders of culturally responsive gifted programs are, at their core, instructional leaders who embrace the servant leadership model of developing the capacity of others to lead and manage change.

Key Points

♦ Culturally responsive leaders serve by listening and building relationships to understand what individuals need to grow and better their organization based on the unique cultural needs of the people in the organization and the community.

♦ Cultural competency occurs along a continuum that has six stages: 1) cultural destructiveness, 2) cultural incapacity, 3) cultural blindness, 4) cultural precompetence, 5) cultural competency, and 6) cultural proficiency.

♦ Liberatory Design is a creative problem-solving approach that is focused on equity and design solutions for the liberation of people from systems of oppression.

♦ Change fatigue is the resistance or passive resignation to organizational changes by stakeholders.

References

Anaissie, T., Cary, V., Clifford, D., Malarkey, T., & Wise, S. (2021). *Liberatory design: Mindsets and modes to design for equity*. Liberatory Design.

Cross, T. L., Bazron, B. J., Dennis, K. W., & Isaacs, M. R. (1989). *Toward a culturally competent system of care*. Georgetown University Child Development Center.

DuBois, M. P., & Greene, R. M. (2021). *Supporting gifted Ells in the Latinx community: Practical strategies, K–12*. Routledge.

Goodwin, M. (2018). *Racial battle fatigue: What is it and what are the symptoms?* https://medium.com/racial-battle-fatigue/racial-battle -fatigue-what-is-it-and-what-are-the-symptoms-84f79f49ee1e

Greenleaf, R. K. (2002). *Servant leadership: A journey into the nature of legitimate power and greatness*. Paulist Press.

Hofstede, G. (1993). Cultural constraints in management theories. *Academy of Management Executive, 7*, 81–94. http://doi.org/10.5465 /ame.1993.9409142061

Jones, K., & Okun, T. (2001). *Dismantling racism: A workbook for social change groups*. ChangeWork.

Minnesota State University. (n.d.). *How to cope with racial trauma and racial battle fatigue*. https://medium.com/racial-battle-fatigue /racial-battle-fatigue-what-is-it-and-what-are-the-symptoms -84f79f49ee1e

National Center for Cultural Competence. (n.d.). *Definitions of cultural competence*. https://nccc.georgetown.edu/curricula/ culturalcompetence.html

National Equity Project. (n.d.). *Creating a world that works for all of us*. https://www.nationalequityproject.org/

United States District Court, N.D. Illinois, Eastern Division. (2013). *McFadden v. Board of Education for Illinois School District U-46*. https://casetext .com/case/daniel-v-bd-of-educ-for-ill-sch-dist-u

4

Creating Sustainable Culturally Responsive Gifted Education Systems

Gifted Program Analysis

Culturally responsive gifted leaders must have a strong understanding of whether their state, district, or even their school is serving gifted learners in a culturally responsive manner so that they can determine if an area of their gifted program(s) may need additional support. The leader's goal is to create a sustainable system with processes, practices, and protocols that are not person-dependent; that is, the process, practices, and protocols become so deeply entrenched that when there is change, diverse gifted learners are not negatively impacted by that change. When determining whether a district is serving learners in a culturally responsive manner, an evaluation of gifted services is vital for recognizing strengths and areas of growth. This chapter serves as a roadmap for leaders in understanding the components of an inclusive culturally responsive gifted education system, including program design, assessment, and identification; programming and services; professional learning; and family engagement at the micro (classroom), meso (school), and macro (district) levels of an organization. The tools used in this book

DOI: 10.4324/9781003293729-4

to guide this understanding are the DuBois Greene Culturally Responsive Gifted Framework (CRGF) (DuBois & Greene, 2021), the Checklist for Culturally Responsive Gifted Best Practices (DuBois & Greene, 2021), and the National Association for Gifted Children's (NAGC) Master Checklist of Gifted Program Elements for Self-Assessment (Neumeister & Burney, 2012).

DuBois Greene Culturally Responsive Gifted Framework

The DuBois Greene Culturally Responsive Gifted Education Framework (Figure 4.1) from *Supporting Gifted ELLs in the Latinx Community: Practical Strategies K–12* (2021) is designed to support identification and programming of gifted culturally and linguistically diverse learners while integrating culturally responsive and equitable practices.

The Framework highlights culturally responsive and equitable practices for diverse gifted learners into four components: assessment, programming, professional learning, and family engagement. Each of these components are essential to providing equitable access to advanced services for diverse learners of color. When applying the Framework to the larger educational system within your work, it is critical to think about what each of these components looks like at the micro, meso, and macro levels within your organization so that you can understand what culturally responsive gifted education looks like to different stakeholders within your system. As a culturally responsive leader, you have to be adaptive and move from the floor (micro level) to the balcony (meso and macro levels) to gain different

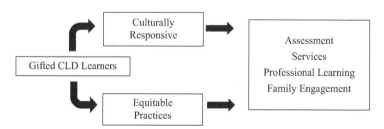

FIGURE 4.1

DuBois Greene Culturally Responsive Gifted Framework. From *Supporting Gifted ELLs in the Latinx Community: Practical Strategies, K–12* by Michelle Pacheco DuBois, Ed.D. and Robin M. Greene, Ed.D., © 2021. Reprinted with permission from the CCC.

perspectives and become objective (Heifetz et al., 2009). This will help you differentiate your approach to solving equity challenges with your stakeholders while informing the entire system and set of structures you have in place.

In most educational systems, students who receive gifted services are selected based upon a cut criterion score on an assessment they took at some point during their school career. Why is this process not equitable for culturally and linguistically diverse learners? Generally, assessments used in the gifted identification process are often a mismatch for culturally and linguistically diverse learners. Additionally, using only one test score is in direct opposition to research-based best practice that instead advocates for building a complete body of evidence that shows the learner's strengths. Too often in gifted education, assessments are commonly the "gatekeepers" that exclude students of color from advanced opportunities and experiences. In order to ensure that our assessment practices are culturally responsive and equitable, we must develop a process that includes collecting both qualitative and quantitative data to develop an expanded body of evidence (DuBois & Greene, 2021), and we must ensure that the assessments, checklists, protocols, etc. that we use are culturally responsive and/or culture-fair and that appropriate personnel have training on how to administer the assessments with reduced bias.

Culturally responsive gifted programming and services are also key components when serving our diverse gifted learners. Students have multilayered identities, and when providing academic and social emotional services to our students of color, educators must take into consideration a student's heritage language and their cultural experiences and intentionally weave that into the everyday experiences of the classroom and into the practices at the district level. Not doing so negates the value of their home language and the student's and their family's pride in their cultural and linguistic heritage.

Culturally responsive gifted programming at both the school level and the district level includes access to and implementation of curricular materials and instructional practices and an environment that is reflective of the culture of the learners and their families within it. There are many approaches to providing culturally responsive gifted programming within the classroom, in school, and at the district level. For example, culturally responsive gifted programming services include, but are not limited to, developing or providing academic, social-emotional, and professional mentorship opportunities within the immediate community as well as outside of the community with mentors of color or who speak the same heritage language. It includes having window and mirror texts in the classroom or in the district library and teaching learners, families, and teachers how to access those texts and incorporate them into lessons; and not only having posters, photographs, and artwork that look like the children and staff in the building and district offices, but also artwork created by the learners and or artists from the cultures within the community.

Incorporating culturally responsive gifted programming into educators' practice does not cost a school, district, or state additional funds. There is the pernicious misconception, however, that investing time and energy into gifted programming will cost more money than the organization has or is willing to spend. It is critical as a leader of culturally responsive gifted programs, however, that you vociferously dispel this myth rooted in anti-intellectualism and white supremacy culture for all of our gifted learners. Allowing this misconception to persist makes leaders complicit in denying quality student-based authentic programming that is asset based and proven to increase student efficacy and student test scores.

Another key component in the Framework is professional learning. Those working with diverse learners need to have opportunities to grow their knowledge and expand their skills to support and challenge gifted students of color. They must have access to ongoing professional learning geared towards culturally and linguistically supportive practices, such as, but not limited to, mindsets, cultural identity, the role of privilege, equitable practices, and culturally responsive gifted education. This type of professional learning is happening across the country and is being recognized for improving identification and mindset shifts in educators towards gifted learners of color (Greene & Honeck, 2022). Family engagement is the final component of the Framework. A strong relationship between families, the school, and the district is essential for the educational success of students of color. Strive to create partnerships with families and offer learning opportunities specific to their students' needs.

Checklist for Culturally Responsive Gifted Best Practices

The Checklist for Culturally Responsive Gifted Best Practices (DuBois & Greene, 2021) encompasses each of the Frameworks components. It is a series of guiding questions that highlights culturally responsive gifted best practices for culturally and linguistically diverse learners. When a student's cultural background is acknowledged and incorporated into their learning experiences, the student feels accepted and supported. This checklist can be used to support a starting point for a conversation or a thorough equity scan for culturally responsive gifted best practices in a school building. As a leader of culturally responsive gifted programs, you can scale the checklist to multiple buildings or across the district where applicable. The complete checklist can be found in Appendix A.

NAGC's Master Checklist of Gifted Program Elements for Self-Assessment

The Master Checklist of Gifted Program Elements (Neumeister & Burney, 2012) is designed to be used as a reference for self-assessment of six core gifted programming elements. These elements are divided into eight main items which are program design, affective needs, identification, curriculum and instruction, professional development, and program evaluation. It is meant to be comprehensive in nature, examining all areas of a gifted program's system. The rest of this chapter continues with a discussion on ways to develop an inclusive culturally responsive gifted education system and provides tools for districts to use in the process.

Developing an Inclusive Culturally Responsive Gifted Education System

The first step in developing an inclusive culturally responsive gifted education system is to examine what is currently in place and evaluate strengths and weaknesses. This requires a systematic approach that may involve multiple stakeholders to support this type of comprehensive work. There are multiple guides currently published for designing services and programs for gifted students. This book is not dispelling any of the work previously published but hoping to add to these rich resources by utilizing culturally responsive best practices within our evaluation guidelines.

The Master Checklist of Program Elements for Self-Assessment developed by NAGC and published in 2012 provides multiple opportunities for inclusion of culturally responsive language. When comparing NAGCs Master Checklist's six main areas (program design, affective needs, identification, curriculum and instruction, professional development, and program evaluation) and the DuBois Greene Framework's four main components (assessment, programming, professional learning, and family engagement), there are ways to overlap and expand to create six overarching categories that frame the Gifted Program Inclusivity Evaluation (G-PIE) guidelines (Figure 4.2). These categories are program design, assessment

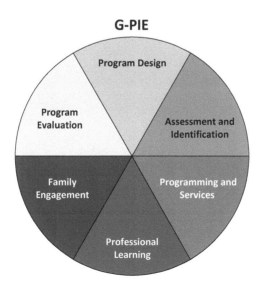

FIGURE 4.2
Gifted Program Inclusivity Evaluation (G-PIE).

and identification, programming and services, professional learning, family engagement, and program evaluation. The rest of this chapter will examine these six categories while synthesizing NAGC's Checklist with the Checklist for Culturally Responsive Best Practices and will provide guidelines for those committed to making their gifted programs inclusive for all gifted learners.

The G-PIE is represented in a pie chart expressing a part-to-whole relationship where each slice represents one component and all slices added together equal the whole. The slices of the pie are equally distributed as each of the elements is equally as important as the others in creating a sustainable equitable gifted education system.

Contemplation Corner

Describe your gifted program's current strengths and opportunities for growth. Which components of your gifted program are culturally responsive?

Program Design

Gifted program design elements should be aligned with state law and district policies, as gifted education is not federally mandated at the time of the writing of this book. Therefore, any state mandate or guidelines for gifted education should be used when reviewing a district's program design. This section will discuss the piece of the G-PIE (Figure 4.3) that examines inclusive culturally responsive program design, including mission statements, definition of giftedness, district gifted policies, gifted programming, and personnel.

Gifted Mission Statement

A gifted mission statement is a brief passage that states the purpose, values, and goals of a school district regarding gifted education. It communicates to stakeholders and the community the importance of gifted learners to the educational system. Eckert (2006) suggests that mission statements should illuminate who gifted and talented children are, why educational services for them are necessary, one or two overarching program goals, and

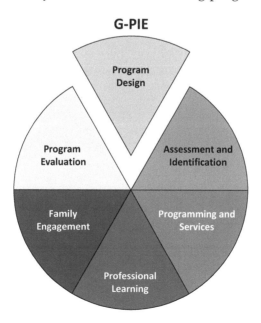

G-PIE

FIGURE 4.3
Gifted Program Inclusivity Evaluation: Program Design.

a clear message about the district's commitment to meeting the learning needs of those students. In addition to this, the authors suggest that the mission statement be framed in terms of social justice and equity, focusing on serving all gifted students, including those of color. Within the mission statement, keywords can be used that are centered around inclusive language that is gender neutral and does not have any exclusionary words. An inclusive mission statement can signify the importance of a diverse body of gifted students and a system that is committed to culturally responsive gifted practices. Culturally responsive leaders cultivate a shared understanding and ownership of the mission, vision, and values among all members of the school community.

Contemplation Corner

Write down key words for a culturally responsive, equity-focused gifted mission statement.

Definition of Giftedness

A school district's written definition of giftedness promotes understanding and provides a description of the students whom the district considers to require specialized services.

As stated in the authors' previous book, *Supporting Gifted ELLs in the Latinx Community* (2021), many definitions of giftedness use common language, including terms such as "outstanding talent," "high academic performance," and "potential" (p. 7). School districts should consider examining different theories of giftedness and selecting a conceptual definition that is consistent with any existing state law defining giftedness, current theory and research, and the values of most of the stakeholders in the district (Moon, 2006).

If the community that the district serves is diverse culturally and linguistically, then the gifted definition should reflect that in the description. When committed to establishing an equity-focused definition of giftedness, one should eliminate any biased language and include specific statements indicating that the program will include gifted students with disabilities and gifted students from various cultural, ethnic, and socioeconomic populations. Included in the definition of giftedness there should be a statement describing the areas in which students can be identified. The concept of giftedness was originally thought of as only intellectual giftedness. Through the years, the concept has changed to extend beyond academic areas, and includes, but is not limited to, the visual and performing arts, world languages, creativity, leadership, and psychomotor abilities. Valdés (2003) suggests expanding the definition of giftedness to include the terms "bilingualism" or "bilingual language abilities" to encompass the extraordinary abilities of young immigrant interpreters. Expanding areas of giftedness for which students can be identified provides opportunity and access for students of color who might demonstrate giftedness in a way that may not be reflected in an academic profile.

Description of Services

A written description of the services to be provided for gifted and talented students at each grade level and in each area served with written goals and objectives for these services should be outlined and examined for equitable opportunity and access for all gifted learners. These services should be designed to meet the wide range of needs of individual gifted students and be constructed so that there is a flexible continuum of services (Neumeister & Burney, 2012). The written description of these services should be available in multiple languages, Braille, or audio versions and delivered to stakeholders in a variety of ways.

The description of services must be included in any overarching policies for gifted education at the district and state level. Highlighting the processes and procedures for best practices for gifted students within policy places focus on these learners and their unique needs. These policies include but are be limited to

- Early entrance
- Grade acceleration
- Subject acceleration
- Early credit
- Early graduation
- Using local and group-specific norms for identification
- Multiple pathways for gifted identification
- Talent development as a pathway towards gifted identification (Neumeister & Burney, 2012)

Policies must be available in multiple languages and accessible for all stakeholders, including students. Limited English language skills should not be a barrier for access to advanced learning opportunities.

Personnel
When developing a culturally responsive gifted program, leaders at the district level supporting gifted education should be trained in gifted and culturally responsive practices. These individuals are the ones involved in creating policy and procedures that schools implement in their gifted programs. They also collaborate with other district departments to develop overall district goals for gifted students. Culturally responsive leaders can infuse conversations with an equity focus, which overall makes a positive impact for culturally and linguistically diverse students and their families.

Demographics

Culturally responsive gifted leaders continuously monitor student demographics to determine if the demographics mirror the student population. If the demographic data demonstrates that the gifted population aligns with the overall demographics of a district, then this indicates that the district selection process for a gifted identification is unbiased and effective in finding students from all racial, socioeconomic, and cultural subgroups (Neumeister & Burney, 2012). If the demographic data does not reflect an alignment, then actions should be put in place to review data and identify areas of inequity.

Stakeholders

A district gifted education advisory committee composed of volunteers from the community who are invested in gifted education can be a driving force in the success of gifted education services within a district. These advisory committees can provide advice and support to important functions, such as:

- Establishing an initial gifted education program
- Revising or expanding services
- Developing new identification guidelines
- Reviewing the extent to which a school district has implemented gifted education services
- Lobbying for appropriate funding
- Establishing public relations
- Disseminating information
- Advocating for comprehensive gifted education services (Leppien & Westberg, 2006)

A district gifted advisory committee should have members that mirror the district's demographics and the types of learners it serves. Committee membership should reflect the ethnic and geographical composition of the school district (Leppien & Westberg, 2006).

Appeals Process

An equitable appeals and exit process should be available to families who are appealing identification decisions or who want their student to exit gifted programming. The appeals and exit procedures should be documented and reviewed by an appeals committee whose job it is to receive and evaluate appeal requests when needed. Recommendations from the appeals committee could include additional testing or student interventions. All of the documentation and meetings with families must be in their preferred language or coding system.

Assessment and Identification

The next section of the G-PIE to be discussed is assessment and identification, which play a key role in providing services to gifted students of color. Generally, students are not given opportunity or access to higher level coursework or gifted services if they have not been formally identified as gifted. This practice hinders the ability of students of color to demonstrate their strengths with higher level work and perpetuates the stigma that students of color are less able than students from the majority culture to participate in advanced academic opportunities. Adverse effects such as risky behaviors may also occur for some students from lower socioeconomic backgrounds who are not challenged in schools to reach their full potential.

Culturally responsive gifted systems recognize that there must be equitable gifted identification procedures in place to develop and reveal talents among all ethnic, cultural, ability, and socioeconomic groups. In order to this, one must also recognize that there are other areas than academics in which a student might demonstrate gifted potential. Many of our culturally and linguistically diverse students demonstrate strengths in areas such as leadership, creativity, performing arts, visual arts, and psychomotor abilities. Assessments used in the identification process should be aligned to students' areas of talent and interests as students exhibit their gifts and talents not only within a specific domain but also within an interest area (Johnsen, 2022). Measures used to determine giftedness should include

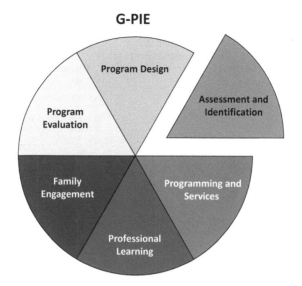

FIGURE 4.4
Gifted Program Inclusivity Evaluation: Assessment and Identification.

assessments that measure the areas of giftedness that a district offers and for which it provides services.

Multiple Measures

Gifted students from culturally and linguistically diverse backgrounds can be challenging to identify and often take an extended amount of time to gather qualifying evidence for a gifted identification. Assessment tools used in the gifted identification process are generally focused on measuring intelligence and achievement from the majority culture. These assessments are often used as single data points in gifted identification processes in school districts across the United States, creating barriers for students whose heritage culture and language may not align with the assessments being given. One way that culturally responsive gifted leaders can challenge inequitable testing practices is to commit to expanding the body of evidence as seen in Figure 4.5. An expanded body of evidence can portray a comprehensive student profile based upon multiple data points, both quantitative and qualitative, that can be analyzed for gifted traits.

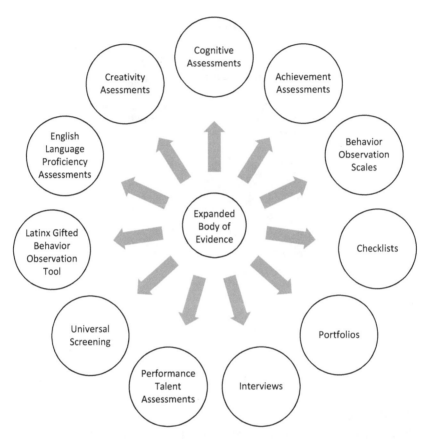

FIGURE 4.5

Expanded Body of Evidence. From *Supporting Gifted ELLs in the Latinx Community: Practical Strategies, K–12* by Michelle Pacheco DuBois, Ed.D. and Robin M. Greene, Ed.D., © 2021. Reprinted with permission from the CCC.

A comprehensive collection of qualitative and quantitative data "casts a wider net," as asserted by Frasier and Passow (1994), and increases the opportunity to discover gifted traits of culturally and linguistically diverse students that otherwise may not be recognized with limited traditional assessment tools. The use of multiple criteria for identification includes a combination of portfolios, authentic and dynamic assessments, performance tasks, teacher rating scales, and other non-traditional assessments in combination with traditional assessments (Missett & Brunner, 2013).

When assessing culturally and linguistically diverse students for gifted traits, it is important to use culture-fair assessments.

All assessments have a cultural bias to some degree, but there are assessments that are designed with the intention of being culture fair. Biased assessments are those that differentiate between members of various groups on the basis of some characteristics other than the one being measured (Johnson, 2022). For instance, if a test is designed to measure math problem solving skills but relies heavily on a student's reading ability, then the test is biased against students who may have limited reading skills but excel at math. Assessments are culture fair when they are equally fair to all cultural groups and there is a lack of bias in the interpretation or use of a test to classify or diagnose (Getz, 2011).

When expanding the body of evidence to include alternative data points, consider including creativity assessments that measure creative and divergent thinking. Look at English language proficiency assessment data of emerging bilingual students for rapid language acquisition. Include performance assessment options for students to demonstrate giftedness in performance and talent domains. Use off-level testing to measure achievement above grade level in each of the areas for which program services are offered. Make sure that assessment tools are accessible in students' native languages and available in a variety of ways which might include paper/pencil versions, online versions, untimed versions, and verbal response versions. Use local norms and/or group norms to evaluate students using a local data sample rather than a national data sample which allows for comparison of students with the peers within their own school or district. All of these tools can increase the opportunity for students from culturally and linguistically diverse populations to be identified and receive gifted services.

Universal Screening

Universally screening students refers to the process of administering a measurement across an entire population of students for the purpose of obtaining data to identify students' strengths and needs. Universal screening at multiple opportunities during a student's school career using culture fair assessments provides increased opportunity for all students, including those from historically marginalized groups, to have access to gifted services. Consider universally screening students as early as kindergarten and first grade.

Early identification practices improve the likelihood that gifts will develop into talents (Johnson et al., 2022). The practice of universally screening students eliminates any teacher bias that might occur during a gifted referral process and creates a level playing field where all students are considered for gifted services.

Contemplation Corner

Describe ways in which you can make changes or adjustments to your current assessment process to increase identification of culturally and linguistically diverse students.

Programming and Services

Programming is a section of the G-PIE that refers to the continuum of services that address the interests, strengths, and needs of students with gifts and talents in all settings (NAGC, 2019).

Several key components create the foundation for culturally responsive gifted programming. There must be true culturally responsive and sustaining gifted pedagogical practices in place as visualized in Greene's (2017) Culturally Responsive Gifted Model (Figure 4.7). This model demonstrates the marriage of multicultural gifted competencies as outlined by Ford

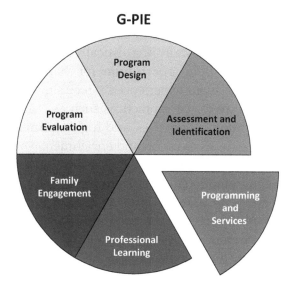

FIGURE 4.6
Gifted Program Inclusivity Evaluation: Programming and Services.

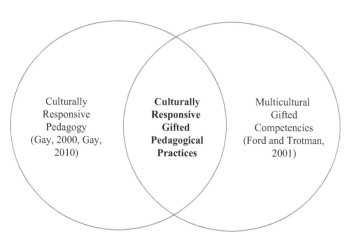

FIGURE 4.7
Greene's Culturally Responsive Gifted Model. From Greene, R. M. (2017). *Gifted Culturally Linguistically Diverse Learners: A School-Based Exploration.* (Doctoral dissertation, University of Denver) and *Supporting Gifted ELLs in the Latinx Community: Practical Strategies, K–12* by Michelle Pacheco DuBois, Ed.D. and Robin M. Greene, Ed.D., © 2021. Reprinted with permission from the CCC.

and Trotman (2001) and Gay's (2010, 2018) culturally responsive teaching (DuBois & Greene, 2021).

Programming for culturally linguistically diverse gifted learners must consist of multiple opportunities for challenging, authentic, and culturally relevant experiences. Green's model spotlights effective culturally responsive practices such as cultural brokering, authentic learning experiences, and high expectations. Other best practices include acceleration and enrichment, varied grouping arrangements, and individualized learning opportunities as well as social and emotional services to meet both the academic and affective needs of students (Johnson et al., 2016).

Culturally responsive gifted programming recognizes the importance of a student's heritage language and culture. It is asset-based, focusing on the value of a student's home language and culture and seeing these gifts as foundational for future learning rather than as obstacles or even hindrances to be overcome (Snyder & Fenner, 2021). Culturally responsive gifted programming incorporates authentic learning experiences that are relevant to students' lives and includes a repertoire of evidence-based instructional strategies to ensure specific student outcomes (Neumeister & Burney, 2012). In addition, it focuses on fostering relationships with students and families while creating safe spaces and trusting conversations to provide an environment in which all students can thrive.

What can a culturally responsive gifted leader do to support culturally responsive gifted programming? A culturally responsive gifted leader reflects on how gifted services can be offered and delivered in a culturally responsive manner. They are aware of opportunity gaps and systemic practices in order to address equity and social justice issues. Culturally responsive gifted leaders are committed to providing equitable opportunity and access to gifted programming and talent development for all populations of gifted students. The remainder of this section outlines gifted services and how they can be provided in a culturally responsive manner.

Curriculum

Generally, gifted students can learn material at a faster rate, process large amounts of information in less time than their peers, and delve deeper into content. These advanced abilities require an appropriately differentiated curriculum to fit their strengths, needs, and interests. Burns, Purcell, and Hertberg (2006) define curriculum as a design plan that fosters the purposeful proactive organization, sequencing, and management of interactions among the teacher, the learners, and the content knowledge, understanding, and skills we want students to acquire. Many teachers have a misconception of the term *differentiated curriculum*. A differentiated curriculum does not need to mean that gifted students have an entirely different curriculum but that the curriculum is modified to adjust to the advanced abilities and needs of these learners. A differentiated curriculum should include complex, abstract, open-ended activities that are multifaceted enough to cause gifted students to stretch in knowledge, thinking, and production (Tomlinson, 2001).

A culturally responsive leader must commit to thoroughly examining all resources and materials used with students for negative representations of specific cultural groups and/or complete omissions from the proposed curriculum (Ford, 2011). Here are a few key biases that Ford (2011) recommends looking for when examining materials used with students:

- *Stereotyping*: Generalizations become inflexible distortions, and diverse groups of people are represented in stereotypical roles such as that Asian students are studious, Black students are athletic, or drugs, violence/crime, poverty, and homelessness are restricted to racially and culturally different groups.
- *Superior–inferior roles*: Materials place racially and culturally different groups in low-level or subservient roles or jobs; for example, whites are in supervisory, prestigious, professional positions, while racially and culturally different individuals are in less prestigious, low-paying jobs and careers.
- *Minimization*: Materials gloss over, ignore, or trivialize the contributions, histories, and strengths of racially and culturally different groups.

A culturally responsive curriculum is multicultural, includes experiences and perspectives from historically marginalized populations of learners, and values diverse cultural and linguistic backgrounds of society. Students learn best when their culture, as well as their language, is represented, affirmed, and used in the curriculum as a valued oral tradition and a bridge for acquiring other linguistic practices (Wright et al., 2022). A culturally responsive curriculum replaces deficit-oriented teaching—seeing language, culture or identity as a barrier to learning—with asset-based approaches (Conrad, 2021). The story below highlights a group of Latinx students who did not see themselves reflected in their school curriculum and the steps they took to make a change to the system of oppression in their high school.

Snapshot: Student-Designed Ethnic Studies

A group of Latinx high school students began noticing in middle school that their culture was not reflected in their school curriculum. These students began discussing with one another that the historical people that they studied in school didn't look like them and when their culture was represented it usually was in a negative way. They started to speak with other students of color in their school and noted that many of their classmates of color were tired of not feeling valued or comfortable in their own schools. After hearing that other students of color were feeling the same way, the students proposed to their school the idea of an ethnic studies course being offered. The group then began working with a local university that had a program where undergraduates help students develop projects on school and community issues, including immigration, racism, and educational equity. The students researched ethnic studies courses in other states and prepared a proposal for the school district supporting their ideas and viewpoints. They believed that the class would improve student engagement and graduation rates, create supportive learning environments for underrepresented students, help students value their own cultural identity while appreciating differences, and foster cross-cultural understanding among students of color and white students. These students were persistent and motivated to make a change to the system to promote racial and cultural awareness and to bring a sense of belonging to students of color and other marginalized populations. The school district recognized the need for an ethics studies course and approved the course.

As noted in the story, students of color need and want to see themselves reflected in the curriculum in positive ways. Curriculum that is culturally responsive acts as a mirror as it reflects the learner's cultural strengths and gives them a sense of value and belonging. It can also act as a window because it offers students a view into someone else's experiences and perspectives.

A culturally responsive curriculum must be accessible in a student's heritage language and include matters of social justice that have authentic connections to self and community for students. By providing culturally and linguistically diverse learners multiple opportunities to draw from and use their home language(s) and culture, teachers validate students' cultural and linguistic backgrounds and elevate the benefits of being multilingual and multicultural (Snyder & Fenner, 2021).

It is important to realize that not only is a culturally responsive academic curriculum vital to gifted students but that there must also be an emphasis placed on students' social-emotional development. Gifted students are just as different from typical students in their social and emotional needs as they are in their cognitive needs (Neumeister & Burney, 2012). Due to the asynchronous development of gifted learners and the intersectionality of their culture with their classroom environment, gifted learners can be more vulnerable to classroom behaviors that are either maladaptive or pathogenic, meaning that if students are not feeling valued or challenged in the classroom, they can become disengaged and find other ways to utilize their time in an unfavorable way. This is different from cultural differences in the classroom that educators might consider less desirable or inappropriate behaviors because of their misunderstanding of a student's cultural background. That is why it is critical for those working with students to know and value their cultural backgrounds and home experiences. Recognition and support of additional differences and issues for gifted students from minoritized populations must be considered (Neumeister & Burney, 2012).

An affective curriculum that is culturally responsive should be grounded in equity and must be accessible to all students. The activities and lessons are culturally respectful and bias-free, and they leverage culture to improve and deepen learning. A culturally responsive affective curriculum will explore social and emotional characteristics, social identities, and cultural identities and will promote cultural competence. Strengthening students' social-emotional competencies can provide an opportunity to acknowledge and buffer trauma experienced by multiple forms of oppression and systemic inequities; develop a sense of positive self-worth and social awareness in connection to race, color, sex, gender identity, religion, national origin, and sexual orientation; and contribute towards dismantling systemic racism and other forms of inequity (Massachusetts Department of Elementary and Secondary Education, n.d.). At this time, affective curriculums for gifted learners are limited. However, any affective curriculum will need to be modified to meet the needs of individual students' cultural and linguistic profiles.

Evidence-Based Service Options

Instructional strategies that work well with gifted students also work for all students. The conceptual idea of teaching to all students as if they were gifted and then scaffolding down is one recommendation that the authors hope that readers will take away with them. All students should have the opportunity to have high-level educational experiences and opportunities to develop critical and creative thinking skills through authentic problems of practice focusing on social justice concepts and topics that are culturally relevant to them. Some evidence-based service options for gifted students include but are not limited to:

- Acceleration opportunities
- Extensions and enrichment

- Advanced programming options
- Interest-based learning
- Flexible grouping arrangements
- Talent development
- Problem-based learning
- Pre- and post-assessments
- Bibliotherapy
- Mentorships

So how can these services be provided to students in a culturally responsive manner? First, you must know who your students are and learn about their cultural backgrounds. Connecting students' cultural knowledge, prior experiences, and frames of reference make learning more relevant and effective for ethnically diverse students (Gay, 2010). Putting it simply, you must connect with your students on a human level and allow them to connect with you and your cultural experiences. Hammond (2015) believes that culturally responsive educators understand the importance of having a social-emotional connection to their students in order to create a safe space for learning. Next, reflect on your own implicit biases and "pobrecito" attitude (translated as "poor little thing") towards your students from culturally and linguistically diverse

backgrounds. Set high expectations for all of your students and operate from an asset-based approach. These steps are vital to creating a culturally responsive environment in which students are respected and valued.

Career Pathways

Culturally responsive leaders hold and communicate an unwavering belief system that all students, regardless of past or current performance, can meet rigorous college and career-ready academic standards (The Leadership Academy, 2022). College and career-ready pathways must be available to all students that engage them to reflect on long-term goals for themselves. Setting goals as early as middle school and revisiting goals often for realigning as needs and challenges occur can create a pathway for students to become successful adults (Adams, 2022).

Many families of color will need additional support to navigate the systemic barriers that result in inequitable access to opportunities for their students. Some of the barriers often include being the first in their families to take advanced coursework; peer pressure from other students of color for acting "white"; and low expectations for themselves and from other teachers. Starting early is the key to success for these students, and acknowledging their strengths is an important step in the process for next steps in career or postsecondary education. Forming a collaborative partnership of educators, families, and counselors can help guide students in identifying their individual strengths and needs. Some programming options include mentorships, internships, and career and technology education programming that match to students' interests, strengths, needs, and goals and introduces them to the world of work or postsecondary education (NAGC, 2019). Additional support should include the distribution of information about these college and career-ready pathways to families and students in a variety of formats and languages.

Professional Learning

Ongoing professional learning is one of the most effective ways to cultivate culturally responsive practices among educational professionals. It allows for educators to enhance and refine their teaching practices, which in effect impacts their student and family interactions. The G-PIE and the DuBois Greene Culturally Responsive Gifted Framework recognize the importance of professional learning in providing intentional and ongoing opportunities to develop culturally responsive gifted teaching practices.

Professional learning must go beyond informational learning towards transformational learning which is active, evolving, self-reflective, and perspective taking and exemplifies the elements of culturally responsive pedagogy (DuBois & Greene, 2021). Through professional learning opportunities focused on social justice and equity, educators can move towards becoming culturally competent.

A culturally responsive gifted leader recognizes the need for developing a strategic plan grounded in equity to intentionally provide professional learning opportunities focused on growing culturally responsive gifted professionals. Figure 4.9 outlines

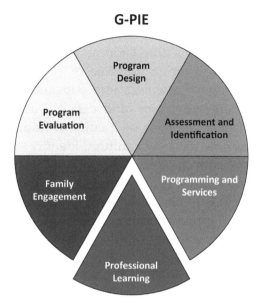

FIGURE 4.8
Gifted Program Inclusivity Evaluation: Professional Learning.

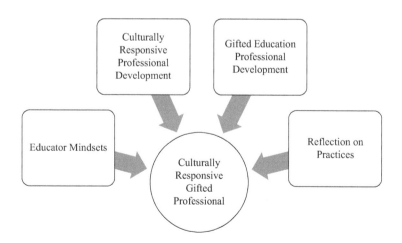

FIGURE 4.9
Strategic Plan for Developing Culturally Responsive Gifted Professionals. From *Supporting Gifted ELLs in the Latinx Community: Practical Strategies, K–12* by Michelle Pacheco DuBois, Ed.D. and Robin M. Greene, Ed.D., © 2021. Reprinted with permission from the CCC.

the four main areas that support the development of a culturally responsive gifted professional. These areas are mindsets, culturally responsive education, gifted education, and reflection.

Any plan focused on an outcome of cultural competency should have training that delves into personal belief systems, implicit bias, microaggressions, and deficit thinking practices. Educators must examine their own cultural frame of reference and understand how their own cultural identity can impact the way they interact with students and families.

Another important piece to being a culturally responsive gifted professional is to have training in both culturally responsive education and gifted education. The combination of both of these provides a practitioner with the necessary knowledge and expertise to work with culturally and linguistically diverse learners in an effective manner. The last area of focus is reflection on practices, which is actually something that culturally competent professionals practice continually. Ongoing self-reflection on daily practices regarding students and families is a continual cycle for educators who are committed to culturally responsive teaching.

Within the strategic plan, considerable thought must be put into the learning environment in which adults will be reflecting on their personal beliefs, biases, and assumptions about students and families that have been historically marginalized. Culturally responsive gifted leaders create courageous spaces to address hard-to-discuss topics with a focus on deficit thinking by modeling vulnerability and help-seeking and being transparent about their own gaps in knowledge (The Leadership Academy, 2022). As a leader, you must be open to reflecting on your cultural identity and how it influences those you lead.

Over the years, the authors have implemented various professional learning plans focused on equity and social justice. In Figure 4.10, a suggested professional learning roadmap is provided as an example of training that focuses on the four main topics previously shown in Figure 4.9.

No matter how you choose to impart professional learning opportunities concentrated on equity and social justice, just choosing to start is critical to providing support for your culturally and linguistically diverse students and their families.

Professional Learning Roadmap	
Year One Suggested Order of Topics	**Years Two and Three** Suggested Order of Topics
Dismantling Systems of Oppression : Begin with Self	Dismantling Systems of Oppression : Students, Families, and Culturally Responsive Gifted Education
Exploring Mindsets	Culturally Responsive Gifted Education
The Educator's Personal Cultural Identity	Cultures in the Classroom and the Community
The Role of Privilege	Seeing and Recognizing Giftedness
White Supremacy Culture and Systemic Racism	Gifted Instructional and Programming Practices
Critical Conversations about Race	Family Engagement

FIGURE 4.10
Professional Learning Roadmap. From *Supporting Gifted ELLs in the Latinx Community: Practical Strategies, K–12* by Michelle Pacheco DuBois, Ed.D. and Robin M. Greene, Ed.D., © 2021. Reprinted with permission from the CCC.

Family Engagement

Parent is a term commonly used to refer to a mother and or father of a child. In this book, the authors use the term *family* to refer to not only the mother and father but also to any other family members who have strong relations with the student. This practice recognizes that many students of color are raised in communal societies where they may have additional family members living with them outside of their parents. Families play a critical role in a student's educational experience. Family engagement is the slice of the G-PIE (Figure 4.11) that refers to supporting families and building cultural bridges between teachers and their students' families. It is the overarching approach to supporting family wellbeing, strong parent–child relationships, and students' ongoing learning and development (Garcia et al., 2016).

The family engagement section of the G-PIE focuses on communication avenues and gifted training for families. Often, culturally and linguistically diverse families are not informed or do not have access to information about gifted identification processes

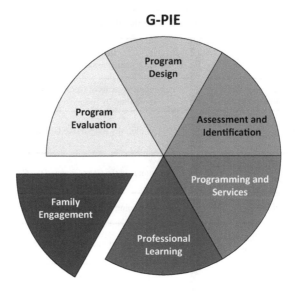

FIGURE 4.11
Gifted Program Inclusivity Evaluation: Family Engagement.

and advanced opportunities that are available to students in their buildings. Some of this miscommunication could stem from language or technology barriers. When communicating with diverse families, you must have the information accessible in their heritage language and available in multiple modalities. Families should be provided multiple opportunities and ways to engage in conversations with school personnel in their native language.

Family engagement is all about relationships and trust between practitioners, students, and families. Communicate clearly and often with families. Be transparent. Provide ongoing learning for families addressing gifted characteristics and needs of gifted learners in multiple languages and multiple modalities. The more the family is engaged, the more likely their student will be successful. Chapter 7 will provide a more in-depth exploration of family engagement and recommendations on how to engage diverse families.

Program Evaluation

The last piece of the G-PIE to be discussed is program evaluation, as seen in Figure 4.12.

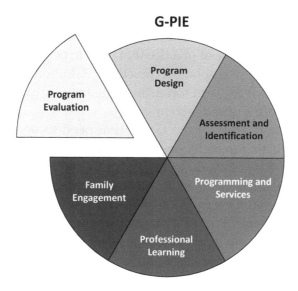

FIGURE 4.12
Gifted Program Inclusivity Evaluation: Program Evaluation.

Program evaluations are critical to assess current systems and evaluate their effectiveness. The evaluation of a gifted program is a systematic process of collecting data from multiple sources to make informed decisions about the effectiveness of the various components of services offered to gifted students (Purcell & Eckert, 2006). These components should be periodically reviewed by individuals knowledgeable about gifted learners and who have competence in the evaluation process. An evaluation process provides a way to continually review gifted services, and the results can be used for continual improvements to gifted programming. All results and plans for improvements to gifted programming should be communicated to the local school board and the stakeholder group and accessible to all constituencies of the program.

How to Use the G-PIE

The G-PIE (Appendix B) can be used as a continuous growth tool to support and guide the development of a strategic action plan focused on gifted programming. This tool can help identify areas of strength and areas that have room for growth. The G-PIE can be used in a variety of ways. It can be used in its entirety to evaluate gifted programs and services for equitable practices by determining problems of practice that need to be refined to allow for more culturally responsive practices. Additionally, any section of the G-PIE can be used as a single focus area to examine practices within a gifted system.

As you find areas of the G-PIE that need to be addressed, remember to be strategic, define the problem of practice, and determine what is in your sphere of control and influence. Then visualize the ideal state that you want and backward design towards the goal. Determine a timeline for implementation and evaluation updates. Progress monitor frequently to adjust, modify, or create a new goal. Celebrate your successes and reflect upon your setbacks. Move forward and make a commitment to being a culturally responsive leader who is a change agent and a warrior for social justice. Remember that change is a constant and continuous cycle. Embrace the hard work and celebrate both successes and setbacks as they are indicators of moving forward.

Contemplation Corner

Use the G-PIE to review your gifted education program. Identify one or two next steps to focus on implementing that will enhance gifted practices within your system to be more culturally responsive and inclusive.

Key Points

♦ The G-PIE is a tool that can be used to evaluate gifted programs for culturally responsive practices.

♦ Culturally responsive gifted leaders are committed to creating sustainable systems rooted in equity and social justice.

♦ All communication should be available in multiple languages and delivered in multiple modalities.

♦ Culturally responsive gifted programming recognizes the importance of a student's heritage language and deep culture.

♦ Culturally responsive gifted leaders are committed to providing equitable opportunity and access to gifted programming and talent development for all populations of gifted students.

♦ A culturally responsive curriculum is multicultural and includes experiences and perspectives from historically marginalized populations of learners and values diverse cultural and linguistic backgrounds of society.

♦ It is important to evaluate gifted systems regularly to determine areas of strength and areas of need.

References

Adams, C. (2022). Programming models and program design. In S. K. Johnson, D. Dailey, & A. Cotabish (Eds.), *NAGC pre-k–grade 12 gifted education programming standards: A guide to planning and implementing quality services for gifted students* (pp. 176–213). Prufrock Press.

Burns, D. E., Purcell, J. H., & Hertberg, H. L. (2006). Curriculum for gifted education students. In J. H. Purcell & R. D. Eckert (Eds.), *Designing services and programs for high-ability learners: A guidebook for gifted education* (pp. 87–111). Corwin Press.

Conrad, L. (2021, September 12). *Culturally responsive and relevant curriculum.* Global #gtchat. https://globalgtchatpoweredbytagt

.wordpress.com/2019/09/19/culturally-responsive-and-relevant -curriculum/

DuBois, M. P., & Greene, R. M. (2021). *Supporting gifted ELLS in the Latinx community: Practical strategies K–12*. Routledge.

Eckert, R. D. (2006). Developing a mission statement on the educational needs of gifted and talented students. In J. H. Purcell & R. D. Eckert (Eds.), *Designing services and programs for high-ability learners: A guidebook for gifted education* (pp. 15–22). Corwin Press.

Ford, D. (2011). *Multicultural gifted education* (2nd ed.). Prufrock Press.

Ford, D., & Trotman, M. F. (2001). Teachers of gifted students: Suggested multicultural characteristics and competencies. *Roeper Review, 23*(4), 235–239.

Frasier, M. M., & Passow, A. H. (1994). Toward a paradigm for identifying talent potential. *Research Monograph* 94112.

Garcia, M. E., Frunzi, K., Dean, C. B., Flores, N., & Miller, K. B. (2016). *Toolkit of resources for engaging families and the community as partners in education: Part 2 - Building a cultural bridge*. http://ies.ed.gov/ncee/ edlabs/projects/project.asp?projectID=4509

Gay, G. (2010). *Culturally responsive teaching: Theory, research, and practice* (2nd ed.). Teachers College Press.

Gay, G. (2018). *Culturally responsive teaching: Theory, research, and practice* (3rd ed.). Teachers College Press.

Getz, G. E. (2011). Culture fair test. In J. S. Kreutzner, J. DeLuca, & B. Caplan (Eds.), *Encyclopedia of clinical neuropsychology*. Springer. https://doi .org/10.1007/978-0-387-79948-3_1186

Greene, R., & Honeck, E. (2022, June 10). Culturally responsive gifted education in Denver public schools. *National Association for Gifted Children Insider*. https://www.nagc.org/culturally-responsive-gifted -education-denver-public-schools

Greene, R. M. (2017). Gifted culturally linguistically diverse learners: A school-based exploration. In *Perspectives in gifted education: Influences and impacts of the education doctorate on gifted education* (Vol. 6). Institute for the Development of Gifted Education, Ricks Center for Gifted Children, University of Denver.

Hammond, Z. (2015). *Culturally responsive teaching and the brain*. Corwin.

Heifetz, R. A., Linsky, M., & Grashow, A. (2009). *The practice of adaptive leadership: Tools and tactics for changing your organization and the world*. Harvard Business Press.

Johnsen, S. K., VanTassel-Baska, J. L., Robinson, A., Cotabish, A., Dailey, D., Jolly, J., Clarenbach, J., & Adams, C. M. (2016). *Using the national gifted education standards for teacher preparation* (2nd ed.). Prufrock Press.

Johnsen, S. K. (2022). The assessment standard in gifted education: Identifying gifted students. In S. K. Johnson, D. Dailey, & A. Cotabish (Eds.), *NAGC pre-k–grade 12 gifted education programming standards: A guide to planning and implementing quality services for gifted students* (pp. 94–127). Routledge.

Johnson, S. K., Dailey, D., & Cotabish, A. (Eds.). (2022). *NAGC pre-k-grade 12 gifted education programming standards: A guide to planning and implementing quality services for gifted students*. Routledge.

Leppien, J. H., & Westberg, K. L. (2006). Establishing gifted education advisory committees. In J. H. Purcell & R. D. Eckert (Eds.), *Designing services and programs for high-ability learners: A guidebook for gifted education* (pp. 292–295). Corwin Press.

Massachusetts Department of Elementary and Secondary Education. (n.d.). *Culturally responsive social-emotional competency development.* https://www.doe.mass.edu/sfs/sel/sel-all.docx

Missett, T. C., & Brunner, M. C. (2013). The use of traditional assessment tools for identifying gifted students. In C. M. Callahan & H. L. Herberg-Davis (Eds.), *Fundamentals of gifted education: Considering multiple perspectives* (pp. 105–111). Routledge.

Moon, S. M. (2006). Developing a definition of giftedness. In J. H. Purcell & R. D. Eckert (Eds.), *Designing services and programs for high-ability learners: A guidebook for gifted education* (pp. 23–31). Corwin Press.

National Association for Gifted Children. (2019). *The NAGC pre-K to grade 12 gifted programming standards*. NAGC.

Neumeister, K. S., & Burney, V. (2012). *Gifted program evaluation: A handbook for administrators & coordinators*. Prufrock Press.

Purcell, J. H., & Eckert, R. D. (Eds.). (2006). *Designing services and programs for high-ability learners: A guidebook for gifted education*. Corwin Press.

Snyder, S., & Fenner, D. S. (2021). *Culturally responsive teaching for multilingual learners: Tools for equity*. Corwin Press.

The Leadership Academy. (2022). *Culturally responsive leadership: A framework for school & school system leaders*. https://www.leadershipacademy.org/resources/

Tomlinson, C. (2001). *How to differentiate instruction in mixed ability classrooms* (2nd ed.). Association for Supervision and Curriculum Development.

Wright, B. L., Ford, D. Y., & Moore III, J. L. (2022). *Black boys are lit: Engaging preK-3 gifted and talented black boys using multicultural literature and Ford' Bloom-Banks matrix*. Information Age Publishing.

Valdés, G. (2003). *Expanding definitions of giftedness: The case of young interpreters from immigrant communities*. Lawrence Eribaum.

5

Data-Driven Approach

Deep Roots

It is vital that leaders in gifted education understand and recognize the root causes of gifted disproportionality for culturally and linguistically diverse students in their systems. The roots run deep in educational disparity for historically marginalized students of color. We have been battling the same fight for more than 100 years to integrate schools and give equitable access to culturally, linguistically diverse learners. In 1868, Iowa became the first state to outlaw segregation in public schools in the United States (U.S.) when the case of *Clark vs. Board of Directors* was tried by the Iowa Supreme Court (Ryan, 2018). It was not until 79 years later in 1947 that California (U.S.) followed with the case of *Mendez vs. Westminster* which outlawed the "separate-but-equal" doctrine in public schools for students of Mexican ancestry (Ryan, 2018). Seven years would pass before the U.S. Supreme Court would rule in the *Brown vs. Board of Education* case that racial segregation of Black children in public schools violated the Equal Protection Clause of the Fourteenth Amendment (History, 2022). These cases propelled the U.S. forward with the integration of all public schools and paved a pathway towards dismantling systemic racism in the U.S.. So why does systemic racism continue to resonate in the U.S.? And what actions can we take as gifted leaders to disrupt this pattern? This chapter examines how data can highlight equity

DOI: 10.4324/9781003293729-5

challenges and areas of growth within educational systems to help guide leaders of gifted education programs towards making systemic changes.

Why Data Matters

Research and national data have shown students of color continue to be underrepresented in gifted education programs across the country, and leaders of culturally responsive gifted programs must be willing to confront the data used when identifying specific areas of concern that continues to create this situation. The distribution of students enrolled in gifted programs across the U.S. is heavily weighted with Asian and white males and females (Fergus, 2017). Changing this pattern requires determining what the factors are creating this disparity in our nation's educational systems. By using data and analytics to highlight patterns of systemic inequality, leaders in gifted education can make data-driven decisions regarding whether gifted students of color are being served equitably across all populations. Interpreting multiple data sets and multiple sources can guide you in aligning resource allocations to impact school, district, and even state-wide gifted services for culturally, linguistically diverse gifted learners. As we look at recruiting and retaining our Black and Brown students in gifted education, data can significantly change the way one looks at gifted and talented disproportionality across schools, districts, and states. This action can transform the way we provide opportunity and can create a pathway for these students towards advanced course work and college readiness. This chapter will help guide you on your culturally responsive gifted journey by expanding upon the traditional data that is collected in schools and districts such as achievement test scores to include discussions of how to collect and analyze student, family, and educator perception inventories, community data, and equity audits that celebrate diversity and inclusion, to help drive decision making. This chapter will explore a variety of ways that data can be used to support systemic change.

Root Cause Analysis

So where do you start? Determine a problem of practice or an equity challenge. What is the basis or the root of the problem? Let's say the current equity challenge your district is facing is that high school–age students of color are not participating in Advanced Placement courses at the same rate as their white peers. As a culturally responsive leader of gifted programs, you may be inclined to try to solve the equity challenge immediately; however, you will need to understand why the challenge is happening first before you are able to move towards any solutions. You will need to collect and review data without forming judgment. Therefore, to understand why and possibly even how to solve an equity challenge in front of you, you need to know the root cause or causes of the equity challenge. In order to determine the root cause or causes, leaders of culturally responsive gifted programs should start by conducting a root cause analysis (RCA). Root cause analysis is a data and research-driven process that names the causes of disproportionate patterns and often points out the presence of bias based beliefs about marginalized populations within policy and practice (Fergus, 2017).

There are several analysis tools that can be used to find the root cause of an identified equity challenge; however, the two tools that the authors have found to be effective in their practice are more commonly known as "the Fishbone Diagram" and the "Five Whys." One of the more popular methods is the Ishikawa Fishbone Diagram (IFD), also known as the Fishbone Diagram. This visual model is considered to be one of the most robust methods for conducting a root cause analysis because it allows for those engaging with the tool to critically think about why something is happening in multiple layers. When completed, it looks like the outline of the bones of a fish.

At the head of the fishbone, the problem of practice, or equity challenge, is noted. Our previous equity challenge stated earlier was that high-school students of color are not participating in Advanced Placement courses at the high school level. So the statement "High school students of color are not participating in Advanced Placement courses at the same rate at their white peers" would be placed at the head of the fishbone. This statement is referred to as the effect. On the top and bottom lines are listed the broader categories that are causing the effect. Examples could include, but are not limited to, material expenses, enrollment process, support systems, communication, racialized tracking, teacher expectations, district resources, or bias. Once you have completed the larger boxes, then you can draw additional horizontal or vertical lines from the diagonal lines and write why those broader categories are causing the effect. Through this process, you will eventually come to the root cause or causes and will then need to determine which cause to address first. Examples of Fishbone templates and diagrams can be found utilizing online search engines. If possible, work on a Fishbone Diagram with someone else so that you can put multiple causes forward.

A second analysis tool that the authors use to help determine root causes of equity challenges is the Five Whys method, an analysis method first developed by Sakichi Toyoda, an inventor and industrialist (Kanbanize, n.d.). The Five Whys method is an iterative way to drill down to a root problem by asking, "why" repeatedly, and answering repeatedly five times (or more) until you reach what you believe to be your root cause. For example,

Example 1—Five Whys:

Equity challenge: Students of color are not participating in Advanced Placement courses.

1. *Why are students of color not participating in our Advanced Placement courses?*
   Possible answer: Students of color are not being referred or encouraged to enroll in advanced courses.

2. *Why are students of color not being referred or encouraged to enroll in advanced courses?*
   Possible answer: Our high-school counselors, the ones responsible for referring students, have a high case load of students and do not have time to communicate with students and families of color about their course options, so they support previous year's recommendations for

advanced placement or work with families who reach out to them seeking high-level coursework for their students.

3. *Why do counselors have high case-loads of students and no time to communicate with students and families of color?*

   Possible answer: Our high school is underresourced and we do not have enough counselors to meet the student body's needs; therefore our counselors spend more time focused on specific state rules and respond to families who reach out to them with their specific student's needs.

4. *Why is your high school underresourced and focused only on families who reach out to those at the school?*

   Possible answer: Our school leader had to make the difficult decision to reallocate resources and they cut one of our counselors, thereby reducing the number of people able to support our most vulnerable populations of learners. The families we hear the most from are historically our white and affluent families.

5. *Why did your school leader reduce counselors instead of cutting funding somewhere else?*

   Possible answer: Parts of the counselor's role can be given to other staff members to take on, and when our counselors are so busy, they are only able to focus on the needs of the students with the most urgent needs. They focus on state-mandated and federally mandated aspects of their work as well as respond to the needs of the students who appear to be most urgent—the ones whose families are calling for support. They just do not have the capacity.

Possible root cause: School counselors do not have the capacity to identify students who should be in advanced courses because they are underresourced and have high caseloads.

When using this model, remember that five is just a number and you can always expand this to more than five questions. As you can see in the example, there are opportunities to ask additional questions. Furthermore, you could go through this exercise again and it could look different based on the variables in your district.

Example 2—Five Whys:

1. *Why are students of color at a specific high school not participating in Advanced Placement courses at the same rate as their white peers? Possible answer: The school counselors are not enrolling them in the courses at the same rate.*

2. *Why are the counselors responsible for placing them in the courses not enrolling students of color in advanced courses at the same rate? Possible answer: The counselors take into consideration multiple factors, including scores in previous advanced courses in middle school. The majority of students of color at this particular high school were not able to access the required middle-school classes for Advanced Placement high-school courses.*

3. *Why are students of color unable to access the required middle school classes for Advanced Placement? Possible answer: The middle school did not offer honors or pre-Advanced Placement courses at this school because the school leader did not think enough students would be able to take the advanced classes.*

4. *Why did the school leader think there would not be enough students to take the advanced classes? Possible answer: The school leader had a school that was majority students of color and achievement was low. He did not want the students to feel bad and did not expect the students to be able to succeed.*

5. *Why did he think the students could not succeed in advanced classes? Possible answer: The school leader had low expectations of his students and implicit bias that was causing missed opportunities for these learners later in their academic career.*

Possible root cause: The school leader at the middle-school level has low expectations of students of color and does not offer advanced courses for them to take, therefore not giving them an opportunity to access the prerequisites needed in high school. The school leader has bias that is harming students of color.

Conducting the Five Whys method when seeking out an answer to a complex equity challenge gives opportunities to multiple stakeholders to give their perspectives on why a challenge is occurring. With this opportunity comes challenges and limitations that culturally responsive leaders of gifted programs must be aware of before they conduct this approach. First, those who are investigating an equity challenge may be tempted to stop at the symptom of the problem and not truly get to the root cause. A symptom in the first scenario is that counselors are overworked and that parts of their job were given away. The larger reason, however, has to do with budget cuts and perhaps even belief systems about whose child deserves to be in advanced classes. Had we asked more than five questions, we could continue to go down that route. In our second scenario, we dug deeper until we learned that there were lower expectations for students of color based on what an administrator stated. In both of these different scenarios with the same effect, the possible root causes give leaders more to investigate to determine where supports are needed.

The Fishbone Diagram and the Five Whys question method can be used together to determine specific causes of the categories within the fishbone. As you can see in these two scenarios, these have two different root causes, and the approach to solving this equity challenge will be different. If the counselors at a high school do not have capacity, you will have to do further analysis and look at what are the systemic reasons behind the lack of capacity and resources and determine with whom you need to speak. If the counselors at the middle school have bias and low expectations for students of color, then that is a mindset shift that you will have to address and approach through professional learning and anti-bias training. You will also need to do much more analysis to determine who else will need help. Either way, as a culturally responsive leader of gifted programs, starting with a root cause analysis tool such as a Fishbone Diagram or the Five Whys is an excellent place to begin as you work to dismantle systems of oppression, both internalized and externalized.

Adaptive and Technical Equity Challenges

Once you have your root causes identified, then it is time to determine whether or not the equity challenges you are facing are technical problems that can be easily solved with authority and are relatively quick fixes, or if they are adaptive challenges that are ambiguous in nature and more complex (Heifetz & Linskey, 2002) and will need a shift in values and mindsets before change can happen. Once leaders of culturally responsive gifted programs have a better understanding of the need, then they can determine how to best approach solving it. The terms *adaptive* and *technical*, first used by Ronald Heifetz and Marty Linsky (2002), refer to the types of challenges leaders face in the workplace. Table 5.1 gives some identifiable examples of the differences between technical and adaptive challenges.

In gifted education, leaders face multiple technical and adaptive challenges. For example, technical challenges like ensuring every student has a math block at the same time on the schedule to allow for subject acceleration can be more easily maneuvered than convincing your staff that they should all embrace having younger students in their classes. This is because subject acceleration is a research-based practice that improves academic and affective

TABLE 5.1
Technical Vs. Adaptive Challenges

Technical challenges	Adaptive challenges
Easy to identify	Difficult to identify
Lead to quick and clear solutions	Solutions are not clear and involve changing mindsets, values, beliefs, and roles
Require change in just one place within the organization, unit, or school district	Require changes across entire systems, in multiple places across the organization
People are receptive to technical solutions because they do not challenge existing belief systems	People resist acknowledging adaptive solutions because they may challenge their existing belief systems
Solutions can be implemented quickly and by direct authority	Solutions can take a longer time to implement and require people to experiment with possible outcomes
Direct authority solves the challenge	People with the equity challenge try to solve it

outcomes for gifted learners. Leaders of culturally responsive gifted programs will face both technical problems and adaptive challenges. In the scenarios above, there were both technical and adaptive challenges intertwined. Your job is to make sure that you have identified the appropriate root cause and the type of challenge you are solving so that you understand how to approach the challenge. Leaders can make the mistake of solving adaptive challenges with technical solutions. Heifetz and Linsky (2002) state, "to make real progress, sooner or later those who lead must ask themselves and the people in the organization to face a set of deeper issues—and to accept a solution that may require turning part or all of the organization upside down." When solving for disproportionality in gifted education, a complex and ambiguous issue, remember that the majority of the challenges you will face are adaptive. You are working to shift mindsets around who deserves gifted education and who should have access to gifted education. You are going to be working on bias, attitudes, and beliefs.

Contemplation Corner

Has your school or district conducted a root cause analysis within the last 3 years? If so, what changes were put in place after the analysis? What types of equity challenges did you face, adaptive or technical?

Data Collection Tools

Equity Audits

There are leadership tools available that can support leaders in evaluating their educational systems for equitable gifted education processes. Leaders engaging in critical and reflective practice utilize tools that assist them in understanding and build trust to work with diverse families and communities and address equity issues. One of these tools is an equity audit. An equity audit is designed to guide school districts in identifying sources of academic and disciplinary disparities using a comprehensive research-based tool (Adjusted, 2022). Utilizing an equity audit approach for analyzing gifted systems for disparities that disenfranchise students of color from access to advanced coursework can reveal areas of need and improvement at the school, district, and state levels. Equity audits have a history of being used in education in the areas of civil rights enforcement, curriculum auditing, math/science reform, and state accountability (Skrla et al., 2009). As we look at recruiting and retaining our Black and Brown students in gifted education, an equity audit can significantly change the way one looks at gifted and talented disproportionality across schools, districts, and states. Equity audits can comprehensively measure equity and inclusivity in an organization in a concrete manner. They can highlight areas that are barriers for students of color to an equitable education and can provide an avenue to allow for authentic discussions and solutions to systemic and prolonged patterns of inequity. The Gifted Program Inclusivity Evaluation (G-PIE) (Appendix B) discussed in Chapter 4 is a tool that can be utilized to collect data for an equity audit highlighting areas of equitable and inequitable gifted practices. By utilizing the data that school systems already have, accountability can be held at school, district, and state levels for gifted education services for students of color. Equity audits can create a staggering amount of data to have to sift through, so determine specific areas that you want to evaluate in your gifted education system. To be able to implement action steps from an equity audit, the results must be clear and manageable in order to be useful for leaders.

Equity audits generally have specific areas that they focus on to get a bigger picture of an organization. Khalifa (2018) suggests that an equity audit relies on four main components when focusing on oppressive practices within an organization: equity trends, survey data, policy analysis, and culturally responsive curriculum, pedagogy, and leadership practices. Skrla, McKenzie, and Scheurich (2009) recommend that a simple equity audit should focus on three main areas of evaluation: programmatic equity, teacher quality equity, and achievement equity. Green (2017) suggests that a community-based equity audit should consist of four phases: disrupt deficit views about community, conduct initial community inquiry and shared community experiences, establish a community leadership team, and collect equity asset-based community data. Some of the data to be gathered for an equity audit focused on disproportionality for students of color would include but are not limited to discipline referrals, discipline policies, discipline practices, enrollment in honors and Advanced Placement courses, enrollment in Special Education and Gifted Education, and referral processes.

As a leader, remember that just because you believe an equity audit is a good tool to use does not also mean your staff will feel the same way. Some people will be on board and think it is a good idea while others might be fearful of the outcome of the audit. As a leader, it is your job to make sure that everyone is willing to move forward with the process and accept that instructional practices and systemic changes may be necessary to facilitate change over time that will suppress educational oppression for students of color.

Leaders of culturally responsive gifted programs see equity audits as an opportunity to focus on equity oriented change. Skrla et al. (2009) outline the traits that a leader needs in order to become an equity-oriented change agent. A leader must have an equity-focused attitude toward their colleagues. This means as a leader with an equity attitude, you treat everyone with respect regardless of their personalities, attitudes, prejudice, or bias. You model the equity attitude behaviors that you want your colleagues to demonstrate as human beings. Avoid demonization, which means characterizing someone wholly by one negative characteristic or characterizing someone as totally negative based upon one experience (Skrla et al., 2009). This is an easy trap to fall into when we judge someone as a whole on the basis of one negative characteristic of the person or by something they might have said that made us angry. This is the danger of a single story and narrative for one person. In order to be an equity-oriented leader, you must create an equity-focused environment, which means that everyone's culture is valued, appreciated, and respected. A leader with an equity attitude initiates and facilitates courageous conversations about equity and antiracism. These are difficult conversations and require leaders to maintain composure and sensitivity to others as well as allowing themselves to be vulnerable as a leader.

Skrla et al. (2009) maintain that equity-oriented change agents demonstrate persistence and are committed to the journey and the challenge of systemic changes that have continued to be perpetuated over decades. Be patient, as it takes time for systems to change. However, do not be so patient that a system remains stagnant. Maintain an assets-based attitude. Discover what strength-based assets are in students and those working with students. Recognize the value in individuals and in yourself. Lastly, Skrla et al. (2009) maintain that equity-oriented leaders require a coherent focus that does not switch from one focus to a different focus frequently but remains focused for the long haul on one coherent focus to make long-term systemic changes.

If you are going to have a comprehensive equity audit for your district or state, you might consider working with a local university or college, or, if resources allow, hiring an educational consultant to help with this process, as the outcome of the audit might be a 100-page document. Many states in the U.S. have had equity audits performed in their school districts. The authors have experienced equity audits as well as participated in equity walks alongside educational consultants conducting equity audits. It is critical as a leader of culturally responsive gifted programs that gifted education is a component of any equity audit that may be taking place in your district. Check with your state to see if they have ever had an equity audit or if they have an instrument that evaluates equity levels in schools and school districts within the state. This could save you some time and give you some already available information to use.

Gap Analysis

Another way to determine where the disparities are in your systems is to conduct a gap analysis. A gap analysis is a way to view your current situation and the objectives that were set. Did you meet the objectives that were set, or is there a gap between where you are and where you want to be? For example, if the objective is to increase students of color in honors and Advanced Placement courses by 15% over a 3-year period and the increase was 5%, then there is a gap between where you are and where you want to be. The basic steps to a gap analysis framework include to

- Identify the area to be analyzed and identify the goals to be accomplished
- Analyze the current state
- Establish the ideal future state
- Compare the current state with the ideal state
- Describe the gap and quantify the difference (Wheeler, 2022)
- Establish a plan with set goals to close existing gaps

Gap analysis can be used at any point in which leaders of culturally responsive gifted programs want to improve outcomes for students (educational experiences, achievement outcomes, family engagement, etc.). It is critical that a plan be established to close existing gaps and that the plan be monitored. A gap analysis alone does not help solve an equity challenge. The data is critical to have, and what you do with that data as a leader is equally of value.

Equity Allowance Formula

Students' experiential and cultural funds are not equally and equitably distributed; therefore, leaders of culturally responsive gifted programs must both be aware of who is not represented within their populations as well as review their data to understand specifically when underrepresentation is significant, and at what point underrepresentation in gifted education within their context becomes discriminatory (Ford, 2013a). Rather than use the already established discriminatory practice of equity quotas (Wright et al., 2017), the authors support the proactive use of Donna Y. Ford's (2013b) Equity Allowance formula to determine and identify underrepresentation of students of color in gifted services. The Equity Allowance formula is designed to quantify equity by calculating the minimal number/percentage of students of color in gifted education programs to rule out bias and discrimination. The 20% equity allowance recognizes that giftedness exists in every racial group and that students' cultural experiences and opportunities to learn are not always equal or equitably distributed (Wright et al., 2017). It is used to indicate the minimal number of students that should be receiving gifted services based upon statistical chance. When the equity allowance formula's percentage of underrepresentation exceeds the designated threshold, it is beyond statistical chance, meaning that human error is operating and that attitudes, instruments, and policies and procedures may be discriminatory (Wright et al., 2017). Using the Equity Allowance formula includes a few steps. An example of how to use the formula is provided in Snapshot 5.2.

Snapshot: Equity Allowance Formula Example

Using the 20% equity allowance formula requires you to have two data sets. The fictional data sets we are using in this example are representative of a school district. The first data set is the percentage of Latinx students in the school district and the second data set is the percentage of Latinx students identified as gifted in the school district.

Overall % of Latinx students—15%

% of gifted Latinx students—9%

Calculate 20% threshold times 15% the overall population of Latinx students in the school district.

20% × 15% = 3%

Then subtract the 3% from the overall % of Latinx students to calculate the adjusted target percentage.

$15\% - 3\% = 14.55\%$

The 14.55% is the equity goal. It is the minimal percentage of Latinx students that should be identified and provided gifted services.

The equity goal is to increase Latinx gifted representation in gifted education in this school district from 9% to 14.55%.

Using the 20% equity allowance formula can provide local, district, and state educational organizations with a concise quantitative metric for measuring underrepresentation of culturally different students in gifted education. It then allows schools and districts the opportunity to review their practices and policies related to identification within these groups.

Types of Data

Generally in educational systems, there are multiple places and platforms in which data is collected and can be used to determine if disproportionality is occurring among a student population. There are also probably data people within your educational system that may be able to gather the data you need and work with you to interpret the data. Some data may be easier than other data to gather and therefore find the results that you need. Either way, data is a useful way to drive equity dialogues and start transformational change within systems that support culturally and linguistically diverse students in gifted education.

There are two types of educational data that are necessary for leaders of culturally responsive gifted programs to collect so that they have a broad picture of their disproportionality: quantitative and qualitative. Quantitative data is considered to be objective, as the data is easily classified or quantified (Gliner et al., 2009). This type of data is often displayed in numbers, percentages, and percentiles, and it usually utilizes some sort of instrument to gather the data. This type of data gives leaders of culturally responsive gifted programs a snapshot of what is going on in the district (e.g., in one school district, Latinx boys are being identified at twice the rate of Latinx girls). However, it does not tell leaders why numbers are trending in a specific way. For those answers, we look to qualitative data. Qualitative data is more subjective and may be interpreted differently by those looking at the data (Gliner et al., 2009) because it focuses on the "why" of the data and is based on user experience and perceptions, rather than numbers alone. Quantitative and qualitative data hold equal value in research and they tell us different parts of a story—both of which are necessary when solving equity challenges and engaging in equity dialogues.

One way to look at data is by dividing data into categories which can then be examined as smaller data sets. These categories could be achievement data, nonacademic data, professional learning data, and perception data (educator, student, family, etc.). All of these categories can help inform leaders in gifted education about patterns of disproportionalities within their educational systems. Culturally responsive leaders use data to discover and track racialized or cultural gaps in achievement, disciplinary trends, graduation, enrichment, gifted education, special education services, and more.

Achievement Data

One of the most readily accessible data sets leaders have available to them is achievement data. In education, leaders typically use achievement tests to measure student progress and growth throughout the year to meet federal and state standards. Annual grade-level testing of students on state assessments in the areas of reading, math, social studies, and science can highlight areas of strengths and growth. This type of data can be disaggregated into multiple demographics and components such as gender, race, migrant status, homelessness, military, language, and socioeconomic status, as well as by performance levels. It can also be used to compare other schools and districts' performances on the same assessment. As a leader of culturally responsive gifted programs, it is imperative that you look at achievement data with a critical eye. Ask yourself: Demographically, which students performed at the higher levels of the assessment? Are these students demographically proportionate to your school, district, or state populations? Why are some schools gaining growth over time while others are stagnant? All of these questions can be answered by diving into the data. Do your achievement gaps mirror poverty and other statistics in your district?

Some states have state assessments that the protocols are in Spanish one year for native Spanish speakers, and then the next year the protocols are in English for the native Spanish speakers. For example, in 3rd grade, the state assessment is administered in Spanish and in 4th grade the state assessment is administered in English. This type of data is useful as you can compare the data between the two years to determine growth over time and trends. So, if a native Spanish speaker is advanced on the 3rd grade assessment in Spanish and then the following year the same native Spanish speaker is proficient on the 4th grade assessment in English, this should suggest that the student has characteristics of rapid language acquisition and should be referred for gifted services.

Another source of achievement data that is important to review is English language acquisition data. Many of our English language learners are given assessments that measure their language acquisition growth. One such assessment is ACCESS for ELLs, which is a suite of English language proficiency assessments for students who have been identified as English language learners (ELLs) (Colorado Department of Education, 2021). These assessments are administered annually to students who are non-English proficient (NEP) and limited English proficient (LEP). This type of data can reveal which students are acquiring English language over time at a rapid rate as compared to other English language learners, which can indicate that a student has superior language abilities even though they may not be proficient in the use of the English language. This type of data would suggest that a student be referred for gifted services and the data added into the student's body of evidence for gifted identification.

Lastly, when students are identified as gifted, achievement data should still be considered and monitored. If students are not continuing to achieve in a content area that is an area of strength for them, then it is critical to review what might be happening to cause a drop in achievement or lack of progress. Is it the curriculum? Is the student having personal or social emotional challenges? Are the material and instructional strategies culturally responsive and authentic? Use the quantitative data of the achievement scores to seek out qualitative information—the "why" behind the scores—so that you can act in a responsive and supportive manner.

Universal Screening Data

As more research is supporting the use of universal screening for giftedness, more school districts are using this approach for gifted referrals; therefore your district may have universal screening ability data available to review. Universal screening means that an entire population of students are assessed using the same assessment tool at a specific grade level for the purpose of identifying high potential or gifted ability. Culturally responsive leaders of gifted programs recognize that screening all students at a specific grade level using a culturally responsive assessment can eliminate teacher bias within the referral process for gifted services. Universal screening tools can be either qualitative or quantitative. Some commonly used tools for universal gifted screening are cognitive assessments that have less of a language load, such as a nonverbal assessment in which students are required to problem solve (DuBois & Greene, 2021).

Other tools used for universal screening are observation tools and checklists that measure the gifted characteristics of students. These tools do not always cost the district more dollars (though they may); however, they will take more time and resources to ensure that the data received from the universal screening is as valid as possible. These tools can be a bit more time-consuming for teachers and might not eliminate teacher bias as teachers are primarily the ones who complete the observations tools and checklists. Leaders of culturally responsive gifted programs can help reduce educator bias and increase understanding of the manifestations of giftedness across cultures by providing training for observation tools prior to having teachers use them in the classroom. Training on how to recognize giftedness across cultures is critical so that educators recognize how culture impacts how giftedness may present in a school setting. No matter which tools you use, universal screening can provide another data point for looking at students who might benefit from gifted services or talent development.

Contemplation Corner

What other achievement or ability data do you have that can be used to find the root cause of cultural gaps within your educational system?

Nonacademic Data

Culturally responsive leaders not only look at academic data but use a variety of data sources to determine disparities in systems. The use of traditionally nonacademic data to pinpoint cultural gaps and potential mismatches within systems is critically important. This is data that relies on factors that affect student outcomes. These factors focus on attendance and the social-emotional wellbeing of students as well as on health and wellness behaviors. When students are socially-emotionally healthy, they are more engaged and able to focus on the cognitive demand that learning requires.

Leaders must recognize the social-emotional and psychological needs of gifted culturally linguistically diverse students.

These students deal with negative peer pressure, prejudice, discrimination, cultural identity, self-esteem, and self-concept on a daily basis (Ford, 2013a). The needs of students of color are different from the needs of students who are not of color.

Research shows that Hispanic and Black students are disproportionately disciplined in schools compared to their white peers (U.S. Department of Education, 2014). By looking at office referrals and suspensions, culturally responsive leaders can identify root causes for why gifted students of color are being disciplined. There is generally an underlying problem such as teacher bias, cultural misunderstanding, or cultural bias on the part of the person referring the student. It is critical to discover the root cause and not dismiss the student as being behaviorally challenged. Many times our gifted students of color can identify when their culture is not being valued in their environment or when their teacher does not respect the deep culture they bring into their classrooms or even understand that their behaviors might look different based upon their culture. This can create student-discourse and classroom-management issues for both the student and teacher. Students want connections with their teachers, especially our students of color who come from collectivist communities which embrace cultural connections as an important part of their racial identity.

Attendance is another source of data that can help leaders understand the reasons students of color may not be engaged in school or may be socially and emotionally unable to get to school. Attendance data can be used to determine if students of color have more frequent absences than other students and if this practice is impacting their academic progress and growth. Looking deeper into data and creating relationships with families can build strong bonds and help avert any attendance issues. When examining attendance data, culturally responsive leaders remember that there are typically deeper reasons behind any student's chronic absences and will seek out resources within the district and outside of the district to support the student getting to school on time.

Examining gifted education referral data is critical in supporting students of color to access gifted services. Are students of color being referred for gifted services or talent development?

Who is able to refer students for gifted services? Is the referral system set up so that only teachers can refer students for gifted services? Are the teachers who are able to refer students for gifted services teachers of color? A review of the gifted referral process and who has access to refer is one of the fundamental steps to providing gifted students of color access to the educational services they deserve.

A primary source of data that should be examined is demographic data. For the past 40 years, Black and Latinx students have been underrepresented in gifted education. Does the gifted demographic data reflect the demographic data of the general population of your school, district, or state? Ford (2013) advises that in order to recruit and retain gifted Black and Hispanic students, all data must be disaggregated by the combination of race, gender, and income. Disaggregated data will reveal patterns and trends that might not be revealed by examining data in larger data sets.

Program Participation Data

Too often when looking at program participation data we discover that culturally linguistically diverse students are disproportionately placed in special education. *Significant disproportionality* is the term used to describe this trend of students from certain racial and ethnic groups being identified for special education and placed in more restrictive educational settings at markedly higher rates than their peers (National Center for Learning Disabilities, n.d.). Research by Grindal et al. (2019) found evidence that the systemic racial biases in our schools and communities led to students of color being identified for special education at higher rates.

The overrepresentation of students of color in special education can create long-term consequences for those students who are misidentified as requiring special education services. These students are more likely to have low self-esteem, a less challenging curriculum, and low expectations from teachers. This practice can be rectified by having cultural and language experts involved in making special-education decisions for students of color and by providing professional learning for educators regarding culturally different learners.

Delve into data that focuses on advanced learning opportunities for students such as accelerated math opportunities, Advanced Placement (AP) courses, International Baccalaureate (IB) Diploma Programs, concurrent enrollment, and the Seal of Biliteracy. Culturally responsive gifted leaders are committed to providing equitable access and opportunity to advanced courses and opportunities for culturally different learners. This begins with providing access at the primary level and supporting these learners throughout their school career to participate and succeed in rigorous coursework. Participation in rigorous courses such as high-school AP courses can involve exponential challenges for students of color and students from low socioeconomic backgrounds. Examination of demographic data of students participating in advanced courses can illuminate inequities and force changes to systems of oppression. What are supports that can be put in place to provide students of color with advanced learning opportunities? The following describe some components of programs that are designed to increase the participation of students from historically marginalized populations in advanced high-school coursework. These components are:

- A culture of high expectations for all students
- Vertical training of all K–12 teachers in recognizing diverse manifestations of talent in a broad range of gifted learners
- Provision of systematic, planned support for students to develop the skills necessary for success in advanced coursework
- Creation of an organized peer support network for students so that they do not feel alone in their pursuit of advanced coursework
- Relentless and individualized recruitment methods (Purcell & Eckert, 2006)

How many students of color are participating in concurrent enrollment or have access to postsecondary courses? Concurrent Enrollment (CE) is a program that provides high-school students with the opportunity to enroll in postsecondary courses and earn college credit at no tuition cost to students or their families (Colorado Department of Education, 2022). This no-cost opportunity can make a significant impact on students with limited financial resources and provide them a pathway for a college education. How many of our families of color know about advanced opportunities for their students? How are advanced opportunities communicated with families who are culturally linguistically diverse? These are all questions that culturally responsive leaders should be asking at the school, district, and state levels.

Language is a strength for many of our gifted Latinx students, and many of these students are bilingual. In the United States, the Seal of Biliteracy is awarded to students who have studied and attained proficiency in two or more languages by high-school graduation (Seal of Biliteracy, 2022). In order to earn the Seal of Biliteracy, students must be able to speak, listen, read, and write at a high level in English and another language. School districts and states who offer the Seal of Biliteracy demonstrate that bilingual and multilingual identities of students are valued. This is an opportunity for students who are bilingual or even trilingual and, in our ever-changing world full of diversity and rich languages, could lead toward a career pathway for culturally linguistically diverse students. The ability to traverse between the English language and another language or multiple languages enhances the cognitive development of students and makes them in high demand for the increasing opportunities throughout the world from companies seeking employees fluent in multiple languages. At the university level, students who have attained the Seal of Biliteracy are recognized for their attainment of high-level skills in multiple languages. As a culturally responsive leader, analyzing data on which students are receiving the Seal of Biliteracy is critical to determine if BIPOC students are seeking out this opportunity or if it is only students from the majority culture. If so, then determine the root causes and implement strategies to encourage and support culturally linguistically students who are interested in this opportunity so that they can be successful and thrive.

Perception Data

Another type of data that can be a useful source of information is perception data. Perceptions are the attitudes and beliefs held about an educational system by people with a vested interest in seeing the system succeed (McGuire, 2022). Perception data involves gathering stakeholders' perceptions through surveys, focus groups, interviews, listening sessions, or other means. This information provides educational systems with a self-evaluation of how well they are meeting the needs of their students, school staff, and families. This type of data is an important source for ongoing improvement planning for schools, districts, and state educational systems.

Many school districts annually distribute climate surveys to their stakeholders. Climate surveys are generally in a questionnaire format using a Likert scale that measures school and work culture in educational systems. They are generally given annually to educators, students, and families to provide feedback on school and work perceptions. These annual climate surveys are a good way to gather information from stakeholders without having to create an additional survey, especially if the survey is centered on equity issues.

When possible, add on questions about advanced or gifted education and family perceptions around programming or identification—or add to the teacher survey questions about the perception of the gifted education department, if you have one, and how they are supporting the teachers and staff. The authors were able to put gifted education on perception surveys aimed at educators and administrators to better understand how their central office was being perceived as being helpful and culturally responsive in gifted education to meet the needs of the diverse learners and schools. The response was overwhelmingly positive and gave the team information to build upon.

Information from these surveys is typically disaggregated into ethnicity and free/reduced lunch. Depending on how small of a group of students fits into each demographic group, you may or may not be able to get specific data. However, examining this data can indicate how groups of students perceive their learning environments and highlight which groups of students, such as students of color, feel differently about their learning environment than students from the majority culture. For leaders of culturally responsive gifted programs, this is an opportunity to gain perspective on how students and families are experiencing gifted education as culturally linguistically diverse learners and families. These surveys can bring to light any disproportionality in services that may exist, or highlight specific examples in which programming is culturally responsive and meeting the needs of the community.

Interviews are generally one-on-one data-gathering sessions, which can be time intensive but can give you a more individual perspective with a human face connected to it. This type of data can be an excellent way to supplement survey statistical data with qualitative anecdotal data. Focus groups and listening sessions are another approach to collecting perception data from stakeholders. Focus groups are similar to interviews except they are not one-on-one sessions but are organized into small group settings with a facilitator. Listening sessions generally involve large groups of people participating in a widely publicized community gathering to express their opinions and perceptions on a specific topic. These sessions can be a way for the community to feel involved and valued for their perspectives and insights into their local and state educational and gifted systems. It is important to have multiple pieces of data that reflect a wide diversity of stakeholder perspectives in order to evaluate whether the current educational practices are effective and impactful for students' academic and social-emotional learning environments.

Professional Learning Data

Professional learning is one of the most important ways that administrators and educators can gain information about gifted students and the characteristics of these diversified learners. In order to develop culturally responsive educators and administrators, a strategic professional learning plan must be grounded in equity. Through ongoing professional learning, administrators and educators can keep up to date on current research, learn culturally responsive practices, and implement changes in their schools and classrooms that can successfully impact students of color.

One of the ways to determine if professional learning is an effective tool for teaching culturally responsive practices is to analyze the participation rates of educators taking courses that focus on culturally different gifted students. One of the ways that the authors have encouraged educators to take professional learning that focuses on culturally diverse gifted students is by offering a Culturally and Linguistically Diverse Gifted course. This course is available for instructional seat time which can be used for licensure hours and for college credit through a local community college upon completion of the course. The authors also collaborated with their district Culturally Linguistically Diverse Education department to promote the course through their communication methods to their English language teachers. Another incentive for educators to take the 8-week course was that the 22 hours earned for completion of the course could be applied to their educator licensure renewal for the required 45 hours of English language learner professional development. The participation in this course has been connected with increased student referrals for gifted identification and a stronger stated rapport across departments.

Contemplation Corner

What other forms of nonacademic data can you think of that might be areas of growth to review for possible disproportionality?

Holistic Data Review Team

Once you have collected your data, it is critical that you have a team of trained individuals reviewing that data with you. Typically when solving complex equity challenges at school, district and state levels, data is collected and reviewed by a team of people invested in the outcome of the data. This team can comprise as many as 20 people or as few as 5, and, in some rural districts, the team might be a team of 2. The number of people does not matter as long as the people on the team are the ones that can interpret and make appropriate recommendations from the data being reviewed. When leading culturally responsive gifted programs, one set of data that leaders must focus on is disparity and proportionality of race, language, income, and gender data in gifted education programming. Disproportionality can be seen across all types of data, and Fergus (2017) suggests that the following roles should be included on a leadership team focusing on disproportionality causes within any educational organizational system:

- Superintendent
- Building leadership
- General education and special education teachers
- Program leadership folks
- Board representatives
- Union representatives
- Local parent groups
- Families
- Local college or university faculty
- Community groups advocating for historically marginalized populations

Once a leadership team has been formed and the root cause has been identified, then solutions can be developed, implemented, and monitored for improvement. This process can create a structure that minimizes the need for a continuous barrage of putting out proverbial fires every time a recurring situation arises. This approach allows the leader to be proactive with data and equity challenges and provides an opportunity for the leader of culturally responsive gifted programs to serve the needs of their community by using data.

Developing an Equity Plan

Now that you have an abundant source of qualitative and quantitative data, the next step is to establish the areas of change that are needed to achieve equitable access and opportunity for culturally linguistically diverse gifted students, their teachers, and their families. This equity plan must involve developing, creating, and/or refining culturally responsive practices and policies, and will involve multiple pieces of change moving at once. Leaders of culturally responsive gifted programs know that they must have a cross-functional team to support them.

Your next step, as a leader, will be to create an equity team with a focus on gifted students of color and develop a 3-year plan, at minimum, including how progress will be monitored. One way to help guide this work that the authors have found useful is the Objective and Key Results framework, or the OKR framework. This type of goal-setting framework was invented by Andrew Grove and was used at Intel from its early years (OKR University, n.d.). The framework is designed to guide organizations to reach their goals in an efficient and timely manner.

OKRs are similar to SMART goals in that they are specific, measurable, and time-bound. The OKRs first part is the objective: this is *what* will be achieved. The second part are the key results: this is *how* you will accomplish your objective and the actions that you will take to obtain the objective (Better Leaders Better Schools, 2019). An example of an OKR can be seen in Table 5.2. The primary focus area is family engagement and the timeframe is year one of a 3-year plan. The objective is to connect Latinx families of gifted students to opportunities that they might not otherwise experience through the support of a district gifted education Latinx family liaison. The events are held in Spanish with English support if needed.

TABLE 5.2
Monitoring Objective Key Results (OKR)

Family Engagement			
Objective **Year 1** *Connect with Latinx families of gifted students to facilitate their learning,* *opportunities, and resources* *Key Person: Gifted Education Director*			
• **Key Results 1st Quarter**	• **Key Results 2nd Quarter**	• **Key Results 3rd Quarter**	• **Key Results 4th Quarter**
Create a job description for a Gifted Education (GT) Latinx Family Liaison	Liaison organizes a Latinx Family Event at the Museum of Natural History	A Hispanic gifted scholar presents to the Latinx families about self-advocacy	Liaison partners with a local science organization to present a series of science events for the Latinx families
Recruit and hire a bilingual Gifted Education Latinx Family Liaison	Liaison presents a Gifted 101 in Spanish to Latinx families	Latinx families are invited to a resource fair	End-of-year gathering with Latinx families to celebrate

How do you measure your OKR for progress and pivots? There are three components: Scoring, self-assessing, and reflection (Better Leaders Better Schools, 2019). Regular check-ins with your equity team are an important part of the OKR process. OKRs are regularly scored during check-ins: Green indicates an OKR is "on track." Yellow means "needs attention" and that something should be adjusted. Red symbolizes "at risk." This kind of OKR might need to be adjusted or eliminated (Better Leaders Better Schools, 2019). During the check-ins, notes are made indicating what action steps have been implemented and what next steps need to be achieved. This is the self-assessment component of the OKR framework. The next part is the reflection, where the leader and team ask questions about the progression of the goals such as:

- How are you progressing on your OKRs?
- What do you need to be successful?
- Is there anything getting in the way of attaining your objective?
- Do we need to adjust, add, or eliminate anything ?

(Better Leaders Better Schools, 2019)

OKRs are a great tool to help leaders and teams reach their goals.

Conclusion

Culturally responsive leaders in gifted education must be committed to using both qualitative and quantitative data to evaluate gifted programming and services for equitable access for culturally different students. Data can pinpoint which areas in your educational system are perpetuating disproportionality and systems of oppression. We must as culturally responsive leaders break the cycle of overrepresentation of students of color in Special Education and the underrepresentation of students of color in Advanced Placement courses. Data can help guide leaders to determine root causes and make sustainable changes within systems to provide equitable access and opportunity for students of color.

Key Points

- ◆ Using data can help leaders to make data-driven decisions about systemic change that can promote equitable practices.
- ◆ Equity audits are an approach that can be used to analyze gifted systems for disparities that disenfranchise students of color.
- ◆ The equity allowance formula is designed to quantify equity by calculating the minimal number/percentage of students of color in gifted education programs.

- ◆ OKRs are a type of framework that can guide educational organizations to set goals and monitor them in an efficient and timely manner.
- ◆ The use of traditionally non-academic data to pinpoint cultural gaps and potential mismatches within systems is critically important.

References

Adjusted. (2022). *Want to conduct an equity audit?* http://ajusted.org/

Better Leaders Better Schools. (2019). *OKRs: A school leader's productivity secret weapon.* https://www.betterleadersbetterschools.com/okrs-a-school-leaders-productivity-secret-weapon/

Colorado Department of Education. (2021). *Using ACCESS for ELLs.* https://drive.google.com/file/d/13KvO3wqyg7W9zXF2riPL9yO6U8nSkke1/view

Colorado Department of Education. (2022). *Concurrent enrollment.* https://www.cde.state.co.us/postsecondary/concurrentenrollment

DuBois, M. P., & Greene, R. M. (2021). *Supporting gifted ELLs in the Latinx community: Practical strategies, K–12.* Routledge.

Fergus, E. (2017). *Solving disproportionality and achieving equity: A leader's guide to using data to change hearts and minds.* Corwin.

Ford, D. Y. (2013). *Recruiting & retaining culturally different students in gifted education.* Prufrock Press.

Ford, D. Y. (2013a). Gifted underrepresentation and prejudice—Learning from Allport and Merton. *Gifted Child Today, 36*(1), 62–67.

Ford, D. Y. (2013b). Gifted underrepresentation and prejudice—Learning from Allport and Merton. *Gifted Child Today, 36*(1), 62–67.

Gilner, J. A., Morgan, G. A., & Leech, N. L. (2009). *Research methods in applied settings: An integrated approach to design and analysis* (2nd ed.). Routledge.

Green, T. L. (2017). Community-based equity audits: A practical approach for educational leaders to support equitable community-school improvements. *Educational Administration Quarterly, 53*(1), 3–39.

Grindal, T., Schifter, L., Schwartz, G., & Hehir, T. (2019). Racial differences in special education identification and placement: Evidence across three states. *Harvard Education Review, 89*(4), 525–553.

Heifetz, R., & Linsky, M. (2002). *A survival guide for leaders.* https://hbr.org/2002/06/a-survival-guide-for-leaders

History. (2022). *Brown v. Board of Education.* https://www.history.com/topics/black-history/brown-v-board-of-education-of-topeka

Kanbanize. (n.d.). 5 Whys: The ultimate root cause analysis tool. https://kanbanize.com/lean-management/improvement/5-whys-analysis-tool

Khalifa, M. (2018). *Culturally responsive school leadership.* Harvard Education Press.

McGuire, D. (2022). *Perception data.* https://study.com/academy/lesson/perception-data-in-education-importance-analysis.html

National Center for Learning Disabilities. (n.d.). *Significant disproportionality in special education: Current trends and actions for impact.* https://www.ncld.org/wp-content/uploads/2020/10/2020-NCLD-Disproportionality_Trends-and-Actions-for-Impact_FINAL-1.pdf

OKR University. (n.d.). *Ultimate guide to objective and key results.* https://www.profit.co/blog/okr-university/what-is-okr/

Purcell, J. H., & Eckert, R. D. (2006). *Designing services and programs for high-ability learners: A guidebook for gifted education.* Corwin Press.

Ryan, M. (2018, November 19). *How Iowa became the first state in the nation to desegregate schools.* Des Moines Register. https://www.desmoinesregister.com/story/news/education/2018/11/19/iowa-civil-rights-history-school-desegregation-muscatine-alexander-clark/1524457002/

Seal of Biliteracy. (2022). *Steps to implement the seal of biliteracy.* https://sealofbiliteracy.org/steps

Skrla, L., Mckenzie, K. B., & Scheurich, J. J. (2009). *Using equity audits to create equitable and excellent schools.* Corwin.

U. S. Department of Education. (2014). *Disproportionality in school discipline: An assessment of trends in Maryland, 2009–12.* https://ies.ed.gov/ncee/edlabs/regions/midatlantic/pdf/REL_2014017.pdf

Wheeler, J. (2022). *The complete guide to gap analysis.* https://www.smartsheet.com/gap-analysis-method-examples#:~:text=For%20example%2C%20if%20a%20company,their%20campaign%20or%20loan%20 application

Wright, B. L., Ford, D. Y., & Young, J. L. (2017). Ignorance or indifference? Seeking excellence and equity for under-represented students of color in gifted education. *Global Education Review, 4*(1), 45–60.

6

Systems of Support

System-Wide Supports

This chapter focuses on system-wide supports that can be put in place to help gifted culturally and linguistically diverse learners thrive. It guides culturally responsive leaders to think creatively about their current practices and reflect on either developing or refining those practices. Generally, schools provide multiple levels of support, varying from language supports to reading interventions, math interventions, and more. However, too often schools provide resources and support to struggling students first while considering high ability students second as these students "will be fine." That is common verbiage that is often heard from teachers and administrators regarding allocating resources to high ability and gifted students. Then consider what this means to culturally and linguistically diverse gifted students who are already minoritized in our school systems. As a leader of culturally responsive gifted systems, you are in a position of power and privilege to interrupt that pattern of thought and shift mindsets.

This chapter will review how leaders can appropriately utilize the Multitiered System of Supports (MTSS) framework focusing on the layered continuum of supports as a way to provide intervention and enrichment for gifted learners, and the Ford-Harris/Bloom-Banks Matrix (Ford, 2011) as a tool for developing multicultural differentiated lessons. Collins' Culturally Responsive Multitiered System of Supports (CR-MTSS) framework (Collins,

DOI: 10.4324/9781003293729-6

2020) will be discussed as a way for servicing twice-exceptional (2e) and thrice-exceptional (3e) learners. Twice-exceptional learners are those students who are gifted and also have a disability as defined by the federal/state eligibility criteria. Thrice-exceptional learners are students who are gifted, have a disability, and are also culturally diverse. The chapter ends with recommendations for building crosscultural competency across school and district departmental systems.

Multitiered System of Supports (MTSS)

In many schools across the United States, MTSS is used as a framework for providing academic and behavioral support to students who need intervention to increase their progress. Prior to MTSS, Response to Intervention (RtI) was the primary approach used for interventions and support of students with learning and behavior needs. RtI was intentionally designed as a framework for supporting struggling students, not for responding to the needs of high-ability or gifted students. In 2004, the reauthorization of the Individuals with Disability Education Act (IDEA) included RtI specifically as part of an assessment process to determine if a child has a disability (Johnsen et al., 2015). This change made way for a new take on RtI as being not just for "students with disabilities" but a process that can be used for "all students." Soon after, the Council for Exceptional Children issued a position paper stating that RtI addresses the needs of children who are "twice-exceptional" and that their needs must be met through the provision of "access to a challenging and accelerated curriculum, while also addressing the unique needs of their disability" (Council for Exceptional Children, 2008). The inclusion of twice-exceptional students within the RtI process led the way for the Association for the Gifted (TAG), a division of the Council for Exceptional Children (CEC), to endorse the idea that RtI should be expanded in its implementation to include the needs of gifted children (Association for the Gifted, n.d.). With this endorsement, the momentum grew for RtI to be used as a collaborative approach requiring educators to think about the child first and match the supports and services to the child's strengths and needs (Coleman & Hughes, 2009).

RtI and Positive Behavior Intervention and Supports (PBIS) are the basis of MTSS. MTSS takes on the whole-child approach by addressing academic, social-emotional and behavioral student needs. The key components of MTSS are:

- Universal screening of all students early in the school year
- Tiers of interventions that can be amplified in response to levels of need
- Ongoing data collection and continual assessment
- Schoolwide approach to expectations and supports
- Parent involvement (PBIS Rewards, n. d.)

The MTSS model has three main levels of support: Universal (Tier 1), Targeted (Tier 2), and Intensive (Tier 3). Universal screening and data-driven decisions determine in which tier students are placed, what continuum of services are needed, and at what rate. Student progress is monitored frequently to examine student achievement and gauge the effectiveness of the curriculum and instruction (RTI Action Network, n.d.). Students may move from one tier to another depending on content and their areas of need.

The MTSS model is typically visualized as a triangle-shaped graphic illustrating the multiple tiers of support with Tier 1 as the foundation and largest tier. Tier 1 is a universal level of support. These are the services provided to all students—basically the curriculum and core instruction. Research shows that 80%–90% of gifted students can have their needs met within the regular classroom setting if there is consistent differentiation (Cox et al., 1985) and if specific learning conditions are met. The majority of gifted students' needs can be met using differentiation strategies based upon student readiness and learning styles. Within Tier 1, all students receive high-quality, scientifically based instruction provided by qualified personnel to ensure that their difficulties are not due to inadequate instruction (RTI Action Network, n.d.). Ultimately, Tier 1 is meant to act as an educational equalizing agent by giving access and opportunity to high-quality instruction for all learners.

Leaders of culturally responsive gifted programs will ensure that their educators understand which data to collect in each tier, how to analyze data and review it with as limited bias as possible, and how to use the data collected to inform instruction and differentiation and to help provide professional learning supports to educators so they can deliver evidence-based instructional practices. Consider conducting a needs assessment to understand what gaps in skills your own educators or service providers may have. They may need their own differentiated supports in understanding how to support the various readiness levels of learners in their classes. As the leader of this work, you must be able to support their ongoing professional learning. Each of these components is critical in every aspect of MTSS; however, they are especially so in Universal instruction where the majority of students receive their instruction, and the majority of culturally linguistically diverse gifted, 2e, and 3e learners sit because they have not been identified for services yet.

Structuring Support for MTSS in the Classroom

As a leader of culturally responsive gifted programs, you must assess all structures and systems within your context. At the school level and within MTSS, you have the ability to help learners and educators receive the appropriate access, scaffolds, and opportunities necessary for advanced culturally linguistically diverse students to thrive. You must set these structures up strategically and with intentionality and attention to learner needs as well as educators' professional learning needs, strengths, and areas for growth.

A relatively simple way to assist with building the efficacy of culturally linguistically diverse gifted learners and their teachers is to support teachers as they differentiate based on content, process, product, environment, and affect for gifted culturally linguistically diverse learners. One way you can help structure differentiation within the classroom for your teachers is by modeling the use of universal ongoing assessment data to determine flexible instructional grouping of students based on their ongoing identified needs. These needs could be interest-based, readiness-based, linguistic-based, learning-style based, socially-emotionally based, or something else entirely. Below are common differentiation strategies found in Tier 1 instruction for advanced learners:

- Most difficult first: Students solve the most difficult problems first rather than starting with the easiest problems. When students can demonstrate mastery of a concept by completing the five most difficult problems with 85% accuracy, then they do not have to complete any more of the problems.
- Choice boards: These boards provide multiple formats and levels for students to choose from to demonstrate mastery of content.
- Compacting: To compact, the teacher must pretest students in the content to be presented. Students master, or nearly master, the content, then move onto an advanced level of difficulty. Pretesting students should occur at all levels of instruction to prevent repetition and reteaching of content that students have already mastered.
- Tiered assignments: All students explore the same essential ideas but work at different levels of depth and complexity (Tomlinson, 1999, 2014).
- Flexible pacing and cluster grouping: This research-based best practice for all learners supports the academic and affective needs of gifted, advanced, and high-achieving learners (Winebrenner & Brulles, 2008).
- School Wide Enrichment Model (SEM): This model allows all students to follow their interests and passions and is constructed around the students individual interests (Renzulli & Reis, 2014).

Rogers (2002) recommends that instructional practices for advanced learners must include or revolve around higher-order thinking and questioning, more open-ended assignments, choice, and proof and reasoning at all levels of learning. As leaders of culturally responsive gifted programs, we believe that all learners should have access to those pieces as a way to help develop talent.

In the MTSS model, Tier 2 support is targeted intervention in which approximately 5%–10% of high-ability/high-potential students will need some type of augmented service (Cox et al., 1985). Tier 2 support in addition to Tier 1 is provided to advanced learners when their needs go beyond the differentiated instruction within Universal Tier 1. Data from ongoing school-wide screenings conducted at the Tier 1 level determine if additional supports are needed for learners. Universal screenings can include but are not limited to:

- Standardized achievement testing administered to specific grade levels
- Standardized norm-referenced tests
- State/local assessments
- Classroom-based assessments
- Cognitive assessments
- Creativity assessments
- English language proficiency assessments
- Gifted behavioral observation tools
- Social-emotional observation tools
- Mental health questionnaires (anxiety, suicide, depression, etc.)

The data collected can show evidence of strengths, needs, and interests to help determine the supports needed to extend instruction for advanced learners. Often, Tier 2 support is depicted as a pull-out group of advanced learners that meets for advanced instruction one or more times a week, or push-in groups. Ideally, these groups should be taught by a teacher who understands giftedness and how to work with gifted learners. Pull-out groups are most effective when the material the gifted learners are engaging with is tied back to the general education classroom and the work is supplanted, not supplemented (Rogers, 1992); that is, students are not receiving work, but they are receiving different work from the general education classroom with their peers and taught by someone who understands best practices in gifted education. In many places around the country, pull-out groups are offered as gifted programming. Opportunities for advanced learners to come together in small groups to extend their critical and creative thinking continues to challenge these learners who might otherwise become disengaged with the material and instead engage in maladaptive classroom behaviors without additional supports. Below are some Tier 2 differentiation strategies that as a leader you will want to ensure exist within your context for culturally linguistically diverse advanced learners:

- Subject acceleration: Students who have demonstrated with their data that they mastered 85% of the curriculum or grade level standards should be considered for acceleration (Belin Blank Center, n.d.). These students may still need linguistic supports or accommodations to access the content.
- Push-in programming: A teacher who is trained in culturally responsive gifted education best practices supports in the general education classroom.
- Pull-out programming: A teacher who is trained in culturally responsive gifted education best practices supports students by pulling them from the general education classroom to work on separate work for a specific amount of time.
- Ability grouping: Students with similar ability levels are put together based on data-driven decisions to access material in a differentiated manner. These groups should be flexible, otherwise you will run the risk of tracking students, and that is the antithesis of equity.
- Competitions or advanced clubs that may typically be reserved for older students: For example, Math Olympiad, Brain Bowl, and Robotics Club. Students must have any linguistic, IEP, and 504 supports available to them.
- Curriculum compacting: This practice allows for students who have mastered or nearly mastered the material to be learned to have new content, enrichment options, or other activities.

- Honors, Advanced Placement, and International Baccalaureate: Students take courses with advanced or accelerated content (usually at the secondary level) to test out or receive credit for completion of college-level coursework. Ensure there is a pathway for students who are not high-school age to engage in these classes should data show they are ready.
- Mentorship: Student(s) are placed with a subject-matter expert or professional, ideally with a cultural and linguistic connection to the learner from their community, to further a specific interest or proficiency that cannot be provided within the regular educational setting (Tomlinson, 1999, 2014).
- Specialized curriculum programs providing advanced content: Curricular materials or curricula are provided that were created specifically with gifted learners in mind.

In your systems of support you will also want to ensure that you have the appropriate gifted intensive Tier 3 interventions designed to be implemented with highly, profoundly, and exceptionally gifted students who need extended services beyond Tier 1 and Tier 2. These interventions are intensive in nature due to the duration and pacing of the intervention. Generally, students who need this intensive type of intervention make up 1%–5% of the population. This small percentage of students may require some of the following Tier 3 interventions to support their unique needs:

- Full grade-level acceleration or multi-grade-level acceleration: This is sometimes referred to as *radical acceleration*. Whole grade or multi-grade-level acceleration must be data-informed. It should also be supported by a school-based decision-making process, or your MTSS process. The Iowa Acceleration Scale is a helpful tool when considering acceleration. It generates recommendations and guidelines for whole-grade acceleration based upon academic, social, emotional and behavioral factors. Using this tool also allows evidence-based decision making for those educators and administrators who have bias towards acceleration.

- Magnet classrooms for gifted learners: These are classrooms of similar peers within school buildings designated for students identified as having intense intellectual and/or social-emotional needs.
- Schools for gifted students: The whole staff and curricula are focused on the nature and needs of identified gifted learners.
- Dual enrollment: This allows current high-school students to take college-level courses,
- Early entrance: This allows students to enter kindergarten earlier than age five.
- Early graduation: This allows students to graduate from high school earlier than their same-age peers.
- Long-term internships: These offer a year-long or greater internship and career, ideally with whom the student has a cultural or linguistic connection.

As with all decisions regarding students, families and schools will need to collaborate together to find the appropriate fit (Iowa Department of Education, 2018, Colorado Department of Education, 2022).

MTSS is a powerful process that can support academic and behavioral practices for all students, including those who are highly advanced and gifted. How can the MTSS framework best serve culturally and linguistically diverse gifted learners? It begins with the teacher's understanding of not only MTSS but also their knowledge and expertise about culturally and linguistically diverse learners. As a culturally responsive leader of gifted programs, you must develop and implement the MTSS framework with representation from experts in curriculum and content as well as from those most knowledgeable about the influences of cultural and linguistic diversity on the implementation of that curriculum and content (Hoover & Patton, 2017).

Consider who within your staff can serve as a part of the MTSS team and can continually focus that team on the intersectionality of culture, ability, and interventions/acceleration. Ideally, your entire MTSS team will be trained in supporting culturally linguistically diverse learners and understanding the manifestations of culture in the classroom and their intersectionality with exceptionality. However, without the cultural and linguistic knowledge in the developing and implementing of an MTSS framework you, or your team, will be making decisions based on data about students of color that may not be culturally responsive and might inaccurately refer a student for special education services, or that may not see the strengths the student has and fail to refer the student for any level of service in general. Additionally, when using the MTSS process with gifted students with limited English proficiency and or disabilities, you will need to address supports for both their strengths and challenges. Some of these students may be twice or thrice exceptional and will need services for their giftedness as well as services for their other areas of need.

Much of the curricula, assessments, and expectations for achieving benchmarks in school are reflective of a white middle-class perspective, which varies significantly from collectivist values, teachings, and expectations of many students of color educated in today's schools. When instruction, interventions, and assessments are not culturally and linguistically responsive to the needs of students, then they fail to show the actual potential or growth of diverse students, which can lead to inaccurate interventions and harmful placement decisions. The MTSS structure you build for learners and the training your provide educators has the potential to create access to and opportunity for gifted education in ways that culturally linguistically diverse learners across the nation lack.

Contemplation Corner

What data is collected in your buildings to measure student growth for multilingual and other diverse learners? Are the assessments used culturally fair?

Social-Emotional Support Structures

While accelerated academic needs are critical for gifted students to reach their potential, leaders of culturally responsive gifted programs understand that culturally linguistically diverse students must have systems and structures in place to nurture social emotional wellbeing. Gay (2018) says that one of the pillars of culturally responsive pedagogy is building positive relationships with your students and families. This means building trust with students and showing that you actually care about them and their families, not just that you care how they manage academically but also authentically care about their emotional and physical wellbeing. This also means showing consistency in your approach to social-emotional wellbeing so that students and families know they are safe to be themselves.

As stated before, many of our students of color come from collectivist community-based cultures where relationships are a foundational piece of the fabric of their lives. Everyone works together for the betterment of the group, not for the advancement of themselves individually. Building trusting relationships with students and families can break down barriers that might be preventing students of color to reach their true potential. Hammond (2015) suggests that through acts of caring, authentic listening, and becoming more authentic with students, educators and administrators can build trusting relationships.

Relationships founded on respect for cultures and racial trust help foster self-efficacy and academic success. In *Raising Voices Above the Silencing in Our Schools: A Critically Compassionate Intellectualism for Latino/a Students*, Cammarota and Romero (2006) share how students and teachers feel disconnected from one another across grade levels and distrustful at times. However, that changes when educators start becoming vulnerable, demonstrate authentic caring, and use a social justice curriculum. As Hamond (2015) notes, "This is especially true when building relationships across racial, ethnic, and socioeconomic lines where implicit bias can get in the way."

When addressing the social-emotional needs of culturally linguistically diverse students, racial identity is a critical topic that must not be dismissed. Our racial identities are deeply ingrained into our self-being and self-worth. Many times students of color do not feel like they fit in or they feel like they are being ignored, especially if they are one of the few students of color in a classroom or in a school. This type of disconnect for these students with their teachers and classmates can create stress that can manifest in behavioral outbursts, a low sense of self-worth, and even prolonged depression, which then impacts achievement. Often, these students feel they need to assimilate to the majority culture in order to feel a sense of belonging and acceptance from others. This is disconcerting as it can have a negative impact on their lives such as losing interest in their ability to speak their heritage language, which can cause stress within the family.

Self-advocating can be an important tool for diverse learners. Teaching students how to advocate for themselves and their needs will give them a voice for themselves and empower them to be the leader in their own educational journey. Those teaching students to self-advocate need to have knowledge and understanding about culturally, linguistically diverse populations so that they can authentically engage them and earn their trust.

A Culturally Responsive Equity-Based Bill of Rights (Ford et al., 2018) outlines additional social-emotional supports that students of color must have access to for their emotional growth and success in schools. Scholars and practitioners have been taking notice of this Bill of Rights as it clearly represents the actions needed to create an equitable support system for students of color. The authors of the Bill of Rights state that "it represents a culturally and equity grounded holistic approach to do what is necessary to desegregate gifted education and advanced learner programs to support and advocate for students of color" (Ford et al., 2018). The Bill of Rights has multiple sections; however, we have chosen to share the section specifically covering social and emotional rights. Gifted students of color have:

- The right to supportive services and programs by school counselors trained in multicultural counseling (theories, methods, strategies)
- The right to counselors familiar with and skilled in racial identity theories
- The right to counselors who understand and promote racial identity development
- The right to counselors and teachers who understand the unique challenges of being a gifted student of color
- The right to pre-service educators, current educators and counselors formally trained in the socio-emotional needs of gifted children of color
- The right to counselors who understand the relationship between racial identity and achievement
- The right to interact and be educated with peers from similar cultural, racial, and linguistic backgrounds
- The right to academic support when they underachieve, fail, and/or make mistakes

- The right to understand the area(s) in which they are gifted and talented
- The right to be taught how to self-advocate to increase their access to appropriate instructional and support services (Ford et al., 2018)

When leading, it is critical to consider how to operationalize the pieces listed within the Bill of Rights so that gifted students of color thrive. Because leaders of culturally responsive gifted programs are attuned to the daily microaggressions, racial battle fatigue, stress, and trauma that culturally linguistically diverse students face, you can use the Gifted Students of Color Bill of Rights to intentionally create school-wide and district-wide systems of support for these learners. The following are suggested social-emotional support systems and structures that we have seen successfully support culturally linguistically diverse learners' social-emotional wellbeing across multiple contexts:

- Hiring and retaining culturally linguistically diverse school counselors, psychologists, and social workers with appropriate caseloads to support diverse gifted learners
  - Providing necessary professional learning to the professionals listed above and supporting their social-emotional needs as adults
- Providing teachers with training to support Tier 1 culturally linguistically diverse social-emotional needs
- Dedicating time in one-on-ones or feedback cycles with educators to addressing the social emotional wellbeing of culturally linguistically diverse gifted learners
- Creating opportunities for student-organized affinity groups focused on concerns for their community, such as Latinx youth groups, African American youth groups, Indigenous student school groups, Gay Student Alliances (GSA) for students of color, and even newcomers' groups, etc.

- Have a mentorship program established in the school, at elementary and secondary levels with community members to support the interests and passions of learners, both academic and nonacademic

Providing the right support to students based upon their needs is essential for students' academic and emotional success. However, providing support to students of color without considering their cultural linguistic diversity is a disservice and can be harmful to students' potential. The cultural mismatches that can occur through poorly planned systems of support can cause cultural mismatches and misunderstandings, leading to increased harm for our students and reinforcing negative stereotypes and perceptions for our educators.

Culturally Responsive Multitiered System of Supports (CR-MTSS)

Another MTSS tool we will explore in this chapter that is both exciting and has the potential to transform how students engage with their learning is Kristina Collins' Culturally Responsive Multitiered System of Supports (Collins, 2020) framework, or CR-MTSS. The CR-MTSS is designed to be used as a tool to create opportunities to include individual student culture in every tier of learning so that students see themselves, are affirmed, and are engaged. The CR-MTSS can help guide students to have culturally responsive discussions about systems of oppression, and can be used to support students who may be considered 3e, or thrice exceptional—that is, a student who has been identified as needing gifted services and special education services, and who is culturally linguistically diverse. The CR-MTSS blends Donna Y. Ford's revised Bloom-Banks Matrix (Ford & Harris, 1999; Ford, 2011), also known as the Ford-Harris Matrix, with an overlay of tiered levels of MTSS. The Bloom-Banks Matrix synthesizes Benjamin Bloom's Taxonomy (1985) and James Banks' (1989) multicultural curriculum reform work.

Ford's Matrix is designed to be used to teach about racially and culturally different groups in an authentic and meaningful way through differentiated multicultural lessons (Ford, 2011). The Bloom-Banks Matrix incorporates the 2001 revised version of Bloom's Taxonomy, which has six levels of knowledge: knowing, comprehending, applying, analyzing, evaluating, and creating (Anderson & Krathwohl, 2001). On the Bloom-Banks Matrix, the levels of knowledge are aligned horizontally at the top of the frame beginning with knowing and ending with creating. Banks' four levels of approaches to multicultural curriculum reform are aligned vertically on the left side of the Bloom-Banks Matrix beginning with contribution, then additives, transformation and social activism. The Bloom-Banks Matrix portrays 24 cells or four quadrants which are based on the six levels of Bloom by the four levels of Banks (Scott, 2014). The four by six matrix can be divided into four quadrants:

- Quadrant 1:
  - Contributions—Knowing, Comprehending, Applying
  - Additive—Knowledge, Comprehension, Application
- Quadrant 2:
  - Transformation—Knowing, Comprehending, Applying
  - Social Action—Knowing, Comprehending, Applying
- Quadrant 3:
  - Contributions—Analyzing, Evaluating, Creating
  - Additive—Analyzing, Evaluating, Creating
- Quadrant 4:
  - Transformation—Analyzing, Evaluating, Creating
- Social Action—Analyzing, Evaluating, Creating (Ford, 2011)

As previously stated in Chapter 2, Ford (2011) suggests that the best use of the Bloom-Banks Matrix for culturally responsive gifted education practices is to focus on Banks' transformation and social action levels *and* on Bloom's analysis, evaluating and creating levels. In *Multicultural Gifted Education* (2011), Ford provides multiple examples of lessons using multicultural literature and concepts that are focused on race and cultural identity.

Using Ford's Bloom-Banks Matrix as a foundation, Collins expands on Ford's work by overlaying Tier 1: Universal Support, Tier 2: Additional Intervention and Enrichment Support, and Tier 3: Intensive Intervention and Enrichment Support for learners with exceptionalities, twice-exceptional (2e) and thrice-exceptional (3e) learners. Twice-exceptional learners are those students who are gifted and also have one or more disabilities as defined by federal or state eligibility criteria. Twice exceptional learners have unique needs both academically and socially emotionally as they are at risk for being misunderstood by both administrators and educators. Collins' (2020a) thrice-exceptional model describes thrice-exceptional students as those who are twice exceptional and have an additional cultural or language component. In the thrice-exceptional model, students who are culturally linguistically diverse are considered to have an exceptionality; therefore, when the student is identified as gifted, they are considered 2e. In this same model, if a student is identified as needing special education services and is also culturally linguistically diverse, then the student is 2e. This is a paradigm shift for gifted and special education and creates an opportunity for leaders, scholars, and practitioners to highlight the strength of a student's diversity and how that diversity manifests.

Collins' CR-MTSS indicates that Tier 1 Universal classroom support for 80%–90% of all gifted learners should incorporate all levels of Bloom's and incorporate Banks' Contribution and Additive Approaches. According to Banks (1989), the Contributions Approach is "the easiest approach for teachers to use to integrate ethnic content" into the curriculum. The Additive Approach also has limited cognitive lift for the teacher and allows educators and leaders to add cultural "concepts, content, themes, and perspectives to the curriculum" (Banks, 1989) without restructuring said curriculum.

In Tier 2 of CR-MTSS, targeted supports highlight Banks' Transformation Approach to multicultural learning. This approach infuses multiple perspectives, frames of reference, and content from various ethnic and cultural groups that move beyond an Eurocentric perspective (Banks, 1989). At this tier, additional specific interventions using the Transformation Approach for students with special education needs are overlaid on Bloom's domains of *remember, understand,* and *apply.* For students who have advanced abilities or gifted needs, Collins' framework offers Tier 2 enrichment interventions using the Transformation Approach by connecting them with Bloom's domains of *analyze, evaluate,* and *create.*

Lastly, in Tier 3, the most intensive level of support for students culturally, and with specific learning needs, Collins' CR-MTSS focuses on Banks' Social Action Approach. The Social Action Approach was specifically designed to teach students decision-making skills to "empower them, and to help them acquire a sense of political efficacy." (Banks, 1989). As in Tier 2, students in need of intervention at a more intensive level will explore the Social Action Approach in Bloom's domains of *remember, understand,* and *apply.* Tier 3 additional enrichment support for advanced learners is overlaid with Bloom's domains of *analyze, evaluate,* and *create.*

CR-MTSS (Collins, 2020)

- Tier 1: Universal Support
  o Bloom—all levels
  o Banks—Contribution and Additive Approach
- Tier 2: Additional Intervention Support
  o Bloom—Remember, Understand, Apply
  o Banks—Transformation Approach
- Tier 2: Additional Enrichment Support
  o Bloom—Analyze, Evaluate, Create
  o Banks—Transformation Approach
- Tier 3: Additional Intervention Support
  o Bloom—Analyze, Understand, Apply
  o Banks—Social Action Approach
- Tier 3: Additional Enrichment Support
  o Bloom—Analyze, Evaluate, Create
- Banks—Social Action Approach

Collins' framework blends the matrices together to create opportunity for growth in cognitive (thinking/intellectual ability), affective (feeling/attitudes, values, and interest toward learning), and psychomotor domains (doing/perceptual ability to interpret and appropriately act/react to environment and situation) by allowing 2e and 3e students the ability to apply their culture wealth, funds of knowledge, and personal strengths (Collins, 2021). It is also a structured way for administrators, educators, and students to discuss race and racism, differentiated by need.

For example, in the Universal Tier of CR-MTSS, students are asked to make meaning of information and cultural themes within their own context. When unpacking information and using the Contribution Approach to culture, this can be done by exploring cultural references, artifacts, events, groups, and other cultural elements across the various levels of Bloom. When utilizing the Additive Approach to culture in the Universal Tier, students will focus on facts and concepts as well as the relationships between concepts and theories. Leaders of culturally responsive programs will ensure that their educators have curricula that offer multiple perspectives other than the Eurocentric perspective in typical textbooks, and have mirror, window, and prism books available to tell counter-narratives.

In the CR-MTSS model, Tier 2 and Tier 3 support both intervention and enrichment for 2e and 3e students. Collins suggests the use of Banks' Transformation and Social Action approaches for both Tier 2 and Tier 3 interventions and enrichments so that students can make personal connections and understand multiple perspectives and strengths of diverse cultures while also taking a social action approach, thus living the tenets of culturally responsive teaching and pedagogy.

Leaders of culturally responsive gifted programs should explore the use of CR-MTSS for their MTSS tiers and will need to dedicate training resources, professional learning hours, and planning time to this process. This will include lesson planning and conversations that intentionally weave in student culture, and it will require intentional work on the part of educators and administrators not to stereotype or generalize cultures.

Leaders at district level and state level organizations set the tone for their entire educational organization by exploring and implementing CR-MTSS, not only for 2e and 3e students, but for all culturally linguistically diverse learners. This integration of culture with rigor and affect is in its essence culturally responsive education. In order to implement this, however, there must be an interdisciplinary group of invested and impacted departments, including, but not limited to, curriculum and instruction, teaching and learning, psychology/social work, special education, gifted and talented/advanced academics, culturally linguistically diverse, response to intervention, family engagement, and communications. These departments may be named something else where you work; however, you will need these groups and their diverse perspectives to obtain stakeholder buy-in, planning, and implementation so that these changes to existing structures are successful.

Culturally Sustaining Systems

The purpose of your work as a leader of culturally responsive gifted programs is to ultimately create systems that not only invite culturally responsive practices of your learners and educators into the school system, but create a system that will maintain those practices after you are gone from your leadership position, because these are the practices that will disrupt systems of oppression. This is going to require strategic planning and seeking out diverse opinions and creating networks of support across your organization. It is going to take a collectivist culture mindset and attitude in the primarily individualistic cultural setting of education.

Professional Learning

As we said in Chapter 2, culturally responsive teaching and culturally sustaining work is not a set of engagement strategies, but it is a value system that you hold and a way of looking at your environment. In order to adopt this mindset so that you can perceive the world in this way and create opportunities for culturally sustaining practices to occur within your context, you will need to develop multiple systems and structures, one of which is specifically focused on training and disseminating information to those people working with students and families. This can be done efficiently by developing a strategic plan that includes ongoing professional learning opportunities focused on culturally responsive gifted education.

Professional learning should be intentional and have supports in place so that leaders do not regress in the practice of being culturally responsive and modeling those behaviors to other members of their team, such as teachers, paraprofessionals, instructional coaches, gifted coordinators, etc. These professional learning opportunities should be provided in various formats such as in person, online, or in hybrid synchronous and asynchronous versions to meet learners' preferences. They should be made accessible at a variety of times to allow for the convenience of participants and be work-embedded so that the experiences are authentic and relevant. A Professional Learning Roadmap was shared in Chapter 4. Additional topics can include, but should not be limited to, the following:

- Identifying and interrupting racism, microaggressions, and macroaggressions
- Understanding one's own cultural identity and frame of reference
- Expanding one's cultural perspectives and building empathy
- Seeking to understand the deep, shallow, and surface culture of your community
- Understanding the impact of white supremacy culture and systemic racism on students within your community
- Considering trauma and the impact on your community
- Establishing culturally responsive academic and affective instructional practices
- Establishing culturally responsive gifted practices
- Creating culturally inclusive classrooms

The list above is not exhaustive, and is just scratching the surface of some of the topics that should be covered to work on developing mindsets and values that support an inclusive environment. As the leader yourself, you will need to make sure that you are creating the conditions for this type of learning to thrive and take place. Therefore, your staff will need to feel safe and feel like they can take risks, and discussing culture and focusing inward to shift mindsets is a risk. Zaretta Hammond (2015) notes that when educators begin to unpack their implicit bias, their amygdalas will send out stress hormones whenever you are talking about "race, racism, classism, sexism, or any other kind of -ism," because the brain thinks it is under emotional or physical attack and prefers that it stay in a neutral state. Cognitive dissonance creates emotional distress.

During these professional learning sessions, you will need to ensure that you are prepared for any cognitive dissonance that occurs with your staff or peers, as you are dealing with emotions of adults whose intent is to help children. Part of your strategic plan for professional learning should include a plan to help them notice when they are dysregulated and include opportunities for breathing exercises or journaling such as the ones we mentioned in Chapter 1. In order to help keep your staff or team members emotionally regulated, ideally your professional learning should be embedded into existing structures such as Professional Learning Communities (PLCs), book studies, and district and state-wide long-term professional learning plans so as not to add more change. However, if you do not have a structure in place to allow for this type of learning, then change is absolutely necessary so that you disrupt the status quo. We have seen culturally responsive gifted education professional learning both successfully implemented and woefully misguided in our own work. One workshop, poorly planned to check off a requirement for equity, will not change minds, hearts, or student outcomes.

Cross-Departmental Connections
It is important that you make connections with other departments in your building, district or state level in order to build capacity and challenge thinking about culturally, linguistically diverse gifted students. These students are the responsibility of multiple departments, not just the gifted department. Often, school, district, or state-level departments are siloed from each other, with each department working on their own initiatives without noticing that there are other departments working on similar projects.

This structure is a holdover of both white supremacy and individualistic cultural attitudes towards education espoused by the very people who created the education system hundreds of years ago. This is one of the reasons we continue to see the same dismal outcomes for students of color. Leaders of culturally responsive gifted programs, however, understand that it is critical to break the traditional educational mold. Reaching out to other departments and having authentic conversations about serving culturally linguistically diverse gifted learners can lead the way to developing strategic plans focused on supporting gifted students of color with cross-departmental resources.

Departmental structures may look different in your district or state, or, as stated earlier, the names of the departments might be different. Regardless of these differences in nomenclature across the educational system, there are specific actions that you can take to build cross-departmental connections to increase awareness and gifted services for culturally and racially diverse students.

Culturally Linguistically Diverse Learner Departments
One of the first sets of stakeholders you must seek out to build systems of support for your learners is the group (or perhaps the lone person) that oversees and manages initiatives with linguistically diverse and or culturally linguistically diverse learners in your district. This may be called a variety of titles, such as Culturally, Linguistically, Diverse Education; Multicultural Education; or Multilingual Education. You may not have a whole department, but you may have one person who oversees and tracks the number of students who are proficient in English. Ask who that person is in your district (rural, suburban, or urban). This department should hopefully already have diverse gifted learners on their radar. However, due to federal and state requirements, sometimes this department is more concentrated on students of color, or students with linguistic differences, who are not achieving at grade level, rather than those who need targeted or intensive support for their giftedness.

Once you determine who this is and are able to meet with them, begin building systems of support by building rapport. Ask about their vision and mission for the learners they serve. Listen for connections to your work that you will be able to use and share with them. Ask them what they know and understand about culturally linguistically diverse gifted learners. Find out how the laws that exist to protect students work in combination with the practices that are in place to support gifted learners. Offer to share resources about the characteristics of gifted students across cultures. If they have a handbook or a website, ask to have a section centered on gifted, twice-exceptional, and thrice-exceptional students. Provide a handout that can be given to those working with these students in schools that offer strategies to use with ethnically diverse gifted students. Work with the department to understand how they are organized at all levels of the organization to determine who needs to know information about gifted learners so that they can be identified and supported.

Seek out ways to establish the collection of data—specifically language acquisition data—that can be used for students who are acquiring English or another language rapidly. Investigate which students are earning a Seal of Biliteracy if your district or state offers this opportunity. To obtain a Seal of Biliteracy award, students must have studied and attained proficiency in two or more languages by high-school graduation (Seal of Biliteracy, 2022). Currently, all of the United States has approved the Seal of Biliteracy for their states except for one state, South Dakota, which is in the early stages of beginning the process. Finally, establish regular meetings with them to discuss the data you see and the needs of the educators in the field.

Curriculum and Instruction

Connect with curriculum and instructional departments such as Literacy, Math, Technology, Social Studies, and the Science Department. As with the culturally diverse learners' department, when you work with curriculum and instruction, you will want to understand their vision and mission for learning for all learners. How do they view students with exceptionalities? Ask them about their views on culturally responsive education and what that looks like for gifted learners and students who are in special education and or receiving language support. This information is important to know as you form a relationship with this key department in your school district or state. Keep them up to date on the number of gifted students that are identified in their content areas categorized by demographics. Determine if the number of gifted students of color align with district or state demographics. Ask for a time to give a presentation on giftedness with a focus on identifying and serving culturally linguistically diverse learners. Create 10–15-minute videos demonstrating differentiated gifted strategies for culturally, linguistically diverse learners. Ask to be part of the team that examines curriculum materials for inclusion of content that reflects people of color in an authentic and positive way. During your time with this team, make sure that you are creating bridges of understanding on how gifted students progress through standards, both academic and affective standards, including the research base of acceleration and the impact of acceleration on students.

For multiple well-researched racist and classist reasons, many gifted learners of color may not demonstrate their talents through traditional academic measures such as standardized achievement tests, but they may shine in a talent domain such as art, music, dance, or psychomotor abilities. Therefore, connect with these departments to explore ways to create portfolios for students nominated for gifted identification. Reach out to art, music, dance, and athletic experts in the community to be part of an expert talent panel who will evaluate student demonstrations in their talent domain, judge portfolios, and determine the criteria for a gifted identification. Ask about local, district, and state competitions where students may have their talents displayed. Connect with the athletic, dance, and arts departments for a list of culturally linguistically diverse students who excel in movement and the arts.

Family Engagement

In some districts there may be a district family liaison and a school-level family liaison. The role of the family liaison is to connect families to resources needed between home and school that will help students be successful in school. Here are some of the tasks they might be asked to do:

- Share information among students, families, and school staff
- Set up home visits and office meetings with families
- Talk to teachers to find out how students are doing
- Organize community events and activities that support families, such as open houses and potluck
- Refer students and their families to services they need
- Run programs for parents, such as parenting classes and English classes (USAHello, n.d.)

The family liaison plays an important role for families of color. Often, the liaison is bilingual and is able to communicate in several languages. Families with limited English skills feel connected and appreciated because the family liaison can speak to them in their heritage language.

As previously mentioned in this chapter, gifted students of color can be twice exceptional or thrice exceptional, and these students will need multiple departments working together to provide the supports needed for their giftedness and learning exceptionalities. Connect with the Special Education department and offer to be part of a collaborative district neurodivergent team of people to support gifted students of color that are twice or thrice exceptional. Ask the Culturally Linguistically Diverse Education department to join the neurodivergent team to support those students who are thrice exceptional. Provide training for administrators, educators, paraprofessionals, and families focused on characteristics of twice- and thrice-exceptional learners and best practices in gifted education to support these learners.

Communication
Communication is an important piece of building trust with families. Communicating with families with transparency and consistency demonstrates to families that you are providing information to them in a timely and respectful manner. Communication to families should be available to culturally linguistically diverse families in their heritage language, in a variety of formats, and with little educator-ese.

Visiting with the Communication department, if you have one, in your school or district can help you better understand what options families have to receive information. Does the school district send things out via text message, by email, on their social media accounts, and/or through robo-calls and paper? Also, what methods of communication are effective with your diverse families? Do your families trust the education system enough to give their phone number or email address? Is their information up to date? The Communication department can help manage your social media gifted page and also give you tips on how to manage your Twitter feed. They can develop a communication and marketing strategic plan to build up understanding of gifted education across the district. If possible, ask them to give you editing access to the different newsletters throughout the different organizations in the district so that you have a variety of platforms on which to send out information about gifted education.

MTSS Teams or Department

As previously discussed in this chapter, MTSS must be recognized and implemented by administrators and educators so that it can be utilized effectively as a system of supports for all learners, including gifted students. Many school districts that embrace MTSS have MTSS leads in each of their schools to support the MTSS process and train administrators and teachers on how to utilize the framework to support students. Connect with these people and provide training for them on how to use the MTSS framework for gifted learners. Share the CR-MTSS with the MTSS leads and demonstrate how CR-MTSS can be used to promote discussions of racism through differentiated multicultural literature (Ford, 2011).

Mental Health Department

Gifted students may require social-emotional support from school counselors or psychologists as they tend to experience the world in a different way than their non-gifted peers. *Asynchronous development* and *intensity* are two of the main terms associated with the emotional development of gifted students (Davidson Institute, n. d.). Gifted students often feel different than their peers and may experience feelings of loneliness and anxiety. Counselors and psychologists working with neurodivergent students must have training in gifted education practices, culturally responsive practices, and special education to effectively serve these students and their families. Establish protocols and referral processes with the mental health providers in the school setting for gifted culturally diverse learners, or at the district level. Discuss what training needs to be in place for psychologists, social workers, counselors, and others to understand the intensities of gifted learners and the intersectionality of culture.

Provide training for mental health advocates and attendance advocates in your district surrounding gifted characteristics and social-emotional intensities for gifted students. Ask for regular meetings with the advocates to discuss the connection between mental health and absences and create a strategic plan to develop supports for at-risk gifted learners.

Equity Department

Now, we know that the word *equity* is taboo and that not everyone is as fortunate as we have been to have worked with districts who have allocated resources to create a team focused on equity across the district. If you do have that opportunity, however, collaborate with the Equity department to promote gifted education practices for diverse students and equitable opportunities for access to gifted services. Work with the Equity department to close the equity gap for gifted culturally linguistically diverse learners. Ask to be part of any equity leadership teams, especially those that will analyze gaps in access to education. This will provide you a platform and resources to advocate for equitable gifted services for ethnically and racially diverse gifted learners. Ask the type of equity they are focused on: racial, gender, sexual orientation, class, educational equity, etc. This knowledge helps inform how you show up to meetings and advocate for your gifted learners and the resources they need to thrive.

In addition to culturally linguistically diverse learners, the Equity department may also work to put supports in place for students who identify as part of the Lesbian, Gay, Bisexual, Transgender, Queer/Questioning, Intransition/Intersex, Asexual community (LGBTQIA). Find out which schools in your district, if any, have a Gay Straight Alliances group. Reach out to their sponsor to set up a time that you can come and meet with them to discuss how gifted LGBTQIA gifted students are supported. Ask the sponsor what they need to feel supported from the district or the school. Offer to come and present to the students about gifted LGBTQIA students' academic and social emotional needs. Sit down and listen to the students share their needs in an empathy interview to help determine what supports you need to put in place for them. Provide training for families covering characteristics and intensities of gifted LGBTQIA students. Include a section in your gifted communications specifically addressing gifted LGBTQIA students and their needs.

Finance and Grants

Reach out to the Grant department at the district and state levels to support you in searching for grant funds that can be applied for to support gifted learners, especially those from diverse backgrounds. Let the Grant department guide you in the application process and have them review the application before sending it off. Talk to the person who supports your budget in the budget office, or accounting, about how your current grant funds can be utilized more efficiently to support gifted culturally linguistically diverse students' academic and affective outcomes. Annually, review your budget and determine what allocations can be shifted to support culturally responsive gifted education practices. Reach out to other departments for funding that can be shared to support culturally linguistically diverse gifted, twice-exceptional, and thrice-exceptional students.

Postsecondary

Connect with the Career and Postsecondary department to learn about what your district provides as pathways for students to enter college and the postsecondary workforce. As with other departments, ask what their vision and mission is for gifted diverse learners. Collaborate with them on creating pathways beginning in elementary for culturally linguistically diverse students to prepare for college readiness. Join the leadership team, or ask to be a part of a committee that is creating these pathways and advocate for early implementation of career planning for students of color so that they are prepared academically by the time they attend high school to take advanced courses. Provide an informational session for families of gifted students of color that informs them about what their students need to prepare for a successful future. Share with families the different pathways that their students can choose early in elementary school.

Contemplation Corner

Think about the departments within your school district or state organization. With whom do you have strong connections and systems of support in place? With whom do you need to connect to establish or strengthen support for culturally linguistically diverse gifted students?

Conclusion

Creating culturally responsive gifted systems of support may seem arduous. It may feel like you are the only one traveling this path of equitable opportunity and access. Do not despair, but look around and notice that there are others who are demanding that culturally linguistically diverse students are provided the same educational opportunities as students from the white majority culture. There are proverbial armies forming all around you, and you are not alone. It just takes one person to begin to take notice of inequities and oppression within systems to become a change agent focused on dismantling these systems. Become that change agent by connecting specialists, counselors, educators, administrators, and families to one another in a strategic manner around a common vision for supporting culturally linguistically diverse gifted learners. In doing so, you will gather your army of people that can support you in this work.

Key Points

◆ The Multitiered System of Supports works for all students.
◆ CR-MTSS is an approach to supporting culturally linguistically diverse twice exceptional and thrice exceptional learners.
◆ Developing systems of support begins with building relationships.
◆ In order to create culturally responsive sustainable systems, you must work with other departments to make cross-departmental connections focused on equity and social justice work.

References

Anderson, L. W., & Krathwohl, D. R. (Eds.). (2001). *A taxonomy for learning, teaching, and assessing: A revision of bloom's taxonomy of educational objectives*. Allyn & Bacon.

Banks, J. A. (1989). Approaches to multicultural curriculum reform. *Trotter Review, 3*(3), 17–19.

Belin Blank Center. (n.d.). *Acceleration institute*. http://accelerationinstitute.org/

Bloom, B. (1985). *Developing talent in young people*. Ballantine Books.

Cammarota, J., & Romero, A. (2006). A critically compassionate intellectualism for Latina/o students: Raising voices above the silencing in our schools. *Multicultural Education, 14*(2), 16–23.

Coleman, M. R., & Hughes, C. E. (2009). Meeting the needs of gifted students within an RTI framework. *Gifted Child Today, 32*(3), 14–17.

Collins, K. H. (2020). *Multicultural curriculum development, teaching approach & learning taxonomy: Using Bloom-Banks matrix* [Unpublished Resource]. CI 5359 Curriculum for Depth and Challenge, Department of Curriculum & Instruction, Texas State University.

Collins, K. H. (2021). *Servicing 2e and 3e learners using Collin's culturally responsive multi-tiered system of supports.* https://www.sengifted.org /post/3e-learners

Collins, K. H. (2020a). Talking about racism in America and in education: The reflections of a gifted Black educational professional and mother of a gifted Black young adult. *Parenting for High Potential, 9*(3), 5–9.

Colorado Department of Education. (2022). *Chapter 6: Multi-tiered system of supports, special education needs, and gifted education.* ttps://www .cde.state.co.us/cde_english/eldguidebook2022chapter6

Council for Exceptional Children. (2008). *CEC's position on response to intervention (RTI): The unique role of special education and special educators.* https://exceptionalchildren.org/sites/default/files/2020 -08/RTI_FIXED.pdf

Cox, J., Daniel, N., & Boston, B. O. (1985). *Educating able learners: Programs and promising practices.* University of Texas Press.

Davidson Institute. (n.d.). *Social & emotional needs of gifted children.* https:// www.davidsongifted.org/prospective-families/social-emotional -resources/

Ford, D. Y. (2011). *Multicultural gifted education.* Prufrock Press.

Ford, D. Y., Dickson, K. T., Davis, J. L., Scott, M. T., & Grantham, T. C. (2018). *A culturally responsive equity-based bill of rights for gifted students of color.* https://www.nagc.org/blog/culturally-responsive-equity -based-bill-rights-gifted-students-color

Ford, D. Y., & Harris III, J. J. (1999). *Multicultural gifted education.* Teachers College Press.

Gay, G. (2018). *Culturally responsive teaching: Theory, research, and practice* (3rd ed.). Teachers College Press.

Hammond, Z. (2015). *Culturally responsive teaching & the brain.* Corwin.

Hoover, J. J., & Patton, J. R. (2017). *IEPs for ELs and other diverse learners*. Corwin.

Iowa Department of Education. (2018). *Advanced learner: Multi-tiered system of support guide*. https://drive.google.com/file/d/1PkxneV AJ88ISzR2jNd7znK4DElXxLrTf/view

Johnsen, S. K., Parker, S. L., & Farah, Y. N. (2015). Providing services for students with gifts and talents within a response-to-intervention framework. *Teaching Exceptional Children, 47*(4), 226–233.

PBIS Rewards. (n.d.). *What is MTSS?* https://www.pbisrewards.com/blog/what-is-mtss/

Renzulli, J. S., & Reis, S. M. (2014). *The schoolwide enrichment model: A how-to guide for talent development*. Routledge.

Rogers, K. (1992). *A best-evidence synthesis of research on acceleration options for gifted students*. https://www.davidsongifted.org/gifted-blog/a-best-evidence-synthesis-of-research-on-acceleration-options-for-gifted-students/

Rogers, K. B. (2002). *Re-forming gifted education: Matching the program to the child*. Great Potential Press.

RTI Action Network (n.d.). *What is RTI?* http://www.rtinetwork.org/learn/what/whatisrti

Seal of Biliteracy. (2022). *State laws regarding the seal of biliteracy*. https://sealofbiliteracy.org/

Scott, M. T. (2014). Using the Bloom–Banks Matrix to develop multicultural differentiated lessons for gifted students. *Gifted Child Today, 37*(3), 163–168.

Tomlinson, C. A. (1999). *The differentiated classroom: Responding to the needs of all learners*. ASCD.

Tomlinson, C. A. (2014). *The differentiated classroom: Responding to the needs of all learners* (2nd ed.). ASCD.

The Association for the Gifted. (n.d.). *Response to intervention for gifted children*. https://www.nagc.org/sites/default/files/Position%20Statement/RtI.pdf

USA Hello. (n.d.). *How to be a school liaison*. https://usahello.org/work/choose-career/education-jobs/school-liaison/#gref

Winebrenner, S., & Brulles, D. (2008). *The cluster grouping handbook: How to challenge gifted students and improve achievement for all*. Free Spirit Publishing.

7

Commitment to Families

Honoring Diversity

Families are the central core of our students' lived experiences. Each one of these experiences shapes and impacts the way students perceive and engage in their school communities and the world. Before children enter school buildings, their families are their teachers. They model and communicate their cultural, educational expectations and values to their children through language, stories, traditions, and beliefs. Our families' cultures are a combination of many factors that influence them: family traditions, countries of origin, geographic regions, ethnic identities, cultural groups, community norms, sexual orientations, gender identities, educational and other experiences, personal choices, and home languages (National Center on Parent, Family, and Community Engagement, n.d.). Being a culturally responsive gifted leader means making a commitment to culturally and linguistically diverse families to ensure equitable opportunity and access to gifted programming and services. Honoring our families' cultural and linguistic heritages is a vital part of this commitment.

The term *family* is used in this chapter to refer to what has traditionally been referred to as a *parent*. The term *family* acknowledges that diverse and multilingual learners may live with and have strong relationships with family members instead of or in addition to their parents (Snyder & Fenner, 2021). Many families are multidimensional and may even reside in multigenerational households

DOI: 10.4324/9781003293729-7

or have extended family members living near each other in the same community (DuBois & Greene, 2021). It is important to recognize and honor each family's distinct cultural backgrounds. The key to any family engagement process is the understanding of the cultural beliefs, values, and priorities of families (National Center on Parent, Family, and Community Engagement, n.d.).

Family engagement refers to the ways in which educators build authentic relationships with families. Positive relationships with families promote strong parent–child relationships, family wellbeing, and better outcomes for children and families (National Center on Parent, Family, and Community Engagement, n.d.). Through family engagement practices, families become partners in their students' education. When families feel supported, valued, and respected in their school community, research indicates that their students have a higher rate of success than those students whose families do not feel supported, valued, and respected.

Unfortunately, in some instances, schools and districts fail to engage families but tend to provide "random acts" of family engagement rather than systemic, integrated, and sustained shifts in practice (Fehrer & Tognozzi, 2018). A random act might appear as holding a gifted family information night in Spanish for Latinx families at the beginning of the school year, but then during the remainder of the school year offering nothing else for these families in their heritage language. How can families be engaged when they do not have opportunities to become engaged? Engaging ethnically diverse families means supporting families throughout the entire school year with intention and a focus on equitable practices that embrace the families' vision of engagement.

Examining Beliefs

Working with students and families of color means that we must examine our own personal belief systems and how we perceive people of color and their family units. Do you make assumptions about students of color and their families? Do you believe that students whose families' heritage language is not English are academically inferior? Do you believe that their families are academically inferior? Do you believe that some families from some parts of the world are more educated than others, and do you place a value on the type of the education (formal schooling, pre-university, home-school, GED, real-world non-academic learning, etc.) the families bring with them? Do you treat ethnically diverse families differently than the white families in your classroom? Do you make assumptions about what families know and understand about gifted education? What do you know about how families view gifted education? Is your vision and idea for family engagement the same as the families'?

In families with multilingual learners, engagement may look less obvious to administrators if they are not familiar with types of engagement that differ from the majority white culture. For example, a culturally linguistically economically diverse family may not be able to attend an event in person; however, they may ensure that their children complete work and encourage them to study (Snyder & Fenner, 2021). What questions have you asked about family engagement with your families? These are some of the deeper questions that you must ask yourself to keep your implicit bias and assumptions in check when working with students and families of color.

Contemplation Corner

Start exploring your beliefs about families. What beliefs and assumptions do you have about your families, and are they asset or deficit based?

Building Rapport

Engaging culturally and linguistically diverse families requires building rapport with them that goes beyond surface level. Culturally responsive gifted leaders recognize the importance of building authentic rapport and trust with students, staff, families and the community, while also affirming the multiple identities of these individuals (The Leadership Academy, 2022). Authentic rapport means creating effective partnerships with families that are grounded in mutual trust. One way to do this is by creating a welcoming school community that values and honors diversity. Allow for all voices to be heard and responded to in a culturally responsive manner.

Recognize that there are certain groups that have more privilege than others and make the shift to allow for all groups to have power and not just one group. Respond to all families' concerns equally and honor their contributions.

Building authentic rapport at the district and state levels also means creating effective partnerships with families that are grounded in trust, which can be more difficult to do when the administrator is not directly connected to a building with families every day. Therefore, culturally responsive leaders of gifted programs at the district and state levels may have to connect with schools or community organizations to find families and build rapport. Families will not necessarily come to them. This work at the district and state levels is critical because family engagement within all levels of education has a powerful impact on student and family outcomes. Consistently, research shows that students with involved families, no matter what their income or background, are more likely to:

- Earn higher grades and test scores, and enroll in higher-level programs
- Be promoted, pass their classes, and earn credits
- Attend school regularly
- Have better social skills, show improved behavior, and adapt well to school

- Graduate and go on to postsecondary education (Henderson & Mapp, 2002)

Building a Cultural Bridge

As a leader of culturally responsive gifted programs, it is important to recognize that families already come to school with assets from their culture that are vital to family engagement and student success. Furthermore, families who are ethnically and linguistically diverse come to school with rich cultural backgrounds and heritage languages. When we embrace these assets and invite families to use their strengths as they partner with leaders of gifted programs at schools and districts, we are helping build a cultural bridge of understanding and empathy. A cultural bridge is a metaphor for connecting cultures together and discovering commonalities and differences, always with the intent of valuing and respecting each other's cultures (Skrefsrud, 2018). This allows for a deeper connection and relationship building with families and students. It also allows us to start to see how the roots of our own cultural trees that we explored in Chapter 2 are connected, so that when there are conflicts due to cultural differences or miscommunication, leaders and families have common understanding of one another and are committed to working out whatever the conflict is together.

In order to build a cultural bridge, leaders must learn what is important to families. Hear their stories. Listen to families with open hearts and nonjudgmental attitudes. Let them tell you what they need for their students to be successful learners. Open communications with families and invite them to express their ideas for creating a more responsive and equitable gifted environment (The Leadership Academy, 2022). Letting families know that you care about them and their cultural assets will help build a stronger connectivity between the gifted program and family. We will share specific examples later in the chapter on how to specifically build cultural bridges with empathy interviews.

Funds of Knowledge

Families bring vast experiences with them into the educational environment; these are referred to as funds of knowledge. A culturally responsive leader of gifted programs can leverage families' funds of knowledge to help shape and create culturally responsive gifted programs with the school and district. The concept of funds of knowledge was originally applied by Vélez-Ibáñez and Greenberg (1992) to describe the historical accumulation of abilities, bodies of knowledge, assets, and cultural ways of interacting that were evident in U.S.–Mexican households in Tucson, Arizona. Funds of knowledge are originally thought to be derived from a Vygotskian perspective that views the everyday practices of language and action as a way to construct knowledge (González et al., 2005). Utilizing students' funds of knowledge as a resource can be a powerful tool to access content in the classroom through building upon students' lived experiences, especially those students from low-income and diverse populations. Researchers have discovered over years of working with funds of knowledge that the implications for students from diverse populations is significant to making connections between teachers, students, and families (Moll et al., 2013). How can a teacher discover a family's funds of knowledge and make deeper connections? They can visit with families outside of the classroom, have families create cultural identity profiles that they share with their class, or have students work on projects that focus on their lived experiences. Embracing families' funds of knowledge and applying this knowledge to classroom activities and content or through district events will create more meaningful and authentic relationships with students and families. In doing so, leaders are modeling culturally responsive gifted education, culturally responsive leadership, and culturally responsive family engagement. Specific family engagement strategies that elicit funds of knowledge, such as home visits and family cultural identity portraits, will be shared later in the chapter.

Cultural Wealth

What cultural wealth does the family bring into the school community? Cultural wealth is the talents, strengths, and experiences that students and families bring with them from their homes and communities into the classroom. Yosso's (2005) idea of community cultural wealth as an asset-based framework rooted in Critical Race Theory (CRT) acknowledges there are at least six forms of cultural capital that communities of color possess. The six forms of cultural capital are:

- Aspirational
- Linguistic
- Familial
- Social
- Navigational
- Resistance (Yosso, 2005)

Cultural wealth utilizes asset-based thinking and maximizes the underutilized assets that students of color bring with them into the school community. As culturally responsive leaders in gifted education, we must challenge deficit thinking and promote asset-based thinking about our learners and families who are ethnically diverse. These students and families are bringing with them aspects of their culture that may be different from yours but they should be valued and respected as part of the strengths that they bring into the school community.

Aspirational capital refers to the ability to maintain hopes and dreams for the future, even in the face of real and perceived barriers (Yosso, 2005). From the author's personal experience, families of color aspire for their children to achieve more than themselves and attain a higher education than they have attained. These families work hard to provide for their children, often working multiple jobs and denying their own needs so that they can give more to their children. This form of cultural wealth is evidenced in those who allow themselves and their children to dream of possibilities beyond their present circumstances, often without the objective means to attain those goals (Yosso, 2005). This rings true with an often-heard phrase in Spanish from our Latinx families "Sí, se puede" translated as "Yes, we can."

Linguistic capital refers to the various language and communication skills students bring with them to the school community (Yosso, 2005). Through rich storytelling, traditions are passed down verbally in many families of color. Yosso (2005) argues that because storytelling is a part of students' lives that they bring with them, "skills that may include memorization, attention to detail, dramatic pauses, comedic timing, facial affect, vocal tone, volume, rhythm and rhyme" (p. 79). Student's rich language and communication skills can be utilized to enhance content and boost academic success in school.

Familial capital is a form of cultural wealth that fosters a commitment to community wellbeing and expands the concept of family to include a more broad understanding of kinship (Yosso, 2005). Many of our diverse families have strong extended family bonds. These families tend to be communal in nature, whereby they value extended family members as part of their familial community. From these extended familial ties, students learn the importance of maintaining a healthy connection to their community and its valuable native resources (Yosso, 2005). This learning is extended into the school as students and families of color build relationships within the school community.

Social capital can be seen as networks of people and community resources (Yosso, 2005). This type of cultural wealth is utilized by families to access resources that they need to survive. It involves peer and social contact networking.

Navigational capital refers to students' skills and abilities to navigate "social institutions," including educational spaces (Yosso, 2005). How do ethnically diverse students traverse between the various social groups in school? Yosso (2005) suggests that navigational capital empowers families of color to maneuver within unsupportive or hostile environments as they pull from their inner resources. Gifted culturally and linguistically diverse learners are more likely to be able to easily traverse between cultural groups in the school community as they can morph from one culture to another.

Resistant capital refers to those knowledges and skills fostered through oppositional

behavior that challenges inequality (Yosso, 2005). This form of cultural wealth is grounded in social justice and equality. These are the skills that students develop while engaged in a community that actively disrupts systems of oppression. Culturally responsive gifted leaders recognize that students and families bring with them their cultural wealth. Understanding that students and families come with their own cultural strengths and valuing these assets can promote strong bonds and deepen surface relationships with families.

Cultural Dimensions

Making authentic connections with students and families means knowing who they are beyond a surface level. What is their culture? What are their lived experiences? Let us delve a little deeper into culture and examine Hofstede's (2011) cultural dimensions theory and some of the differences in cultures globally and the way these behaviors might appear in a school environment or within a family interaction. Hofstede originally had four dimensions, but in 1988 Michael Harris Bond added the fifth dimension with Michael Minkov adding a sixth dimension in 2010 (Kobiruzzaman, 2019). The six dimensions are:

- Power Distance Index (PDI)
- Individualism vs. Collectivism
- Masculinity vs. Femininity
- Uncertainty Avoidance Index (UAI)
- Long Short Term Orientation
- Indulgence vs. Restraint

As we explore these dimensions, reflect upon your practices and think about how understanding the cultural dimensions might change the way you interact with ethnically diverse students and their families.

Power Distance Index

The first dimension is the power distance index. Hofstede (2011) defines power distance as the extent to which the less powerful members of organizations and institutions (like the family) accept and expect that power is distributed unequally. Power distance index scores tend to be higher for East European, Latin, Asian, and African countries and lower for Germanic and English-speaking Western countries (Hofstede et al., 2010). How does this permeate with our Brown and Black families? The high index scores indicate that these families expect to be treated unfairly and do not question the majority authority. How do we as culturally responsive gifted leaders shift this index and change this dynamic within our school and district communities? One way is to provide multiple opportunities for our diverse families to have a voice in school and district decision making and empower them to recognize that they are valued members of the school community. Give them a platform where they can be heard and seen.

Individualism vs. Collectivism

Although discussed in Chapter 2, it is critical to review the role of individualism and collectivism in our schools. Individualism refers to the individualistic culture of a society where people prefer to work separately as opposed to working in groups. In individualism, everyone is supposed to take care of him or herself and his or her immediate family only (Hofstede, 2011), whereas in collectivism, people prefer to work in groups. In collectivism, people from birth onwards are integrated into strong, cohesive in-groups, often extended families (with uncles, aunts, and grandparents), that continue protecting them in exchange for unquestioning loyalty (Hofstede, 2011). Individualism and collectivism can be seen in students' work preferences. A student from a collectivist culture may appear in the classroom as noncompliant when working individually on a project. In a collectivist culture, children are taught early on to work collectively with other people, so working individually is not their preferred learning style. They are social beings that welcome the collaborative process. Individualism tends to prevail in developed and Western countries like the United States while collectivism tends to prevail in Latin American and African countries as well as others. Collectivistic cultures are prevalent in Guatemala, Ecuador, Venezuela, Indonesia, Pakistan, Taiwan, South Korea, China, Bangladesh, and Malaysia (Hofstede, 2011). Understanding your students' work preferences and acknowledging the cultural differences and similarities between your students is an important aspect of being a culturally responsive gifted educator and understanding how to interact with students' families.

Masculinity vs. Femininity

Knowing from which country families come from can help us understand their behaviors. In this cultural dimension, masculinity represents a preference in society for achievement, heroism, assertiveness, and material rewards for success (Hofstede Insights, n.d.). Its opposite, femininity, stands for a preference for cooperation, modesty, caring for the weak, and quality of life (Hofstede Insights, n.d.). Some countries are high in the masculinity dimension while others are high in the femininity dimension. Hofstede's research determined that masculinity is high in countries like Japan, Italy, Mexico, and English-speaking Western countries. And Sweden, Norway, Netherland, Denmark, Costa Rica, and Finland are considered as the most feminine countries in the world (Kobiruzzaman, 2019).

Uncertainty Avoidance Index

The uncertainty-avoidance dimension is to what extent a culture programs its members to feel either uncomfortable or comfortable in unstructured situations (Hofstede, 2011). In the face of the unknown or the future, different cultures experience stress in more or less extreme ways. High uncertainty avoidance societies prefer to follow routines and make plans to prevent unpredictable moments (Kobiruzzaman, 2019). People in low uncertainty avoidance countries are relaxed and open-minded (Kobiruzzaman, 2019). They tend to be more flexible when things do not go as planned. Greece, Guatemala, Russia, Portugal, Belgium, and Japan are considered to be high uncertain avoidance countries (Kobiruzzaman, 2019).

Long vs. Short-Term Orientation

This dimension is time oriented. Some societies maintain time-honored traditions and norms while viewing societal change with suspicion (de Bruin, 2017). Other societies favor more short-term thinking and focus on the future. Asian countries such as China and Japan are known for their long-term orientation whereas Morocco is a short-term oriented country (de Bruin, 2017).

Indulgence vs. Restraint

Indulgence stands for a society that allows relatively free gratification of basic and natural human drives while restraint stands for a society that suppresses gratification of needs (Kobiruzzaman, 2019). This dimension speaks to how desires and impulses are controlled or freely indulged. Some of the most indulgent countries in the world include Mexico, Colombia, Germany, and Nigeria (Kobiruzzaman, 2019).

The overview of these cultural dimensions reminds us to recognize that our culturally and linguistically diverse families may come to our schools and districts with global behaviors based upon their native country. Being cognizant of these behaviors and how they might portray in school communities can help guide us to make informed decisions for our families. Knowing the various cultural dimensions of our families guides us to a deeper understanding and opens our minds up to appreciation for cultural similarities and differences.

Contemplation Corner

Take a moment to think about cultural dimensions. What are your cultural dimensions and what do you know about the cultural dimensions of your families?

Family Engagement Strategies

In this chapter thus far we have examined how the cultures of students and families are an important part of school communities. Not only do families have their own culture but schools also have a culture and a hidden curriculum of their own. So how do we recognize the rich culture of our families and infuse their culture so that it is affirmed in the hidden curriculum? And how do we engage families in a culturally responsive manner? In this next section, family engagement strategies that the authors have found to be successful in their own work are described.

Home Visits
Home visits can provide an incredible opportunity to learn more about your culturally linguistically diverse learners and their

families (Snyder & Fenner, 2021). Families know information about their children that may not be revealed at a traditional parent–teacher conference held once or twice a year focused on academics, or that a child will reveal to the teacher or school leader themselves, and home visits are an excellent way to engage families outside of school and deepen relationships with families. The information shared at home visits has been documented to increase the connection families have with schools and school districts, increase educator morale, increase family and student sense of belonging, and increase academic growth (Faber, 2016; Kronholz, 2016).

Even though it is called a home visit, that does not mean that the visit must be conducted in the home. Some families may not want a home visit in their home due to a variety of reasons. Let the family choose which environment works best for them. The family could choose to meet at the local library, a community center, a religious center, a park, or somewhere else that they feel comfortable. Make a note of the family's home language and inquire whether an interpreter is needed. Also ensure that you share your desire to conduct a home visit to learn about the families' hopes and dreams for their child. Assure families that you and or your staff are not there to talk about academics, unless they want to discuss that; your purpose is to build a relationship with them and know how to best support their family.

The concept of a home visit is simple—to build relationships. The visiting educators, paraprofessionals, and administrators focus on the family's hopes and dreams for the child and what school was like for the family members themselves. These are open-ended questions that build empathy and understanding and enable families and school personnel to relate to one another throughout the year. Typically the home visit is made twice a year and is a part of an overall family engagement strategic plan that includes continued opportunities for involvement.

The first meeting should be made at the beginning of the school year and can be as short or as long as the family can afford. It is critical to have the home visit at the beginning of the year, not focused on academics, so if any challenges occur during the year you will already have made a relationship with the family during the initial home visit. It is important to come with positive strength-based anecdotes about their child. You may also consider bringing a small token or gift for the family from your culture as one way to show respect to the family you are visiting. Additionally, you can also bring a cooperative game, and if there is time, ask if the family wants to play together during the visit (ensure instructions and interpretation are available in heritage language if applicable).

While the concept of a home visit is simple, the skills involved in conducting a successful home visit are complex, and culturally responsive gifted leaders must ensure they and their staff engage in training to ensure that the visits do not unintentionally create harm and impede a positive visit. Training must include conversations about confronting microaggressions, implicit bias, cultural faux pas when interacting with families, positive and negative stereotypes about the families' culture, and how to repair harm if harm is done. Leaders must ask those conducting home visits to step into conversations about the assumptions they hold about families. For example, if the family is living in poverty, what assumptions are the staff making about the families and their engagement with school? Do staff members only view family engagement as what is happening directly in the classroom, or would they consider the way in which families encourage their children or support with homework as engagement (Fenner, 2014)? What assumptions do you, as the administrator, have about families? It is your job as a culturally responsive leader of gifted programs to model the challenging of any assumptions you have and then hold your team, and yourself, to the same standard.

Finally, remember that not all families will welcome a visit from the school or the district. They may see a visit from the school as intrusive, or perceive it as a threat (e.g. undocumented families, families with past trauma caused by school, etc.). That is okay because home visits are optional. The point is that you as the leader make the offer and attempt to reach out to them. If they do not want to meet, do not make assumptions about why. Ask again in the spring and perhaps consider some of the many other family engagement strategies we have listed below. Your goal is to build relationships and cultural bridges, and this is only one strategy.

Crosscultural Communication

Communicating with full transparency with families is critical in building relationships with families. Schools and districts should engage in crosscultural communication to establish trust and support for family engagement. Hanover Research (2017) notes that "cross cultural communication is a must to minimize the confusion and frustration that people may experience when they enter an environment where not only their language, but also their attitudes, values, and behaviors differ from that of others." For communication to be effective it must be two way and crosscultural so that it is truly authentic and valuing of the family. Examples of evidence-based two-way and crosscultural communication strategies that we have used in our practice are listed below:

Two-way communication:

- Host family events in the community such as a community center, library, religious center, park, etc.
- Translate materials into the heritage language.
- Use bilingual staff members and family liaisons to communicate with families and staff.
- Provide transportation for families to bring them to events if needed.
- Create and utilize family support groups who speak the same language, or are from the same community, and are able to offer support to one another at family events.
- Create family support groups that network with one another at family events to help educate one another.

Crosscultural communication:

- Begin conversations relationally and personally—not transactionally. Do not begin with academics or district policies immediately.
- When speaking with families, mix personal conversation with professional—stay relational.
- Use the pronoun "we" instead of " you" and "I" to create a sense of caring, common purpose and belonging. For

example, "*We* are here today to work together to support Vishali."

- Discuss how the student's achievements are within the context of the whole classroom, school, or district and how they are contributing to the wellbeing of the entire community.
- Discuss how the family's contributions are positively impacting the entire community.
- Explain the goals and expectations of the school or the district and work together with families to find ways they are comfortable supporting their children's learning.
- Ask for feedback from families and show them how you are using what they tell you to change systems and structures for their families and their children.

Crosscultural and two-way communications are some of the tools you will use to communicate with families; however, there are additional considerations related to communication that must be considered so that families stay engaged. Culturally responsive leaders of gifted programs know that what you communicate to families, the purpose of your communication, how you communicate, when you communicate, and through what modalities you communicate are the driving questions that will guide your communications. If you do not know the answers to some of these questions, you can gather this information at the beginning of the year through family interviews or surveys. For example, will families want weekly, monthly, or quarterly updates? What are your families' preferred methods of communication (phone, text, email, paper, video call, etc.)?

Additionally, you as the leader must consider accessibility to the information you are providing, including, but not limited to, how all families will have access and the ways in which families can communicate with you if they do not understand the information. It is important to provide multiple modals for families to receive information in family-friendly language. That is, communication should be free of educator-ese and acronyms when possible. Additionally, leaders should provide interpreters at family meetings and parent–teacher conferences if linguistically diverse families need them for translation of information. Make note of a family's home language and provide communication to the family in their home language every time something comes home. Also, as stated in Chapter 2, ensure that the families' heritage language is visible in the classroom, or in district and state offices, so that if and when they are in those spaces, they have a sense of belonging.

Offer multiple ways to connect with culturally and linguistically diverse families that include tech and non-tech options, formal and informal. Options for communication can include updates about what is happening in the gifted program at the school or district through physical papers, physical or virtual newsletters, emails, postcards, etc. that are sent home. Or they can be more informal through quick face-to-face conversations if you see the family at drop off or pick up, in the hallway, or in the before- or after-care program.

Many of your families will communicate with their smartphones, if they have one, or with school-authorized tablets. Use texting apps like Talking Points, Class Dojo, School Messenger, and others to create an optional family group and keep connected in this way in the families' heritage languages. Investigate if your school district has an app for phones or tablets that is already available. If not, advocate for this technology. For those who do not have access to smartphones, make sure that you send home a paper copy of whatever it is you sent via text or email and time those high-tech and low-tech messages to be sent out at the same time. By sending messages out at the same time, you are not placing a specific value on any one type of communication method, thus establishing a hidden curriculum. Again, ask your families ahead of time how often they want to receive messages because some families will stop reading information if they receive too many texts or emails.

Another tech option that many schools and districts leverage is social media. Create a gifted social media page or pages that can be accessed in a variety of languages to communicate information with families and the community. Again, you will need to consider what information needs to be on the page and what is appealing to families, and ensure that is accessible to people with disabilities as well. Have families review the social media pages to give you feedback on the page and help you make changes, or even ask if they will help design the page or pages.

Finally, you and your staff can also reach out to families the "old fashioned way" and have a phone conversation. Ensure that the phone conversation and as many of your communications that you have with families are crosscultural and two way at minimum. There are multiple ways to communicate with families. Remember that whatever form of communication you use, make sure the information is accessible to all families including those families that are ethnically diverse.

Contemplation Corner

What aspects of your communication with families are crosscultural and two way?

Empathy Interviews

Empathy interviews are one way in which administrators can help create culturally inclusive family engagement while shifting mindsets, recognizing bias, and re-shaping systems and structures to support some of the most vulnerable students they serve. While there are multiple research-based strategies that administrators in education use to seek out information from learners and their families about their experience in education, such as surveys and focus groups, these strategies do not yield the depth of information that can come from an empathy interview that is a direct and personal approach to working with families. When wanting to dismantle systems of oppression and create a more inclusive environment, this approach is critical to include among your family engagement strategies because it directly elicits responses about the lived experiences of students and families who are often marginalized and excluded from traditional data and research methods.

Empathy is both a mindset and a skillset to continue to practice and develop (Nelsestuen & Smith, 2020). Empathy is the ability to share and develop a deep understanding of the feelings and experiences of another person. While it is not possible to completely understand every experience the families within your classroom have had, or even the experience of another educator in the building or system, it is essential that you try. The goal of an empathy interview is to find out what your families and learners need so that you can create culturally inclusive spaces where they feel welcomed, seen, and valued.

By their very design, empathy interviews create cultural bridges with families from a culture that is different from your own. During empathy interviews, the interviewer listens deeply to understand the experience of the family, student, or person being interviewed to help uncover what they may need to feel valued, successful, or supported. These are typically one-on-one conversations with open-ended questions that elicit personal stories about specific experiences from the interview participants and "help uncover unacknowledged needs" (Nelsestuen & Smith, 2020). Therefore, those approaching empathy interviews must do so with humility and be open to listening to experiences without forming judgments. Educators must also be aware of potential power dynamics and how the family's culture may view the role of the educator in the conversation. Empathy interviews will take time and effort, and there is much planning involved so that they are successful and will not cause unintentional harm. The overarching components of an empathy interview include planning for an empathy interview, designing questions, and preparing a team of people to help you conduct the interviews, if possible (Nelsestuen & Smith, 2020). The following five steps will help you plan to conduct an empathy interview:

- Identify your "why?"
- Determine with whom you need to speak
- Assemble an empathy interview team (if possible)
- Plan the logistics of the interview
- Prepare for analysis

The first step in developing an empathy interview is identifying your "why?" What is the purpose of conducting an empathy interview? What is your question? What do you want to know? Are you collecting the stories of families in your class or building to refine or identify a problem of practice? Are you trying to identify a root cause? Are you designing change ideas together with the families? Depending on your reason for conducting the interview, it could be possible that another way to solicit information from your families is more appropriate, such as a survey or focus groups.

The second step in planning for an empathy interview is determining from whom you need to hear. Which families do you need to ensure you speak with first? Do you need to speak with all families? Choosing to listen to families who have been historically marginalized is a way to build equity and challenge systemic oppression with your building, classroom, or larger state organization. You will want to listen to those families who have had different experiences from you in order to help form a robust picture of what they are experiencing.

The third step in planning is determining who will conduct the interviews. If you are a team of one, then is it possible to ask educators in your building, district, or other organizations to help support you? The empathy interview team will not go out as a big group together because that creates an uneven power dynamic. However, this team can spread out and help conduct multiple interviews if needed. If possible, you will want to assemble a team that is broad and diverse in role, perspective, thought, background, and experience. As you are building the team, consider the following:

- Relationships: How will you or the interview team build relationships with families and what are the relationships that already exist? Are they positive, negative, or neutral?
- Impact of power dynamics: Consider how race, gender, ability, language, and position may unintentionally impact conversation and proactively plan to reduce harm.
- Language: Ensure that you have interpreters and translators available in multiple languages with the heritage language of the families whom you are interviewing.
- Community: How are you able to involve students, family members, and/or community members as interviewers? Students, families, and community members may already have trust established, and this could be an untapped resource worth investigating.

The fourth step in planning your empathy interview is to determine the logistics of the interview. When will the interview take place? How? Again, with whom will you speak? How long will the interview take? Where will the interview take place? When working with families of color and those from historically marginalized populations, it is recommended that you go into the community and interview them. This can be done at a recreation center, a community center, at their home if they are comfortable with that, at a library, or at a place of worship (temple, mosque, church, etc.) if you have a largely religious community and you know your families use the house of worship for activities. If you are unsure of where to go, you can always ask the family where they are most comfortable. Furthermore, how many questions will you ask? Do you have an interpreter ready to support as needed, or a heritage language speaker conducting the interview? What is the interview protocol establishing relationships and notifying confidentiality?

The fifth step in planning your empathy interview is to prepare for the analysis of the data. How will you analyze themes? How will you bring stories back together? How will you and your team do all of this without judgment? Once themes have been analyzed, you will need to begin thinking about the areas of change that are needed and how you will make and implement change and who is needed to implement change with you (including those from the community).

After you have conducted this type of human-centered planning for empathy interviews, you will design your questions. Remember that the point of these questions is to have families share their experiences, and therefore you will need to ensure that you have open-ended questions. We recommend between four and eight open-ended questions with the ability to add in follow up questions that are nonjudgmental. You can use question stems such as:

- Tell me about a time when...
- What are your best/worst experiences with...?
- Tell me about your experiences with...
- Can you share a story with me that would help me better understand...?

For example, you may lead an interview with a family wanting to better understand their sense of belonging to the school. You could ask a question like "Tell me about a time when the school has made you feel included?" If you want to know something more specific about how families' voices are used in shaping policies, then you might ask, "Tell me about your experiences working with administration." As interviewees are relaying their experiences to you, you can prompt them to continue speaking by saying phrases like, "Tell me more," or "What emotions or feelings did you have when that happened?" Notice that these follow-up questions remain neutral and are not value statements about the interviewee's feelings. Depending on your relationship with the interviewee, cultural norms, and power dynamics within cultures, these follow-up questions can be crucial by helping to elicit more information. Observation notes should be taken about how the interviewees respond if they do seem hesitant and if/when they have any emotional reactions to the questions. The questions may elicit both positive and negative emotional responses from families as they share their experiences with you, and if they do, your role is to actively listen and empathize. If needed, you may have to suspend the interview and reschedule at the participant's preferred time.

In order to have successful empathy interviews in which you walk away with quality data, the following should be considered when designing your questions:

- Establish an interview protocol that maintains the relationship with families by allowing families to end the process at any time and explain how the data will be used.
- Ensure questions are free of bias.
- Use between four and eight open-ended questions that can be applied across a range of contexts and settings (Nelsestuen & Smith, 2020).
- Ensure empathy interviews are positive and affirming.
- Exclude educational acronyms and jargon.
- Ask for stories and not solutions because you will use their stories to help drive solutions with them at a later date.
- Include additional follow-up questions such as "Tell me more" as needed.

Finally, when considering empathy interviews as a culturally responsive leader, you will need to invest time in preparing your interview team and yourself with training in how to conduct the interviews. While the list we have provided and the steps we have shared may sound rather straightforward, empathy interviews require specific mindsets, technical skills, and openness to experience that must be practiced and nurtured so that harm is reduced or is not incurred at all.

Consider the following topics that will need to be addressed during your professional learning and training on conducting empathy interviews:

- Empathy interviews may become emotionally charged because they can bring up past traumas for the families or the interviewees. Because of this, it will be critical for the interviewer to know that they must give emotional and physical space to the interviewee and be prepared to stop the interview at any time.

- It is crucial for the interviewer to remain neutral when answers are given so that families do not feel as if they are led to a "right" or "wrong" answer. Families may change their answers based on how they perceive the interviewer's response. This is called the Hawthorne effect and can impact the reliability of the data, thus not helping you truly understand the needs of the community (Cherry, 2020).
- Understand and be cognizant of your own biases and how they may shape your reactions and your questions. Maintain awareness of your biases throughout the conversation and take note of anything that surfaces.
- Finally, write or type notes as the participants are sharing their stories. Nelsestuen and Smith (2020) note that this is an important safeguard against bias as it can act as a check and balance for the interviewer's own perceptions.

Empathy interviews are also an integral component of design thinking for leaders of culturally responsive gifted programs. Design thinking uses empathy interviews to determine which problems or, in this case, systemic barriers are in place that can be addressed in a culturally responsive manner. A culturally responsive leader understands the power of empathy interviews for their gifted programs and their school overall to help build knowledge with their community and in the end design a culturally inclusive school system and community together, a liberatory design for learning (National Equity Project, n.d.) As the authors have seen, empathy interviews can serve to help culturally responsive gifted leaders work within a Liberatory Design Model and change the systems and structures in which they exist for learners who identify as BIPOC.

Gifted Family Advisory Committee

Another way culturally responsive gifted leaders can purposefully and authentically engage families in support of improving education and creating inclusive spaces for gifted learners is through a gifted advisory committee. If you do not have one already, consider forming a gifted advisory committee or gifted advisory council with a focus on equity at whatever level of the educational organization you serve: school, district, or state. This committee is invaluable when examining gifted practices and their efficacy in supporting ethnically diverse students as well as students from poverty and students from other marginalized groups. The committee gives a voice to those families who are often overlooked in gifted education and should have members that reflect the diversity of the community. Because this is a family advisory committee, anyone who has a child or is the guardian of a child in the school, district, or state could participate. You could expand that definition to include anyone who has grandchildren, nieces, or nephews or is listed in the household as someone who participates if they have a vested interest in gifted education and will support the vision and mission of the committee. When determining who should serve on the committee, ask the following: "Whose voice is missing?" and "Whose seat is missing from the table?"

The gifted family advisory committee can play a critical role in providing perspective to school administrators, district administrators, and or state administrators as well as school committees or school boards on the impact of gifted education policies and practices. Culturally responsive leaders of gifted programs can leverage this group proactively by having them review policies and practices that will impact gifted learners and their families before they are released to the greater community. The family advisory committee can then discuss the impact on their children and give advice on ways to communicate information that is both family friendly and culturally responsive. They will also be able to share what will not be received well by the families.

The gifted family advisory committee can be a powerful partner in co-designing school, district, and state-level procedures with administrators. When culturally responsive gifted leaders engage in this type of co-creation, they actively seek liberatory collaboration (Anaissie et al., 2021) in complex systems and transform power dynamics within the organization by sharing power with members of the community. An example of a family advisory council working at the district level with district leadership to inform practice is shared here.

At each level of the educational organization, the focus will be the same, but the scope will be slightly different. For example, in a school, the scope of the advisory committee will be focused on culturally responsive gifted education practices at the school and the impact on the immediate community. Families at the school level will focus specifically on the school's needs and make suggestions and give advice to the school leader on the impact of curriculum choices and the hidden curriculum for gifted learners. At the district level, the focus will be on district-wide gifted policies and practices that are impacting all gifted learners, regardless of the school the family's child attends. This larger group at the district level is critical to helping provide perspectives to the gifted education leader and to one another. This larger group can discuss the implementation of district-wide policies and practices and allows the leader of gifted programs to identify strengths and opportunities for growth across the district. Finally, at the state level, a gifted advisory council with families has the opportunity to be incredibly impactful as they come together and learn about the diverse needs of diverse learners spanning the geography of a state. This type of council will review any policies or practices that exist and make recommendations to the gifted team at the state level, if there is one. Or, the council could provide recommendations to the State Board of Education. Not all states have gifted departments at the state level, nor legislation; however, the perspectives of diverse gifted families need to be heard and feedback analyzed at every level of education. Knowing that the advisory group will continue to change over time, it is imperative that the advisory group have equity and bias training and have a deep understanding of the school, district, and/or state's overarching equity mission and vision.

Affinity Groups

Another critical strategy that we have used in our practice to help create a sense of belonging and a deeper level of family engagement is to create advisory councils and family engagement events for only families of color and/or only multilingual families. These are additional events and opportunities to for families within the same ethnic, racial, linguistic, and even gender/sexual orientation group to connect in addition to the larger events held with families from the dominant culture. There are multiple reasons to differentiate and honor the culture of the diverse populations in your group and hold separate events (Gardner, 2019). First, you are creating a safe space for culturally linguistically diverse families that have unique needs. For example, families of immigrant and refugee gifted learners may need specific support on the introductory aspects of how gifted education and even school "works" in your system (Gardner, 2019). Having an event with other immigrant and refugee families with interpreters speaking the heritage language creates a safe space for those families to ask questions that they may not ask if they think someone else in the group who they perceive to have a stronger proficiency with English or has been in a part of the American or specific local school system understands (Gardener, 2019).

Holding specific opportunities for families of color, specifically within the same racial or ethnic group (e.g. Family Night for Families of Black Children) allows families and administrators to break down power dynamics and allow the unofficial stories that challenge the narrative of those in power, or counterstories, to be told (Snyder & Fenner, 2021). Additionally, when holding these events, it is critical to also have speakers of color who are experts in the topic you are discussing to help support conversations when possible.

GiftedCrit, or Gifted Critical Race Theory (Greene, 2017), based on the work of Critical Race Theory, holds that all relationships for gifted learners are structured around power, and that within these relationships, certain groups, typically white middle-class families of gifted learners and their administrators and teachers, have privilege while others do not. Mainstream practices of gifted classrooms and instruction as well as the mainstream practices of central offices and even state-level organizations "often reinforce oppressive systems that are organized around class, race and gender" (Snyder & Fenner, 2021, p. 233) Counterstories have the ability to help families share how they have been excluded, challenge systemic racism and the status quo of daily operations, highlight and stereotypes that exist, and by their nature support a shift in power dynamics. Listening to counterstories also helps create a cultural bridge for administrators and creates opportunities for empathy and understanding to drive systemic change.

Snapshot: Creating Brave Spaces

One large urban school district held a series of events for Black families of gifted learners over a period throughout multiple school years. Events throughout the year included a panel of Black families speaking with other Black families about how to navigate the gifted education system and was facilitated by district-level staff. Another event included bringing a renowned Black author and scholar in gifted education to a community center in a historically Black neighborhood to talk with Black families about being bright, talented, and Black. The room was packed! The district level team took notes from both events and listened deeply to the families. We listened for inconsistencies in our systems that were impacting our gifted Black learners disproportionately. We asked: What can we do to repair harm? We heard the joy, pain, and frustration in our families. So we started acting. We began reviewing policies, practices, and procedures. We reviewed data. We continued with more nights in the Black community. We worked together to change the way our website looked and the way in which we communicated in our Black schools. We saw an increase in Black family nominations for gifted education and we heard families say after both events that they had never had an opportunity to talk about Black excellence this way and that they felt safe.

Gifted Family Liaisons

A gifted family liaison is someone at the school or district who can help families of gifted learners bridge communication from home to family. The gifted family liaison acts as an additional layer of support for academic and social success for the gifted learner and their family. Ideally, they are someone who lives within the community they are serving already so that they can quickly establish a relationship and rapport. We have utilized family liaisons in different ways to help support gifted education, and they are another conduit of communication for us as leaders in our districts. They can help disseminate information such as who to talk with about gifted education, how to fill out paperwork, how to get identified, and how to advocate for gifted programming and services. A gifted family liaison can also be utilized as someone who connects families together, as described in the next snapshot.

Other supports from gifted and talented (GT) family liaisons included working directly with a Family and Community Engagement department in a large school district and training all 100 plus liaisons on the myths of gifted learners, the characteristics of gifted learners from culturally linguistically diverse backgrounds, and how to get gifted learners the supports they needed at the school and district level. It included asking the liaisons what they needed from the leaders of the gifted programs and taking the time to hear the concerns arising at individual schools and the barriers that were in place, including the fact that the liaisons did not know the names of the gifted teacher nor the time of the universal assessment, so they could help families who may not have received timely communication due to unintended barriers know when testing was going to occur and what it would entail. Family liaisons are all too often untapped resources who have a wealth of knowledge and the ability to connect with families that we need.

Authentic Family Engagement and Education Events

Another way to engage families is to have schools and districts hold events throughout the school year that are intended to get families in the door of the school building, because school and district partnerships help improve student outcomes. However, as Donna Y. Ford (2011) noted in the second edition of her book *Multicultural Education*, "many of our families do not know how to be involved. They may lack the cultural capital, educational experiences, and sense of empowerment so important to creating family–school partnerships." Therefore, it is critical that culturally responsive leaders of gifted programs help enfranchise families with the educational tools necessary to truly impact student achievement and belonging.

Typically, these events include, but are not limited to, School Fairs, Back to School Nights, Literacy Nights, College Fairs, Math Nights, Gifted and Talented Information Nights and other district or school-sponsored events. In our experience, school and district leaders have lamented that they have low attendance from families of color at times. Given that families may not feel enfranchised, families may be working multiple jobs, and families have other priorities, this is not surprising. Consider the following strategies to increase attendance and engage families authentically:

- Coordinate events tailored to the family's schedules and offer multiple opportunities for events to occur at different times during the day, including on the weekends.
- Have interpreters and translators available if needed for any and all heritage languages present.
- Have interpreters for sign language if needed.
- Consider holding events at a recreation center, community center, library, park, religious center, Boys and Girls Club, or other place that is considered a hub of the community.
- Have childcare options available, or ways in which to engage all members of the families.
- Have food and drinks available, or let families know ahead of time what food and drink will be provided at the event.
- Ensure accessibility as required under the Americans with Disabilities Act (ADA).

Family Learning Opportunity Workshops—F.L.O.W.

Professional learning is a tool that is often used to support educators and administrators in their school roles. However, this type of learning opportunity can also be provided to families as a way to educate and train families on various topics that pertain to gifted education. These family workshops are a way to bring the gifted community together and let families know that they are not the only ones experiencing the same scenarios with their children.

These are a couple of tips you should know when providing professional learning to culturally and linguistically diverse families. Many of these families will bring their entire family, including their kids, to the training. Consider providing food and childcare for these events so that families can focus on the learning without having to manage their children at the same time. Think about the time of day that works best for families. Try a variety of times, and offer online meetings so that families can access the learning from their homes. Offer families book study options. Let families empower their own learning by letting them choose what they would like the professional learning topics to be.

Community Partnerships

Finally, get to know the community surrounding your school. Do a community walk of not only the neighborhood, but of the surrounding businesses. Are their businesses that would want to partner with your school or with your central office? Is there a local church, temple, or mosque frequented by the community that might want to provide adult mentors for students after school once a week? Are there local bookstores that would want to provide free books to classroom libraries? Is there a local restaurant that would provide food to your family conferences, GT Advisory Councils, or other family engagement opportunities? Building strong partnerships within the community creates a sense of belonging for both community members and families.

Conclusion

There are multiple ways that families can be engaged in their school communities. Remember that as a culturally responsive gifted leader, you must be committed to learning about families beyond the surface level of their cultural tree. Get to know the hopes and dreams that these families have for their children. Understand the cultural wealth that they bring with them every day to school and have at home. Make a commitment to value and respect the cultures of the various families that are in your school community.

Contemplation Corner

What other ways might you engage culturally and linguistically diverse families?

Key Points

◆ The understanding of the cultural beliefs, values, and priorities of families is a critical part of any family engagement process.

- Families who are ethnically and linguistically diverse come to schools with rich cultural backgrounds and heritage languages.
- Provide multiple opportunities for diverse families to have a voice in school and district decision making, and empower them to recognize that they are a valued member of the school community.
- Home visits are an excellent way to engage families outside of school and deepen relationships with families.
- Empathy interviews can create cultural bridges with families from a culture that is different from your own.
- A gifted family advisory committee can play a critical role in providing perspective to school administrators, district administrators, and/or state administrators as well as school committees or school boards on the impact of gifted education policies and practices.

References

Anaissie, T., Cary, V., Clifford, D., Malarkey, T., & Wise, S. (2021). *Liberatory design: Mindsets and modes to design for equity.* Liberatory Design.

Cherry, K. (2020). *The Hawthorne effect and behavioral studies.* https://www.verywellmind.com/what-is-the-hawthorne-effect-2795234

de Bruin, L. (2017). *Hofstede's cultural dimensions.* https://www.business-to-you.com/hofstedes-cultural-dimensions/#google_vignette

DuBois, M. P., & Greene, R. M. (2021). *Supporting gifted ELLS in the latinx community: Practical strategies, K–12.* Routledge.

Faber, N. (2016). Connecting with students and families through home visits. *The Education Digest, 81,* 32–39.

Fehrer, K., & Tognozzi, N. (2018). *Cultural & linguistic responsiveness and meaningful family engagement: Why it matters in early education.* https://files.eric.ed.gov/fulltext/ED594175.pdf

Fenner, D. S. (2014). *Advocating for English learners: A guide for educators.* Corwin.

Ford, D. Y. (2011). *Multicultural gifted education* (2nd ed.). Prufrock Press.

Gardner, L. (2019). *Separate or together: Unpacking the "EL family event: vs.: All-school family event" debate.* https://www.immigrantsrefugeesa

ndschools.org/post/separate-or-together-unpacking-the-el-family
-event-vs-all-school-family-event-debate

González, N., Moll, L. C., & Amanti, C. (2005). *Funds of knowledge: Theorizing practices in households, communities, and classrooms.* Lawrence Erlbaum Associates.

Greene, R. M. (2017). Gifted culturally linguistically diverse learners: A school-based exploration. In *Perspectives in gifted education: Influences and impacts of the education doctorate on gifted education* (Vol. 6). Institute for the Development of Gifted Education, Ricks Center for Gifted Children, University of Denver.

Hanover Research. (2017). *Authentic and proven family engagement strategies.* https://dm0gz550769cd.cloudfront.net/shape/bf/bfd 5045dda80180d39fba7b4abf4d815.pdf

Henderson, A. T., & Mapp, K. L. (2002). *A new wave of evidence: The impact of school, family, and community connections on student achievement. Annual Synthesis 2002.* Southwest Educational Development Laboratory.

Hofstede, G. (2011). Dimensionalizing cultures: The Hofstede model in context. *Psychology and Culture.* http://scholarworks.gvsu.edu/orpc /vol2/iss1/8

Hofstede, G., Hofstede, G. J., & Minkov, M. (2010). *Cultures and organizations: Software of the mind* (3rd ed.). McGraw-Hill.

Hofstede Insights. (n.d.). *National culture.* https://hi.hofstede-insights.com /national-culture

Kobiruzzaman, M. M. (2019). *Hofstede's cultural dimensions-Hofstede's 6 cultural dimensions examples.* https://newsmoor.com/tag/ hofstedes-cultural-dimensions/

Kronholz, J. (2016). Teacher home visits: School-family partnerships foster student success. *Education Next, 16*(3), 16+. https://link.gale.com /apps/doc/A455093021/OVIC?u=colosprings&sid=summon&xid =38673540

Moll, L. C., Soto-Santiago, S., & Schwartz, L. (2013). Funds of knowledge in changing communities. In K. Hall, T. Cremin, B. Comber, & L. Moll (Eds.), *International hand-book of research on children's literacy, learning, and culture* (pp. 172–183). Wiley-Blackwell.

National Center on Parent, Family and Community Engagement. (n.d.). *Family engagement and cultural perspectives: Applying strengths-based attitudes*. https://childcareta.acf.hhs.gov/sites/default/files/public/family_engagement_and_cultural-perspectives-508_2-20-18.pdf

National Equity Project. (n.d.). Introduction to liberatory design. https://www.nationalequityproject.org/frameworks/liberatory-design

Nelsestuen, K., & Smith, J. (2020). Empathy interviews. *The Learning Professional, 41*(5), 59.

The Leadership Academy. (2022). *Culturally responsive in-person observation guide.* https://www.leadershipacademy.org/resources/culturally-responsive-in-person-observation-guid/

Skrefsrud, T. A. (2018). Barriers to intercultural dialogue. *Studies in Interreligious Dialogue, 28*(1), 43–57.

Snyder, S., & Fenner, D. S. (2021). *Culturally responsive teaching for multilingual learners: Tools for equity.* Corwin Press.

Vélez-Ibáñez, C. G., & Greenberg, J. B. (1992). Formation and transformation of funds of knowledge among U.S. Mexican households. *Anthropology & Education Quarterly, 23*(4), 313–335.

Yosso, T. J. (2005). Whose culture has capital? *Race, Ethnicity and Education, 8*(1), 69–91.

8

Engaging in Equity Challenges and Charting a Course for the Future

Equity Challenges

This chapter explores leadership problems of practice, or equity challenges, that the authors have experienced both as classroom teachers and as school and district administrators. These shared equity challenges focus on professional learning, identification practices, family engagement, and specific administrative challenges. Each challenge is described in enough detail to set context for the reader and then we outline the in-the-moment or *immediate strategies* that we have implemented to create more equitable educational opportunities and access for gifted culturally linguistically diverse students and families. Each challenge also offers what we have named *refinements*, or additional changes to our initial immediate strategies that were made upon further reflection. It must be noted here that a solution to any equity challenge should be thought of as a point of entry, not the final destination. Each solution can be reexamined and refined multiple times using the practice of reflection, introspection, and having honest conversations with stakeholders about the impact of the solutions you implement. Furthermore, the solutions that

DOI: 10.4324/9781003293729-8

we offer are meant to be examples, and they may not work in the exact same way in your setting.

As you read this chapter, think about examples within your system that you have encountered and the immediate solutions and further refinements that you implemented. Review the solutions that we have implemented and ask yourself the following questions: What could work in your setting? What would not work in your setting? What might work in your setting if specific understandings about equity, race, and culturally linguistically diverse gifted students and families were in place? What additional work, relationship building, and support must be in place for any solutions to be implemented and sustained? With whom do you need to partner?

As stated earlier, the equity challenges below are categorized into four levels: school, administrative, professional learning, and family engagement. We have also categorized them as either technical challenges that have a quick fix, or adaptive challenges that are more ambiguous in nature, or a combination of both. You may notice that some of the challenges could fit into multiple levels because these challenges are complex and intertwined. As you peel back the proverbial layers of each challenge, you will notice that, yes indeed, they can fit into multiple levels. We have listed the ones that felt the most appropriate at the time. The majority of the equity challenges we share are at the school and administrative levels, and if you look further into them, there are elements of professional learning and family engagement opportunities embedded into almost every single one. For each equity challenge, the type of equity challenge faced (adaptive or technical in nature) is listed; next, the problem of practice is stated, followed by a description of the scenario highlighting the problem of practice. Each of the scenarios are from the authors' lived experiences and how they responded to each of the equity challenges. Also, note that the refinements are not permanent solutions; they are merely refinements made within the authors' scope of time working with each equity challenge.

Equity Challenge One

Level: School

Type of equity challenge: Adaptive

Problem of practice: Gifted demographics do not mirror the demographic population.

Description: A neighborhood elementary school is experiencing decreasing enrollment due to white families choosing to open enroll into other schools. The families' stated reasons are that the school does not have gifted services, and that these services would provide more rigorous instruction to students who are more academically advanced. The school is 86% percent Latinx, and white families have been voicing that the educational services at the school are not as rigorous as in other schools where the population is primarily white. The families have stated that this must be due to the large majority of students who have limited English language skills, so the teachers have to scaffold down the curriculum to meet these students' needs, thus limiting the time they have to meet the needs of more advanced learners.

The school surveyed the neighborhood to find out what programs they could offer to entice the neighborhood families to enroll back into their neighborhood school. The white families in the neighborhood responded that gifted programming would bring them back to their neighborhood school. It should be noted that none of the students of families who unenrolled were formally identified as gifted at the time the families were surveyed.

The school and district were committed to bringing back those students whose families were choosing to enroll into other schools other than their neighborhood school. The school created a part-time gifted teacher position and provided professional learning focusing on gifted education for the teacher. Over time, some of the white students began attending the school, and their families began nominating them for gifted services. The equity challenge arose when it became apparent that the only students being nominated and identified for and receiving gifted services were all white and not of the majority culture at the school, which was Latinx.

Immediate Strategies
- Take a deep breath.
- Implement a one-time, all grade level, school-wide universal screener using a nonverbal assessment to increase diversity in the gifted population.
- Increase communication to Latinx families in their heritage language regarding gifted nomination, identification, and programming.
- Provide professional learning to teachers and administration about the characteristics of culturally linguistically diverse gifted students.

Refinement
- Implement universal screening annually for students in kindergarten for gifted services using a nonverbal assessment.
- Implement universal screening annually at second grade for gifted services using a creativity or observational tool.
- Establish a mandatory requirement for all teachers at the school to participate in the district Culturally, Linguistically Diverse Gifted 8-week course within the next 3 years.
- Create pathways for culturally, linguistically diverse students to participate in talent development opportunities for exposure to advanced learning practices.

Contemplation Corner

What are some additional ideas that you would have implemented for this scenario?

Equity Challenge Two

Level: Professional Learning

Type of equity challenge: Adaptive

Problem of practice: Students of color are not receiving gifted services equivalent to their white peers.

Description: A school district's examination of student participation data confirmed that students of color are not receiving gifted services equivalent to their white peers, and teachers are not referring students of color at the same rate as other students. After surveying and interviewing educators and administrators at schools throughout the district, it was discovered that the root cause of the problem was the limited or lack of knowledge about culturally linguistically diverse gifted learners at the teacher and administrator level. This created a system where teachers were not referring students of color for gifted services because of their limited knowledge about these students and the way they manifest gifted abilities.

Immediate Strategies
- Take a deep breath.
- Collaborate with the professional learning department and the culturally, linguistically diverse education department to discuss the implementation of learning opportunities for teachers and administrators focusing on gifted traits of culturally different learners.
- Develop an hour-long presentation focusing on characteristics and behaviors of culturally linguistically diverse gifted learners to be offered to schools both online and in person.

Refinement
- Develop a multi-week course focused on culturally linguistically diverse gifted learners with a case study component to be offered to anyone in the district.
- Offer recertification credit, professional learning hours, or as a college course for credit.
- Used course hours towards specific teacher licensure state requirement such as English Learner Professional learning hours.
- Engage teachers and administrators in cultural identity training and microaggression training to identify the impact bias has on themselves and their perceptions of learners as related to gifted education.

Contemplation Corner

What are some action steps that you have taken to provide professional learning focused on culturally linguistically diverse gifted students at school, district, or state level?

Equity Challenge Three

Level: Administrative

Type of equity challenge: Adaptive

Problem of practice: The district gifted education coordinator or specialist is not represented in district-level discussions involving educational services for gifted students, which allows for decisions to be made without the input of the person with the expertise on gifted practices.

Description: In many school districts, decisions are made about educational services for gifted students by individuals who may not have expertise and knowledge about giftedness. Often, school districts have the district gifted person designated to a coordinator and not a director position, which often limits their participation in important conversations about gifted students; or, they might have the person covering two roles, such as gifted and MTSS (Multitiered System of Supports) coordinator. In some cases, a director of a content area might also be given the additional job of gifted education without having the associated expertise and knowledge.

Immediate Strategies
- Take a deep breath.
- Identify ways to elevate district leadership's knowledge about gifted students.
- Execute a deep data dive into all district data surrounding gifted students and present the importance of these students to the district upper level administration team.
- In the data, point out the disproportionality of gifted students among the subgroup populations within special education, culturally linguistically diverse education, and gifted education.
- Identify which areas of the district strategic plan pertain to gifted students and focus on those to create a strategic gifted plan that is aligned with the district plan.
- Find your allies at the district level who believe in and support gifted education practices.

Refinement
- Examine your budget for funds that might not be serving gifted students and that can be distributed in a different way that can effectively impact and serve gifted students.
- Connect with other district-level departments such as special education, culturally linguistically diverse education, academics, and student support services to share the district data on gifted students.
- Make an implementation plan with these departments to ensure that gifted students are a subgroup of the district population that they are aware of and provide services for.

Contemplation Corner

What are other strategies that can be put in place to increase conversations about gifted students at the district level and help other district-level departments to understand that these students are also their responsibility?

Equity Challenge Four

Level: Family engagement

Type of Equity Challenge: Technical

Problem of Practice: Cultural faux pas

Description: A school district scheduled a gifted family event night in the month of December which specifically focused on Spanish-speaking Latinx families, with interpretation in English as needed. There was food and childcare provided at the event for families. Two hours before the start of the event, district personnel received a message that the day chosen for the event is one of the holiest days celebrated by many Latinx families in the community and honors La Virgen de Guadalupe.

Immediate Strategies

- Take a deep breath.
- Send Latinx families immediate district-wide communication regarding the error.
- Send an authentic apology letter to the Latinx families in the district regarding the error, admitting your mistake.
- Reschedule the event and send communication to the Latinx families regarding the new date.
- Place communication on the door of the event in case there are families who show up, and as the leader of the program, be at the location to share with families what happened and apologize.
- Give food to any families who do show and donate the rest to local organizations.

Refinement

- Enter the dates for national holidays and cultural celebrations on the district calendar.
- Cross-check the district calendar with the family event dates for conflicts and then schedule accordingly.
- Invite various cultural family groups to share with you which national holidays and cultural celebration days should not have school or district events occurring on those days.
- Invite families to review the days you have chosen for engagement opportunities to determine if there are any major conflicts with the dates that they foresee that will be problematic for the communities at large (not just their own individual concern).

Contemplation Corner

It is two hours before a multilingual family night event, scheduled in a neighboring community, is about to begin. What do you do when the event has to be canceled?

Equity Challenge Five

Level(s): Administrative

Type of equity challenge: Technical and adaptive

Problem of practice: Recognizing oppression through identification practices

Description: Data trends show that the universal screening assessment used in the gifted identification process is not effective in identifying Black and African American gifted learners. The screener you are using is effective at identifying white students at a rate proportional to the demographics in your district. However, as you review the data more closely, the data reveals that Black and African American students are not being recognized on this particular assessment that you use.

Immediate Strategies

- Take a deep breath.
- Examine the assessment tool that is being used for universal screening. Is the assessment tool culturally fair? How do you know?
- Examine the process for administering the universal assessment. Are students being given extra time if their IEP (Individualized Education Program) or 504 denotes the required support?
- Examine how educators are being trained to deliver the assessment.
- Review the additional assessments and portfolio work you can gather to identify students for gifted programming.

Refinement

- Ensure that educators and administrators understand that building relationships prior to giving assessments is key to helping students feel safe in a testing environment.
- Prior to administering the test, provide two or three sessions in which you have all students, specifically students from culturally linguistically and economically diverse backgrounds, engage with the types of questions and thinking asked on the universal assessment. Remember that questions asked on general intellectual ability assessments or creativity assessments are not typically asked in class and require students to think differently than they do in their typical school day.
- If needed, administer the universal screening assessment individually to students of color to provide more support and a differentiated learning environment.
- Look at local and school norms rather than national norms on the universal screening data.
- Include collection of qualitative data as part of your universal data collection.

- Ensure that all educators and administrators who administer assessments are trained in culturally assessment practices prior to the next administration of the assessment.
- Consider the use of another universal assessment that focuses on behaviors of culturally linguistically diverse gifted learners as a way to begin an initial screening for giftedness and provide appropriate training for educators, administrators, and families.

Contemplation Corner

What other ideas can you think of when administering a universal screening assessment that might increase the identification of gifted Black learners?

Equity Challenge Six

Level(s): School/administrative

Type of equity challenge: Adaptive

Problem of practice: English language learners are not participating in Advanced Placement courses at the high-school level.

Description: While examining district student data, it is discovered that gifted English language learners, specifically Latinx students, are not participating in Advanced Placement courses in high school. Counselors have encouraged these students to take the Advanced Placement courses, but the students have voiced that they do not think they will be successful in these courses and that the courses are often not reflective of their culture.

Immediate Strategies
- Take a deep breath.
- Survey families of middle and high-school Latinx students to determine if they know about the Advanced Placement courses and the trajectory that these courses would provide for their students towards college and career advancement.
- Interview high-school Latinx students to determine the root causes of why they are not participating in these Advanced Placement courses.
- Interview counselors to discuss what communication is going home about Advanced Placement classes and how information is being communicated.

Refinement
- Use the surveys and interviews to determine root causes for the lack of participation of Latinx students in Advanced Placement courses.
- Partner with the counselors and the curriculum and instruction team to review the data to determine what appropriate next steps might be to create an inclusive environment.
- Review with the curriculum department, or on your own, the content in the Advanced Placement courses for culturally responsive materials and messaging to students.
- Develop a partnership, if one does not already exist, with the team responsible for Advanced Placement courses to discuss infusing ethnically diverse materials and

Latinx-specific stories and curriculum into the Advanced Placement coursework.

- Provide ongoing student support for Latinx students such as peer mentors, study hall, check-ins with teachers, and family communication.

Contemplation Corner

What other support can you think of that would support Latinx students so they can be successful in Advanced Placement courses?

Equity Challenge Seven

Level: Administrative/family engagement

Type of equity challenge: Adaptive

Problem of practice: Black, Latinx, and Indigenous families express that Black and Brown students are not being given equitable opportunities to access gifted services in their local schools.

Description: At a district board meeting, families of BIPOC students expressed their frustration and disappointment that their students were not being given equitable access to gifted services. They shared that in their schools, their children were being overidentified as needing special education services in the school district and gave specific statistics to the school board. The families then shared that they have a hard time finding out when gifted education testing is happening in some schools but not in others, or even understanding the process for gifted education identification. Specifically, one family mentions they have a child at two different schools, School A and School B. The family learned about gifted testing from School B a week before School A shared the information with them. School B is predominantly white, Black, and middle class. School A is predominantly Black and Indigenous, and has a majority of students on Free and Reduced Lunch. Both schools were testing on the same day, and the family could have chosen to have their child at School B tested on another day, but found out too late. Other families nodded their heads as the family shared their story. When other BIPOC families stood up to speak, they shared similar stories and then shared their concerns with the quality of programming and types of services happening at schools across the district that have higher identified gifted learners and that some school leaders have shared that they do not "believe in gifted education" so they do not send out the flyers notifying families of testing because they "do not want families to leave their schools."

Immediate Strategies

- Take a deep breath.
- Set up meetings with BIPOC families, conduct empathy interviews, and listen to families tell their equity challenge stories. Make notes about the challenges. Work to repair the harm that was done.
- Ask families what they would need immediately from the district to help make them feel as if their children's needs were being met.
- Offer testing at a time that will work for them, or consider reviewing your policies to re-test students whose families were caught off guard.

- Set up empathy interviews with the school leaders to understand why communication may not be going out. Try to get to the root cause of why they do not believe in gifted education or their fear that students may leave. Do not make assumptions—go straight to the school leader.
- Work within the fear and discomfort of the school leaders, families, and educators.
- Review the data at each of the schools to analyze trends.
- Review the communication structures at the schools to determine what could have caused the delay in communication between schools.
- Create a Families of Color District Advisory Council, or affinity group, to offer families the opportunity to become involved with the improvement of the educational system and a place where they can voice their concerns.

Refinement

- Establish a communication strategy for disseminating information regarding gifted testing and programming options—work with your Advisory Council to ensure that the messaging is culturally responsive and available in multiple modalities (district website, robo-calls, texting, paper sent home) and that the information is sent home at the same time.
- In places where communication is not going out because someone does not believe in gifted education, work on developing a relationship with the school leaders to understand their perspective. Develop training on the characteristics of culturally linguistically diverse gifted learners and why they need different learning opportunities.
- Continue empathy interviews and have school leaders conduct empathy interviews with one another to understand why some leaders support gifted education in the district and others do not. Have them talk with one another about what gifted education is and move past myths around high achievement.
- Pull district data on advanced courses and which students are in these courses. Present data to district leadership and

make a 3-year plan for implementing changes to increase access, beginning with access starting in elementary school.

- Create a district Equity Youth Council where students from marginalized populations can express their challenges within the educational system and promote ideas for change.
- Utilize the Family of Color District Advisory Council to get their ideas on practices and policies.
- Utilize the Advisory Council to advocate for culturally linguistically diverse gifted learners and their needs at school board meetings.
- Utilize the Advisory Council to review current practices.
- Share budget and be transparent with families about where monies are going and how funds are being distributed equitably and for what purposes.
- Bring in community experts to help build understanding of the needs of gifted culturally linguistically diverse gifted learners.

Contemplation Corner

What other avenues have you implemented that allow BIPOC students and families to voice their concerns regarding equitable access to gifted services?

Equity Challenge Eight

Level: School/administrative

Type of equity challenge: Technical

Problem of practice: There is an overreliance on standardized achievement and ability measures for identification.

Description: The current assessment tools being used for gifted identification at the school level measure standardized academic achievement and general intellectual ability only. They are quantitative tools that are nationally normed, but they seem to be yielding the same results year after year with identification: underidentification of gifted students of color and well-represented numbers of white high achieving learners. The criteria used at the school and district are limited to these pieces, thus creating disproportionality.

Immediate Strategies

- Take a deep breath.
- Review the Expanded Body of Evidence (DuBois & Greene, 2021).
- Determine what tools you already have in place other than standardized achievement and ability tests to support identification.
- Determine which qualitative tools, such as interviews and observations, you can implement immediately that will not cost additional dollars.
- Review your data to determine which areas students are identified (Reading, Math, etc.) and compare that to your district's definition of giftedness to determine if there are other tests you might be able to administer to find different areas of giftedness.
- Meet with the assessment team and discuss the trends they are seeing in achievement testing for students. Are the trends similar? Are they already working on gathering some different assessments? Is there a way to partner with them when looking at assessments?

Refinement

- Train educators on what culturally fair assessment practices, including collecting a body of evidence, look like.
- Develop a plan to train educators and families on how to use qualitative data such as interviews, observations, and anecdotal notes, and developing portfolios to aid in identification of culturally linguistically diverse gifted learners.
- Train educators and administrators to understand how giftedness manifests in collectivist cultures and not necessarily on standardized achievement and ability tests.
- Ensure you are doing bias microaggression trainings as you review bodies of evidence when identifying culturally linguistically diverse students.
- Ensure that your practices and policies for identification include developing a body of evidence, and then implement those practices as soon as possible.
- Explore talent tests and creativity tests to identify gifted learners.
- Work with other departments such as Special Education, Assessment, Psych, Social Work, and Arts/PE to determine what other assessments could be used to find students who need gifted education.

Contemplation Corner

What nonstandardized measures do you use now to support the identification of gifted culturally linguistically diverse gifted learners?

Equity Challenge Nine

Level(s): Administration

Problem of practice: Resistance to equity plan and white fragility

Type of equity challenge: Adaptive

Description: The equity vision you have created with various stakeholders is being met with resistance by some white educators. The concern from the educators is that it looks like you have called out too many specific vulnerable populations that are underidentified and they would prefer that you say "all" students. They feel as if it seems as if they have not been doing a good job working with diverse gifted learners. Two educators state they are worried they will lose their jobs.

Immediate Strategies

- Take a deep breath.
- Ask the educators to tell you more about their concerns.

- Listen for the reasons behind the concerns and demonstrate empathy regarding the concern that they have not been doing "a good job" or will "lose their job."
- Attempt to understand the fear so that you can help them become regulated.
- Remind them that the equity vision is not a personal attack on them and that it is a vision for the entire organization that will set how you move forward with policy, practices, and actions in your work.
- Share any data you have as to why you developed the equity vision in that way and why you named specific groups.
- Be honest that gifted education has worked well for one type of student, but that the majority of our learners do not fit into a stereotypical mold.
- Do *not* state that you are changing the equity vision; be definitive in taking a stand for these learners and do so with humility.
- Follow up with a separate meeting with the educators to unpack any additional white fragility in a one-on-one setting rather than in a large group.

Refinement

- Be transparent from the beginning stages of your equity plan development.
- Develop a communication plan with your stakeholders that includes how you will roll out the equity vision, including how to manage any resistance.
- In the communication plan, include messaging around the development of the equity plan and the reasoning behind an equity plan.
- Share data multiple times and in multiple ways about all of your demographic groups and discuss what that data means to you and why it is important to review for equity.
- Develop and implement professional learning around microaggressions, cultural identity, and bias and explicitly connect that to the equity vision.

Contemplation Corner

Have you met similar resistance when discussing race and equity for gifted learners? How have you navigated the conversation? If you have not, what might be some ways in which you will prepare for resistance?

Equity Challenge Ten

Level(s): Administration/family engagement

Problem of practice: Recruiting and retaining culturally linguistically diverse gifted learners at a mostly white school

Type of equity challenge: Adaptive and technical

Description: A school leader wants to recruit and retain culturally linguistically diverse gifted learners. When you dig deeper into what is happening at the school, you learn not everything is what it appears. As the leader of gifted programs in a large district and working in a very diverse district with multiple schools that have their own culture and dynamic approach to learning, you get excited because a school leader broaches the subject of wanting to recruit and retain more students of color in their school for gifted learners. They state that they believe in your equity mission and vision and they are confused why more families are not enrolling and staying. They share that they are able to recruit one or two culturally linguistically diverse families a year, but they cannot keep them in the building and they don't not understand why. Your district at the time is primarily BIPOC; however, this school's enrollment is majority white and identified as gifted. Excited at the prospect of supporting change, you arrange a time to meet. On the same day that you go to the school to talk with the school leader about their goals for recruiting and retaining Black and Brown learners, you receive a phone call from a parent who is upset that their child is not receiving language supports in their heritage language at this particular school. The parent expresses their child is failing, and they are not receiving any communication from the school. When you ask the school leader about this, the school leader shares that all communications go home in English and she does not understand how the student has even qualified for gifted services.

Immediate Strategies

- Take a deep breath.
- Address the concerns around translation right away by getting the school leader in contact with interpretation services.
- Ask the school leader how their school is nurturing and fostering culturally linguistically diverse gifted learners and their families.
- Identify with the school leader that there are multiple concerns around equity.
- Ask the school leader about their vision for equity for students and what that means for them.
- Share characteristics of gifted multilingual learners who are not proficient in English yet and ask how the school is supporting the learner in question so he can thrive.
- Give concrete examples of how to support the learner and his family and provide a connection to the English Learner Department.

- Work with the parent and set up a communication between the family and the school about how the school will nurture the child's giftedness and get him language supports.
- Set up a one on one with the student's teacher to determine what the teacher understands about the student's culture and how the student learns best as well as how to support his giftedness in class.
- Work with a family liaison to support the family and the school.

Refinement

- Create a partnership with the English Language Learner Department to develop and implement training for their teachers as well as school leaders regarding how to support gifted language learners.
- Work with the communications department and or translation/interpretation to ensure that all school leaders know of their supports.
- Conduct an equity scan of the school to see how student culture and language is seen throughout the school and if students are able to see themselves in the curriculum.
- Implement a district-wide training on creating inclusive learning environments. Begin with administrators and then share with general education teachers.
- Give specific case studies and instructional practices for teachers and administrators to utilize during trainings to better understand how to help students who are gifted and culturally linguistically diverse.
- Develop a Family of Color Advisory Council and utilize it to support their understanding of giftedness and the school's understanding of their students' culture.
- Identify schools and tier supports for them for culturally responsive gifted education.
- Train family liaisons to support gifted culturally linguistically diverse learners.

Contemplation Corner

What would you have done in Equity Challenge Ten? Where would you start with the school leader? What does she need to know, and what do her teachers need to know? What else do you need to know about the school leader and the school before making assumptions? What would you say to this family? What does the mother need for support?

Future Practices

Throughout this book, we have given specific examples and tangible actions for how to lead culturally responsive gifted programs. Being a culturally responsive leader requires a long-term commitment to staff, students, and families from culturally linguistically diverse backgrounds. This book has offered multiple ways in which a leader of gifted education programs can make systemic changes at their school, district, and state levels. Change is hard and hard work. You will have pushback and resistance from some.

You will need to decide which practices make the most sense to commit to in your individual work in the future. Some of the specific strategies and suggestions described in detail in earlier chapters in the book include but are not limited to:

- Creating culturally inclusive learning environments that are psychologically, environmentally, and physically safe for culturally diverse gifted learners.
- Creating culturally responsive gifted learning environments.
- Implementing professional learning that focuses on cultural identity.
- Implementing professional learning that focuses on the impact of cultural identity on perceptions of culturally linguistically diverse gifted learners and teaching.
- Utilizing the Liberatory Design Model to solve for complex equity challenges.
- Becoming a servant leader.
- Conducting empathy interviews to gather data for change.
- Using data to better understand the current state in your district.
- Conducting equity audits to ensure that your space is inclusive of all learners and their needs.
- Using CR-MTSS to support culturally linguistically diverse thrice-exceptional learners to engage in learning in an authentic way by bringing in culture into every aspect of Bloom's Taxonomy.
- Creating strategic partnerships with departments such as Special Education, Communications, Curriculum and Instruction, Multilingual Learners, Postsecondary, etc.
- Engaging authentically with families in their heritage languages.
- Creating Family Advisory Committees and Youth Advisory Committees to inform administration.
- Creating affinity groups so students, families, and educators feel safe to take risks and be themselves.

Where will you start? Who will join you as you begin to make change?

Mapping Your Course

Gifted education, as a field, has the potential to lead the education system by righting the wrongs of its past and creating environments where culturally, linguistically, and economically diverse learners thrive by design. Leaders have the opportunity to operationalize equity in a way that will disrupt systems of white supremacy. How do you injure a system badly enough that it cannot return to its original state? Racial inequities and disparities will continue to exist unless leaders are willing to make radical systemic changes. School, district, and state leaders in education do not have the privilege of waiting on someone else to repair the educational system; we must actively work on disrupting systems of oppression daily. Leaders within gifted education have a brilliant opportunity in front of them to lead culturally responsive gifted programs.

We cannot be performative in our educational activism. To read this book and put it aside without exploring any changes in your context would be just that—performative. We cannot say that we want equity in education and then not be willing to make the specific organizational and systemic moves necessary within our positions of privilege and power to change the course of education for learners. We know this can be done because we have done this work. We also know that it is not perfect and it is going to take time. You will have to change minds and hearts, and you will continually feel as if you are fighting a battle to prove that BIPOC deserve access to culturally responsive gifted programs— that Black and Brown minds matter. This means that those with whom you work will be uncomfortable as you challenge existing paradigms and thinking. Remember this: Black and Brown students and adults have been more than uncomfortable in white supremacist structures for years.

We ask that you take something from each chapter and try it out. Take a risk and make a mistake. Invite your families in and share what you are doing with them. Use the Gifted Program Inclusivity Evaluation (G-PIE) to review your programs; ask questions of leaders within your system about access and opportunity to culturally responsive accelerated options for culturally linguistically diverse gifted learners. Create a relationship where one does not exist. Remember, you cannot take on a system by yourself, and you need allies and co-conspirators to help do this work. It will be important to build relationships along the way with people with common interests for gifted culturally linguistically diverse learners and know that this will not be easy work. Remaining silent and not acting is not an option for antiracist leadership.

As Derald Wing Sue (2016) stated, silence and inaction only serve to perpetuate the status quo of race relations. Will we, as a nation, choose the path we have always traveled, a journey of silence that benefited only a select group and oppressed others, or will we show courage and choose the road less traveled, a journey of racial reality that may be full of discomfort and pain, but offers benefits to all groups in our society?

Will we, as a gifted education community, continue to choose the path we have always traveled? Or will show courage for our students, families, and fellow educators? The choice is ours, and the time is now. Let us not be satisfied with a band-aid to a solution when we can heal the wound.

References

DuBois, M. P., & Greene, R. M. (2021). *Supporting gifted ELLs in the latinx community: Practical strategies, K–12.* Routledge.

Sue, D. W. (2016). *Race talk and the conspiracy of silence.* Wiley.

Appendix A

Checklist for Culturally Responsive Gifted Best Practices

Culturally and Linguistically Diverse Learners

Assessment
❏ Are there multiple assessment options that are culture fair?
❏ Are the assessments available in the student's native, or heritage, language?
❏ Does the body of evidence contain both qualitative and quantitative data?
❏ Are there opportunities for students to be universally screened?
❏ Are there performance assessment options for students to demonstrate giftedness in the arts, creativity, and leadership?
❏ Is there an opportunity to demonstrate outstanding performance through academic and/or talent portfolios?
❏ Are language proficiency data reviewed for students demonstrating gifted potential throughout the school year? When and how often is data reviewed?
❏ Is the option to use local norms available?
❏ Are group-specific norm data available to use for either gifted identification or talent development opportunities?

Programming
❑ Are gifted _____ able to see and hear themselves in the curriculum?
❑ How is heritage language intentionally valued and incorporated?
❑ Do gifted _____ have access to advanced linguistic supports?
❑ Are there opportunities for gifted _____ to develop critical and creative thinking?
❑ Are _____ students provided with authentic learning experiences that reflect their native culture?
❑ What opportunities exist for gifted _____ to access advanced programming and acceleration throughout their school career?
❑ What available grouping and pacing opportunities for advanced academic and social emotional needs exist?
❑ How do gifted _____ participate in advanced programming options such as Advanced Placement, International Baccalaureate, and concurrent enrollment?
❑ Are there talent development opportunities provided for gifted _____?

Professional Learning
❑ Does your school district have a strategic plan for developing culturally responsive gifted professionals?
❑ Are there professional learning opportunities for educators and administrators to explore and reflect upon their own cultural identity, including the role of microaggression and implicit bias?
❑ How do educators and administrators actively learn about the values and cultures of their school and classroom community?
❑ Are there gifted education professional learning opportunities for educators and administrators?

Family Engagement
❑ How is information about gifted identification and advanced programming being communicated to _____ families?
❑ Are _____ families being given multiple opportunities and ways to engage in conversations with teachers and administrators about their child? Are these conversations asset-based?
❑ In what ways are _____ families engaged in the school community?
❑ In what ways is the school inviting _____ families in?
❑ How does the school recognize and incorporate the strengths of _____ families into the classroom?
❑ Is there a partnership with _____ families and teachers to promote the education of the child?

From *Supporting Gifted ELLs in the Latinx Community: Practical Strategies, K–12* by Michelle Pacheco DuBois, Ed.D. and Robin M. Greene, Ed.D., © 2021. Reprinted with permission from the CCC.

Appendix B
Gifted-Program Inclusivity Evaluation (G-PIE)

Program design items	No evidence	Some evidence	In place	Comments
1. There is a written philosophy and/or mission statement framed in social justice and equity related to serving all gifted students.				
2. There is a written expanded definition of giftedness that extends beyond academic areas and includes a statement about inclusion of students with disabilities and students from different cultural, ethnic, and socioeconomic populations.				
3. There is a written description of the services to be provided for the gifted and talented students at each grade level and in each area served.				
4. There are written goals and objectives for these services, and they align with how giftedness is defined.				

(Continued)

5. Services are constructed so that there is a continuum of services to meet the broad range of needs of individual gifted students.				
6. Policies are in place to allow early entrance, grade acceleration, subject acceleration, early credit, and early graduation for all populations of students according to individual student need.				
7. District policies include local and group-specific norms, multiple pathways for gifted identification, and talent development as a pathway towards identification.				
8. There is an inclusive acceleration policy for learners with limited English language skills that allows for subject and grade-level acceleration regardless of English proficiency.				
9. The roles of personnel at the district, the building, and the classroom levels are clearly defined, and these personnel should have gifted and culturally diverse education training.				
10. The gifted student demographics of the district should reflect the diversity of the community they are serving.				
11. A district-wide culturally and linguistically diverse multi-stakeholder group exists and meets on a regular basis to review the district services for gifted students.				

(Continued)

Assessment and identification items	No evidence	Some evidence	In place	Comments
12. The appeals process is accessible in a variety of ways and languages to families.				
13. There are equitable gifted identification procedures designed to develop and reveal talents among all populations of students.				
14. The procedures ensure that all students have an opportunity to be nominated for screening by publicizing the process and receiving nominations from all stakeholder groups.				
15. Multiple assessment options that are culture fair are available in the gifted identification process and the use of alternative assessment measures to support placement in gifted programs.				
16. Assessments options are available in a student's heritage language.				
17. The district uses multiple norm-referenced measures of ability in a student's heritage language in each of the areas for which program services are offered.				
18. The district uses multiple norm-referenced measures of achievement in a student's heritage language with adequate ceilings to assess achievement above grade level in each of the areas for which program services are offered.				
19. Multiple performance assessment options are available for students to demonstrate giftedness in performance and talent domains.				

(Continued)

	No evidence	Some evidence	In place	Comments
20. The district uses qualitative and quantitative indicators of ability in each of the areas for which program services are offered.				
21. Students are given multiple opportunities to be universally screened for gifted using culture-fair assessments.				
22. The formal identification process is repeated at targeted grade levels including (but not limited to) kindergarten, second grade, prior to placement in middle school, and prior to placement in high school.				
23. Students are identified from all ethnic, cultural, ability, and socioeconomic groups.				
Programming and services items	*No evidence*	*Some evidence*	*In place*	*Comments*
24. There is equitable opportunity and access to gifted programming and talent development for all populations of gifted students.				
25. There is a written curriculum in core subject areas and other areas served by the district that is specific to students identified as gifted K–12, culturally relevant to students, and accessible in multiple languages.				
26. There is clear evidence of extensions and enrichment of curriculum in areas served provided in multiple languages.				
27. A written, differentiated, affective curriculum in multiple languages is available and used by teachers that addresses the social-emotional needs of gifted students.				

(Continued)

28. There are specific examples of research-based gifted instructional practices that are inclusive of students' cultures; including, but not limited to, critical and creative thinking, depth and complexity, problem based learning, concept based learning, etc.				
29. Pre-assessments and post-assessments are used to determine flexible learning groups and demonstrate student growth and attainment of stated learning goals.				
30. Gifted students are grouped together for instruction in their area(s) of talent.				
31. Learning environments should foster personal and social responsibility, multicultural competence, and interpersonal and technical communication skills for leadership.				
32. There is evidence of student use of technology for creating content, learning content, and communicating content that is easily accessible and provided to all students.				
33. Documentation of differentiated career guidance for gifted students is available (e.g. field trips, independent study projects, mentors, speakers, or shadowing experiences pertaining to college exploration).				

(Continued)

Professional learning items	No evidence	Some evidence	In place	Comments
34. Personnel working with gifted students are provided with opportunities for continuing professional development in the areas of gifted education and culturally linguistically diverse education.				
35. The district provides professional learning opportunities for personnel to explore and reflect upon their own cultural identity.				
36. The district has a strategic plan for developing culturally responsive gifted professionals.				
Family engagement items	No evidence	Some evidence	In place	Comments
37. Families of gifted students are provided with opportunities for professional development about the characteristics and needs of gifted learners in their native language.				
38. Information about the gifted identification process and gifted services are communicated to families in their native language.				
39. Families are provided multiple opportunities and ways to engage in conversations with school and district personnel in their native language.				
Program evaluation items	No evidence	Some evidence	In place	Comments
40. All components of the gifted program are periodically reviewed by individuals knowledgeable about gifted learners and who have competence in the evaluation process. The results are used for ongoing program improvement.				

(Continued)

41. The results of the program evaluation are presented to the local school board and the stakeholder group, and are accessible to all constituencies of the program in their native language.				
42. The evaluation report for all educational services involving gifted students includes both strengths and areas of challenge of the program and is accompanied by a plan with implications for improvement and renewal over time.